Table of contents

Imprint:

Bibliographic Information of the German National Library: the German National Library lists this publication in the German National Bibliography; detailed bibliographic data are available on the Internet at www.dnb.de.

Production and publishing house: BoD – Books on Demand, Norderstedt
ISBN: 978-3-75782-133-3

History(s) of the Via Claudia Augusta: The paths before the Romans

Even before the Romans, roads led across the Alps. However, the Raetians and Celts did not need wide, comfortable roads. They did not have a common, tightly run state, but were organized tribally. They also did not produce and transport in masses, as the Romans did. The roads in prehistory and early history may therefore be imagined in valleys as cart paths that connected the settlements with each other, over passes often only as mule tracks on which pack animals transported the goods.

This is how one may imagine pre-Roman mule trails.

The Etruscans, Venetians, Raetians and Celts were already in contact with each other and used the Fern and Reschen Passes for this purpose.

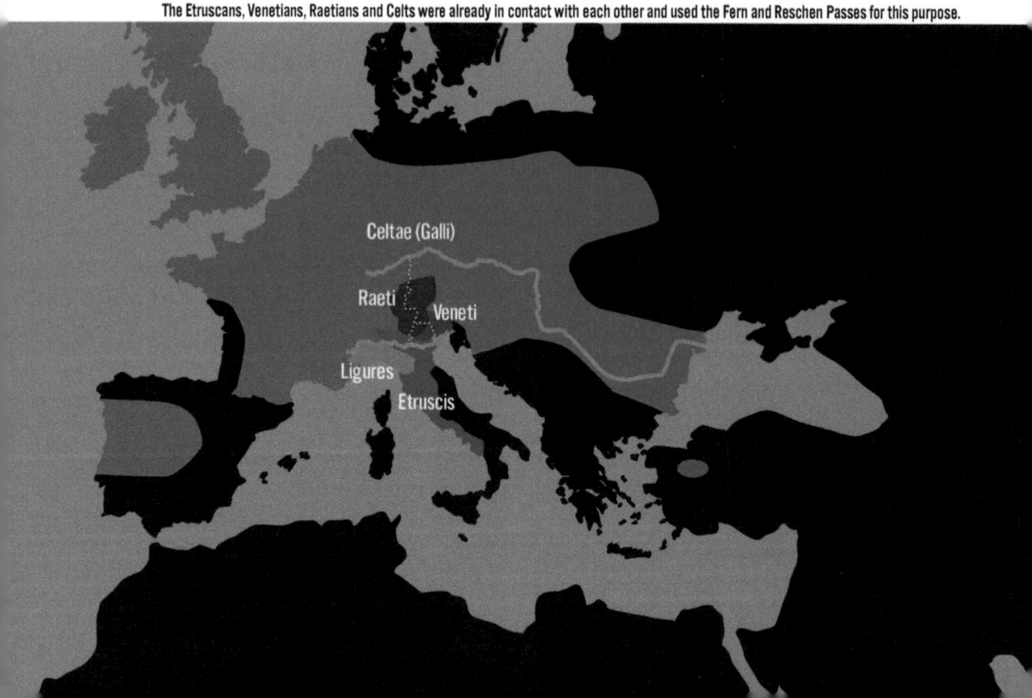

History(s) of the Via Claudia Augusta: The development into the ancient alpine highway

Already during the Alpine campaign, Augustus' stepsons Drusus and Tiberius began to expand the existing routes for the military convoy. Until 46 AD, the Via Claudia Augusta was improved again and again. The first Europe-connecting road across the Alps was finally 6 - 8 meters wide as a rule and thus also allowed two-way traffic. At narrow places there were even traffic regulations. It was curved in the middle and sloped downwards to the outside, to the road graves on the right and left. Thus it was quickly dry again after rain or snow. This was important, as it served the rapid movement of troops. The ancient Alpine highway also enabled and encouraged lively trade without customs duties and tolls. If you like, the Imperium Romanum was the first European single market. The Via Claudia Augusta was not for nothing the most important road across the Alps for a long time. It connected the extreme north with the south of Europe, and even with the south and east of the empire, which reached as far as North Africa and the Near East. When Claudius Paternus Clementianus, who worked in North Africa before he was governor in Noricum, traveled to his homeland in what is now Epfach / Denklingen / Bavaria, he probably crossed by ship to the then Adriatic port of Altinum and then traveled on the Via Claudia Augusta across the Alps. When Emperor Claudius conquered Britain, he probably returned to Rome on the Via Claudia Augusta. And also to the Balkans and further to the Middle East traveled the first part via the Via Claudia Augusta.

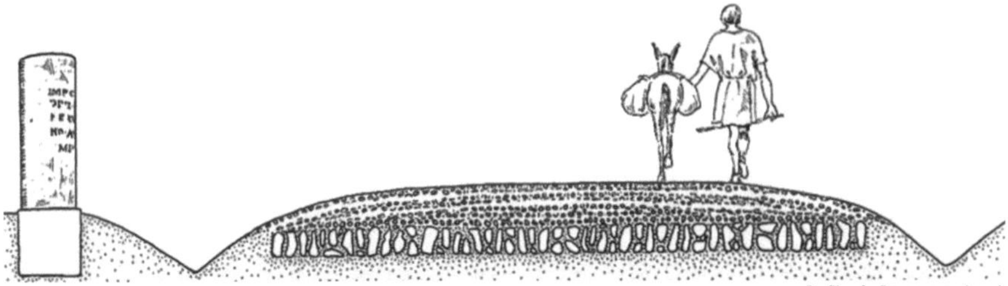

Profile of a Roman gravel road.

The course and importance of the Via Claudia Augusta

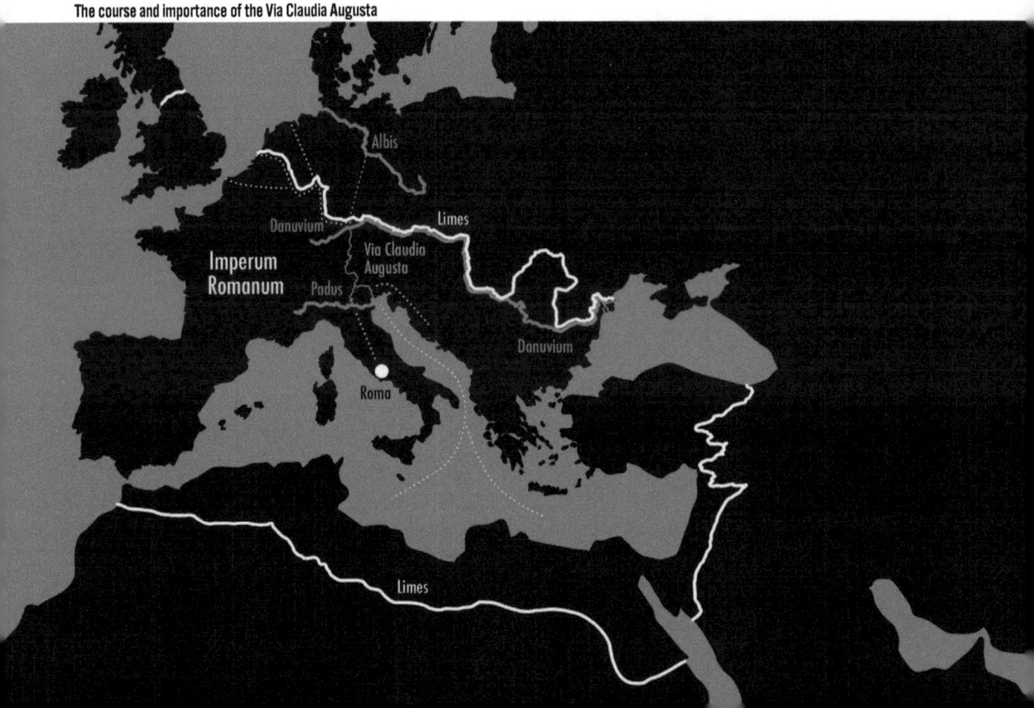

History(s) of the Via Claudia Augusta: Continued use until it was no longer possible

After the decline of the Roman Empire, the Roman roads continued to be used. However, they were no longer regularly maintained and repaired as they had been in Roman times. Accordingly, the condition of the roads was poor. Due to the wagons sliding downhill with the brakes on, the roads of the Romans, which were curved in the middle, gradually became hollow roads. Elaborate road sections, such as the „beating road" between Lermoos and Biberwier, which ran floating on wooden logs, were abandoned. The road through the narrows of the valley north of Bolzano, which had made the Brenner route the easiest and busiest road across the Alps for the first time from 200 AD, fell into disrepair. Travelers again had to conquer a third pass, the Ritten, and the Via Claudia Augusta was again the most important road across the Alps for centuries. In addition to the bad condition and the danger of the roads, there was also the insecurity of being robbed. Accordingly, trade was sparse. The economy languished.

Mugging of travelers by muggers.

Typical hollow way at Fernpass

History(s) of the Via Claudia Augusta: New investment in roads

Towards the end of the Middle Ages and at the beginning of the modern era, nobles and merchants began to invest again in improving the roads in order to stimulate the economy and develop tax revenues. The merchant Kunter from Bolzano took care of the renewal of the road through the Talenge north of Bolzano. In contrast to Roman times, it was customary to collect tolls for the use of the roads. The Starkenbergs, an important family from Tyrol, who invested in the renovation of the Via Claudia Augusta between Fernpass and Landeck, were considered „robber barons" because they recouped their investments through tolls. In addition, the princes collected tolls. Certain goods, such as salt, were even subject to the rules of the so-called Rodfuhrwesen. They could only be transported by local hauliers and had to be unloaded and reloaded at places with the right to lay them down. This was a completely different system than the first European single market, without tolls and customs duties, of the Romans. In both systems, however, many people along the route lived from and with the road. The Via Claudia Augusta was no longer the most important and busiest road, but continued to be an important Alpine crossing. It was finally overtaken by the Brenner route only with the construction of the Brenner railroad and then with the Brenner freeway.

At the hermitage in the south of the Piave Valley.

The salt road near Fernstein Castle.

Carriage along the salt road.

The travel guide for a successful trip across the Alps

The travel guide for a successful trip along the Via Claudia Augusta is designed to be as simple and clear as possible.

The route

The route is presented with
- map-pages
- text-pages and
- picture-pages.

MAP-PAGES

The map pages at a scale of 1:50,000 are for orientation and finding the route. 2 centimeters on the map correspond to 1 kilometer in reality. Intersections are not described with confusing „left and right“, but are evident in the map and also highlighted. In addition to the attractive, varied route, the maps also show the original route of the Roman road, so you know when you are directly on the Roman road or near it. Sights and inns can also be found directly on the map and are explained in a legend. So during the day you will find quite with the maps alone the display, which you can also download on the Internet platform of the Via Claudia Augusta and print out in A4. This increases the scale to about 1:35,000 and the map contents are even easier to see as well as read. Downloading the map pages, driving with the self-printed maps and leaving the guide in your pocket is also a good tip for rainy days or if your guide should have as few traces of use as possible.

TEXT-PAGES

The maps are sufficient for orientation. The text pages for each subsection are for reading and reference. They describe the area and the bike route in the section. In addition, the text pages contain supplementary information on some sights, for which there is not enough space in the legend of the maps.

PICTURE-PAGES

The picture pages complement the text with pictorial impressions and are thus ideal for getting in the mood for the bike tour or individual stages.

Hosts

The host section in the appendix also suggests places to stay that have adapted to the millennia-old tradition of hospitality for bike travelers along the Via Claudia Augusta.

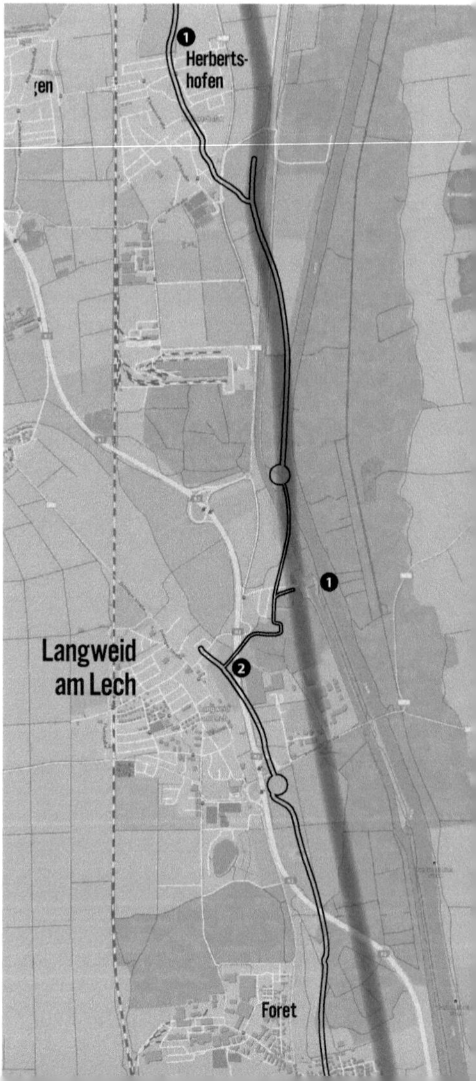

Route description

❶ Romantic Bavaria

From Donauwörth, the route leads through the Lech Valley to the former Roman provincial capital of Augsburg. The route continues over the Lechfeld to Landsberg am Lech and then via the Roman military base at Epfach to Schongau and the Villa Rustica in Peitingen. Finally it goes over the Auerbergland to Füssen and the royal castles.

❷ Picturesque Tyrolean mountain valleys

As if through a gate, the route leads between the mountains into the nature park region of Reutte in Tyrol. The route continues through the Ehrenberg Castle Worlds, over the foot of Germany's highest mountain, the Zugspitze, and the Fernpass mountain pass to Imst. Through the Inn Valley you finally reach Landeck and through the villages of the Tyrolean Oberland up to Nauders and the roof of the tour, the Reschen Pass.

❸ From the Reschenpass along the Etsch river to Trento

From the tower in the Reschensee lake, the route goes steadily downhill. The Etschtal, which is characterized by apple and wine growing, also impresses with places like Laas and Schlanders in the Vinschgau or Algund and Marling at the Therme Meran. In Bolzano there is the possibility to follow the Adige river or the wine road to Caldaro on the lake. Through the vineyards of the Piana Rotaliana you finally reach Trento.

4a Via Claudia Augusta „Altinate „via Feltre to Altino near Venice

Through the Valsugana and the Tesino plateau, the route leads to the historic town of Feltre. Finally, over the Praderadego Pass, you reach the vast plain of Veneto, which begins with the wine hills of Altamarca. The destination of the tour is the Archaeological Museum on the site of the Roman port in Altino.

4p Via Claudia Augusta „Padana „via Verona to Ostiglia on the Po

Alternatively, in Trento you continue to follow the Adige river . First it goes through the vineyards of Vallagarina with its center, the former city of silk, Rovereto. The end of the Adige valley is marked by the Ceraino hermitage, where a detour to Lake Garda is tempting. After Verona with its arena, the route continues through the largest rice-growing area in Europe to Ostiglia on the Po, the former Roman river port.

Fact sheet of the route "Via Claudia Augusta" for car, camper, bus, ...

In 15 BC, the Romans moved north along the paths of the Etruscans, the Raetians and the Celts and began to develop them into the first real road across the Alps. After 60 years, the epoch-making structure was completed in 45/46 AD and named, after the reigning emperor, the „Imperial Road of Claudius". The trans-European road connection continued to exist after the Roman Empire. Goods were exchanged along it. People from many countries and their cultures met on it. The itinerary on the traces of the road founded by the Romans leads over picturesque country roads and mountain passes from the Danube over the Alps to Altino near Venice or Ostiglia on the Po. On the way you will find varied landscapes, tranquil villages, lively towns, many sights and special features that the road has helped to shape. More than 200 hosts have prepared for travelers along the Via Claudia Augusta. Some even have a dish on the menu as it might have been eaten 2000 years ago along Europe's cultural axis.

2 VARIANTS

From Trento, the route splits into the Via Claudia Augusta „Altinate" via Feltre to Altino near Venice, and the Via Claudia Augusta „Padana" to Verona and Ostiglia on the Po. Each variant has its charm. Therefore, it is best to travel south on one route and north again on the other.

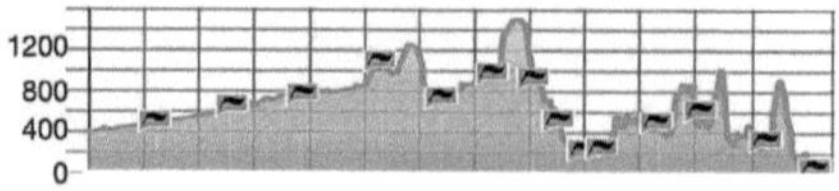

Via Claudia Augusta "Altinate" from the Danube to Altino near Venice

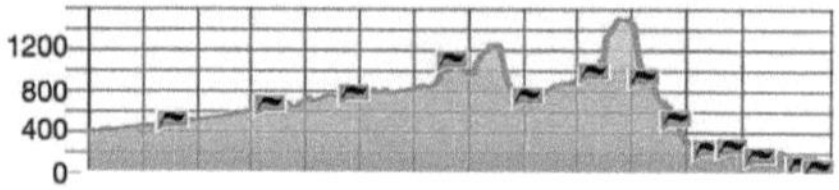

Via Claudia Augusta „Padana" from the Danube to Ostiglia on the Po River

ROUTE

about 600 km from Donauwörth (Bavaria) over the Alps to Altino near Venice or Ostiglia on the Po River

PROFILE

on picturesque country roads and mountain passes, through pretty villages and lively towns.

TRAVEL DOCUMENTS

In addition to tour books, there is an interactive map for individual travel planning on www.viaclaudia.org and apps with which you can navigate along the route according to the individually planned itinerary and also have all the information about places of interest.

CAMPING AND BUS

Additional information for caravans, trailers and buses at www.viaclaudia.org.

History and culture

At the beginning of the introduction of this book there is a brief introduction to the history of the Via Claudia Augusta, which spans several thousand years. If you are interested in the history of the Via Claudia Augusta, the regions and places along the first trans-European road across the Alps, as well as the cultural diversity, which has shaped the Via Claudia Augusta, then we recommend the corresponding pages on www.viaclaudia.org. There you will find for each section, historical and cultural features, as background information but also as an impetus to deal with one or the other closer. Some like to get in the mood for what awaits them before the journey or a stage. Some like to read up after the trip or a stage to understand one or the other better. On the history page there is also a historical database where successive historical knowledge about the Via Claudia Augusta can be found. Finally, „4 maps through the millennia" are in preparation for each region along the Via Claudia Augusta.

29 issues „4 cards through the millennia"

The 4 maps through the millennia depict each region along the first Europe-connecting road across the Alps at four different points in time. 3 of the 4 maps are dedicated to the history of the regions. In each case, the points in history that are particularly interesting in the respective region have been selected. Thus, you can quickly get an overview of how the region has developed over the millennia. The fourth of the 4 maps shows the region in modern times. The 4 maps are not only exciting for those who are interested in history a little closer than it can be presented in a cycling guide, but it is also exciting to discover the differences in the maps together with children. The „4 maps through the millennia" are available in digital form at www.viaclaudia.org. In printed form, they are available at the respective tourist information offices in the region, among other places. Gradually, the maps will also be offered collectively at a special price via the online bookstore.

1 map for each of the 30 regions

Trip planning with the interactive map & navigation with the app

Romans and modern technology are not a contradiction. Even in ancient times, all the things that made life easier, more comfortable, safer and more rational were used. For all those who would like to use modern media to get an impression of the trip from home or to plan the trip, an interactive map is available at www.viaclaudia.org, which can be used to plan an individual trip. The itinerary can either be downloaded as a PDF or transferred to the navigation app on the iPhone or Android phone.

How to plan your individual trip

Open the interactive trip planning tool, which is located on several pages of the homepage www.viaclaudia.org. Select your trip type so that you have the correct one of the different routes on the screen. Then choose approximately how many kilometers a day you want to cover and right-click to set a start and end point. The trip planning tool calculates a corresponding stage suggestion on this basis. As overnight stops, you can choose places where you will find accommodations that are specially adapted to travelers along the Via Claudia Augusta. However, you can also set your own stage locations. An altitude profile informs you about the topography. To get a better impression of the areas and places you have traveled through, you can now zoom into the map. From a certain zoom level, the inns, sights and other special features that you have selected in the menu will appear on the map. If you want more information about a guesthouse, a place of interest or a special feature, simply click on the symbol in the map. The information will appear in the right margin. If you want to make a note of something for your trip, then simply put the respective item on the watch list. When you have finished planning your individual trip, you can download the itinerary as a PDF and print it out, download the route as a GPX file or transfer the map to your smartphone by entering an abbreviation or using a QR code.

On the road with the navigation apps

The Via Claudia Augusta navigation apps for iPhone and Android phones also work offline. You will have fewer zoom levels available and no images will be displayed for the points of interest due to capacity reasons, but you do not need an internet connection and no data will be downloaded. As soon as you have an Internet connection available, all zoom levels and images are available to you, which are subsequently available in their cache for further use up to a certain extent without Internet.

Download guide maps

The maps in this guide are also available for download at www.viaclaudia.org. This allows you to print the maps larger. If you use the printouts during the trip, your guide will be less stressed and there is also no risk that it will be damaged in the rain. Some people also like to take notes, but do not want to do it in a guide.

Other printed guides

Cycling Guide (1) "Altinate" and (2) "Padana"

One hiking guide each for (1) Bavaria, (2) Tyrol, (3) Reschen to Trento, (4) Trento-Altino and (5) Trento-Ostiglia

01 Donauwörth in Donau-Ries, the starting point of the first road across the Alps (map 1)

The Via Claudia Augusta starts in the town of Donauwörth. This has two reasons: the Danube, which allowed the Romans to transport heavy goods, and the northern border of the Roman Empire, which was located here before and after the first retreat of the Roman Empire from the Germanic tribes. The northernmost part of the Roman road runs through the modern district of Donau-Ries, which nearly reaches the Limes in the north. Apart from the Danube, the area is characterized by the Ries crater. It has a diameter of 25 kilometers and was created by a meteorite 14.5 million years ago. The name 'Ries' is said to be derived from the Roman province of Rhaetia. Donauwörth, the town where the Roman road ends, did not exist during Roman times. Instead, the area was frequently flooded by five rivers whose confluence lies in the Donauwörth region: the Danube, Wörnitz, Zusam, Schmutter and Lech. The town began as a fishermen's settlement on the island of Ried in the Wörnitz river. Today, most of the old town is located to the north of the river. It offers one of Germany's most beautiful streets, the Reichsstraße.

A walk through Donauwörth

The Tanzhaus on the Reichsstraße houses the archaeological museum, a fitting start to a journey along the historical road. Do not miss the impressive town hall on the same street. Head through the Rieder Tor gate, which houses the local history museum (Haus der Stadtgeschichte), and visit the old town on the island of Ried. This is where the town first began to develop. Another local heritage museum (the Heimatmuseum) is located here. Back on the Reichsstraße, walk past the Liebfrauenmünster church and the Fuggerhaus. Your walk ends at the Käthe Kruse Doll Museum, which is dedicated to the history of the famous dolls from Donauwörth. The tourist information office offers many guided tours.

■ Archaeological museum: Reichsstraße 34,
+49 (0)906789-170, open on Sat, Sun and public holidays: 2 pm–5 pm.

■ Haus der Stadtgeschichte in the Rieder Tor: Spitalstraße 11,
+49 (0)906789-170 or -151, opens upon request.

■ Heimatmuseum on the island of Ried: Museumsplatz 2, +43 (0)906789-170 or -151, May to October: Tue–Sun, 2 pm–5 pm, November to April: Wed, Sat, Sun and public holidays, 2 pm–5 pm.

■ Käthe Kruse Doll Museum: Pflegstraße 21a, +43(0)906 789-170 or -151. May to September: Tue–Sun, 11 am–6 pm; October to April: Thu–Sun, 2 pm–5 pm; 25 December to 6 January: every day 2 pm–5 pm; closed on 24 December and Good Friday.

Getting out of the city

There is a footpath at the edge of Nordheim. You will see it on your left just after you pass the bridge. It leads to a replica of a milestone of the Via Claudia Augusta, which marked the location of the Roman road.

Special: Ries National Geopark

14.5 million years ago, an asteroid about 1 km in size, accompanied by a 150 m satellite, raced towards the Earth. They hit the Alb plateau with more than 70,000 km/h and created two craters with diameters of 25 and 4 km, the Nördlinger Ries and the Steinheimer Becken.

At the impact point a pressure of several million bar and a temperature of more than 20 000 ° C was generated: The asteroid and some of the rocks even melted or vaporized. A shock wave raced supersonically through the deeper rocks, altering them and leading to the formation of high-pressure minerals such as coesite, stishovite, and diamond. In the first seconds after the impact, a hollow crater was formed, reaching a depth of 4.5 km. The ejected rock masses formed a closed debris blanket reaching to a distance of 50 km. At the same time, a hot cloud of embers shot into the high atmosphere above the crater. The deep crater persisted for only a few seconds. The crater floor bulged up inside the crater. In the process, rock clods slid from the steep crater rim, making the original rim more and more indistinct. Eventually, the crater collapsed and became flater. After a few minutes, all rock movement ceased. The pyroclastic cloud deposited as a hot blanket of rock several 100 m thick.

Everything about the Ries crater can be learned in the museum of the same name in the medieval town of Nördlingen with its completely preserved and walkable city wall. The cosmic catastrophe not only left behind a fascinating almost circular landscape that can be experienced on theme trails and guided tours. It also created the conditions for the crater basin to become the granary of Bavaria. Ice-age drifts then left behind fertile soils. Historical grain varieties and other specialties can be enjoyed with Geopark Ries culinary.

■ RiesKraterMuseum, 86720 Nördlingen, Eugene-Shoemaker-Platz 1, +49 (0)9081 84710, open May - Oct. Tues. - Sun. 10 a.m. - 4:30 p.m. and Nov. - Apr. Tues. - Sun. 10 a.m. - noon and 1:30 p.m. - 4:30 p.m. www.rieskrater-museum.de

■ Ries National Geopark, 86609 Donauwörth, Pflegstraße 2, +49 (0)90674 140,
www.geopark-ries.de

History(s)

Wherever possible, the Romans transported heavier loads by water. That is why the Via Claudia Augusta connects the Danube and Po waterways and the Roman Adriatic port of Altinum. In addition, the Roman road followed various rivers over long stretches: Lech, Inn, Adige, Brenta, Piave and Sile.

The northernmost point of the Via Claudia Augusta is close to the Limes. The Limes was not an impermeable border. The Romans traded with Germania. However, the Romans controlled who entered and left the empire.

The road, which received its name after its later final extension under Emperor Claudius, is said to have originally led to the Elbe River, 60 km from Berlin. However, the Romans were defeated in the Teutoburg Forest and therefore decided to abandon the wooded and marshy area and to move the originally planned border at the Elbe to the Danube. Accordingly, the Via Claudia Augusta ended at the Danube when it was named after Claudius in 46 AD.

With an average water flow of about 6855 m3 and a total length of 2857 kilometers, the Danube is the second largest and second longest river in Europe after the Volga. It drains large parts of Central and Southeastern Europe and flows through a total of 10 countries, and thus through more than any other river: Germany, Austria, Slovakia, Hungary, Croatia, Serbia, Bulgaria, Romania, Moldova and Ukraine.

The Swabian Alb, formerly also called the Swabian Jura or Swabian Alb, which ends here at the Ries, is a low mountain range that stretches across Baden-Württemberg to Switzerland. It is about 180 to 200 km long 35 to 40 km wide, 5887.35 km^2 in size and up to 1015.7 m high. The mountain range consists of Mesozoic Jurassic limestone.

In the area of Donau-Ries the Limes was a border wall, which ran in the north of the district. Over large parts, however, the river itself was the border. One also speaks of the wet Limes.

Regional cuisine like 2000 years ago

■ Gasthaus Alte Brauerei Mertingen, Hilaria-Lechner-Str. 21
0049(0)9078 912 32-0

■ Restaurant Guava, Mertingen, Gewerbep. Ost 15
0049(0)163791 82 43

Overnight and camping possibilities in the maps and in the appendix

Questions and information about the subsection

■ Städtische Tourist-Information Donauwörth, Rathausgasse 1, 0049(0)906 789 151

■ Hotline Ferienland Donau-Ries, 0049(0)90674 211

■ Hotline Via Claudia Augusta, 0043(0)664 27 63 555

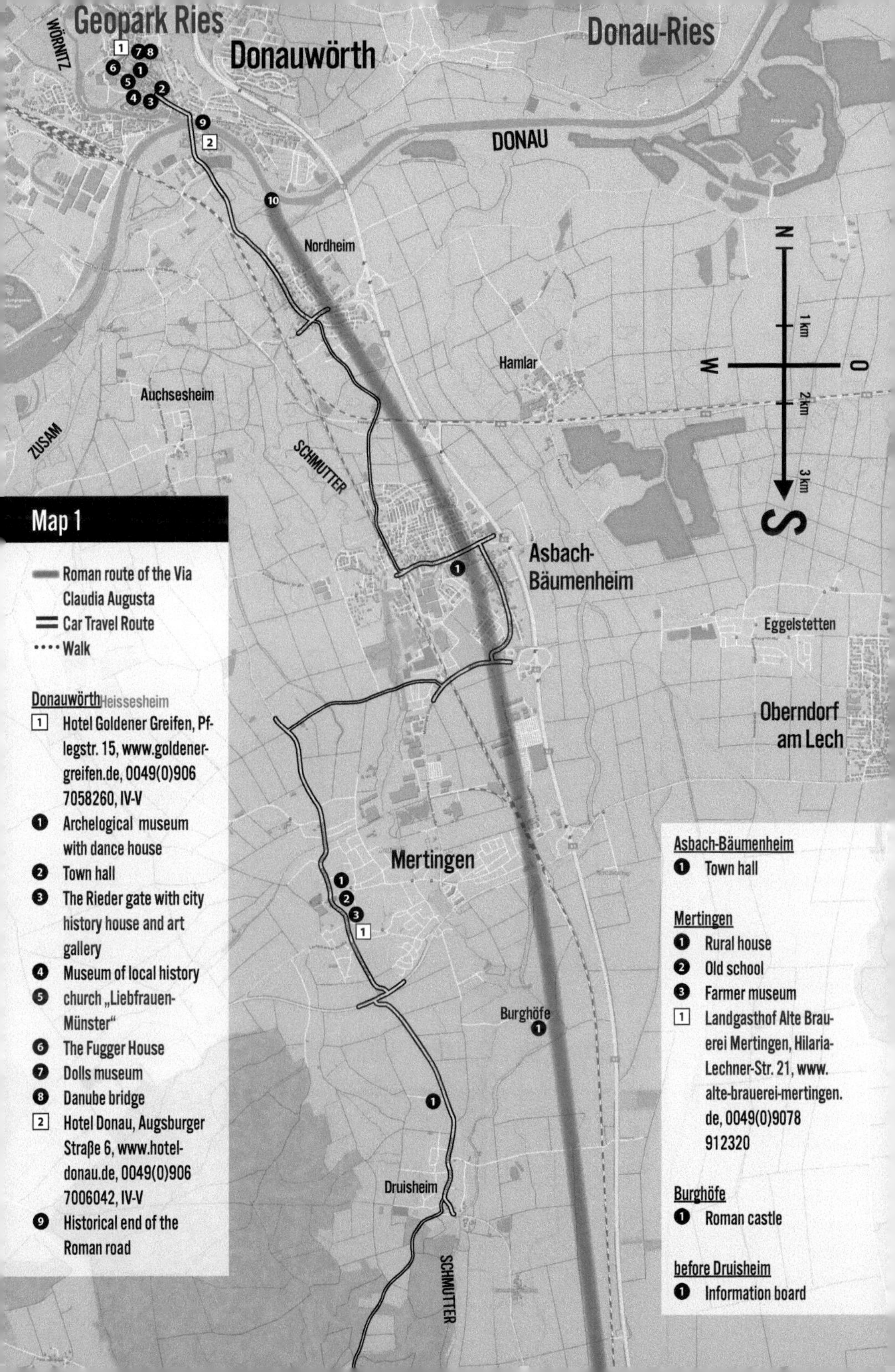

Geopark Ries
Donauwörth
Donau-Ries
WÖRNITZ
DONAU
Nordheim
Hamlar
Auchsesheim
ZUSAM
SCHMUTTER
N
S
W
O
1 km
2 km
3 km
Map 1
Roman route of the Via Claudia Augusta
Car Travel Route
Walk
Donauwörth
Heissesheim
1 Hotel Goldener Greifen, Pflegstr. 15, www.goldener-greifen.de, 0049(0)906 7058260, IV-V
1 Archelogical museum with dance house
2 Town hall
3 The Rieder gate with city history house and art gallery
4 Museum of local history
5 church „Liebfrauen-Münster“
6 The Fugger House
7 Dolls museum
8 Danube bridge
2 Hotel Donau, Augsburger Straße 6, www.hotel-donau.de, 0049(0)906 7006042, IV-V
9 Historical end of the Roman road
Asbach-Bäumenheim
Eggelstetten
Oberndorf am Lech
Mertingen
Burghöfe
Druisheim
SCHMUTTER
Asbach-Bäumenheim
1 Town hall
Mertingen
1 Rural house
2 Old school
3 Farmer museum
1 Landgasthof Alte Brauerei Mertingen, Hilaria-Lechner-Str. 21, www.alte-brauerei-mertingen.de, 0049(0)9078 912320
Burghöfe
1 Roman castle
before Druisheim
1 Information board

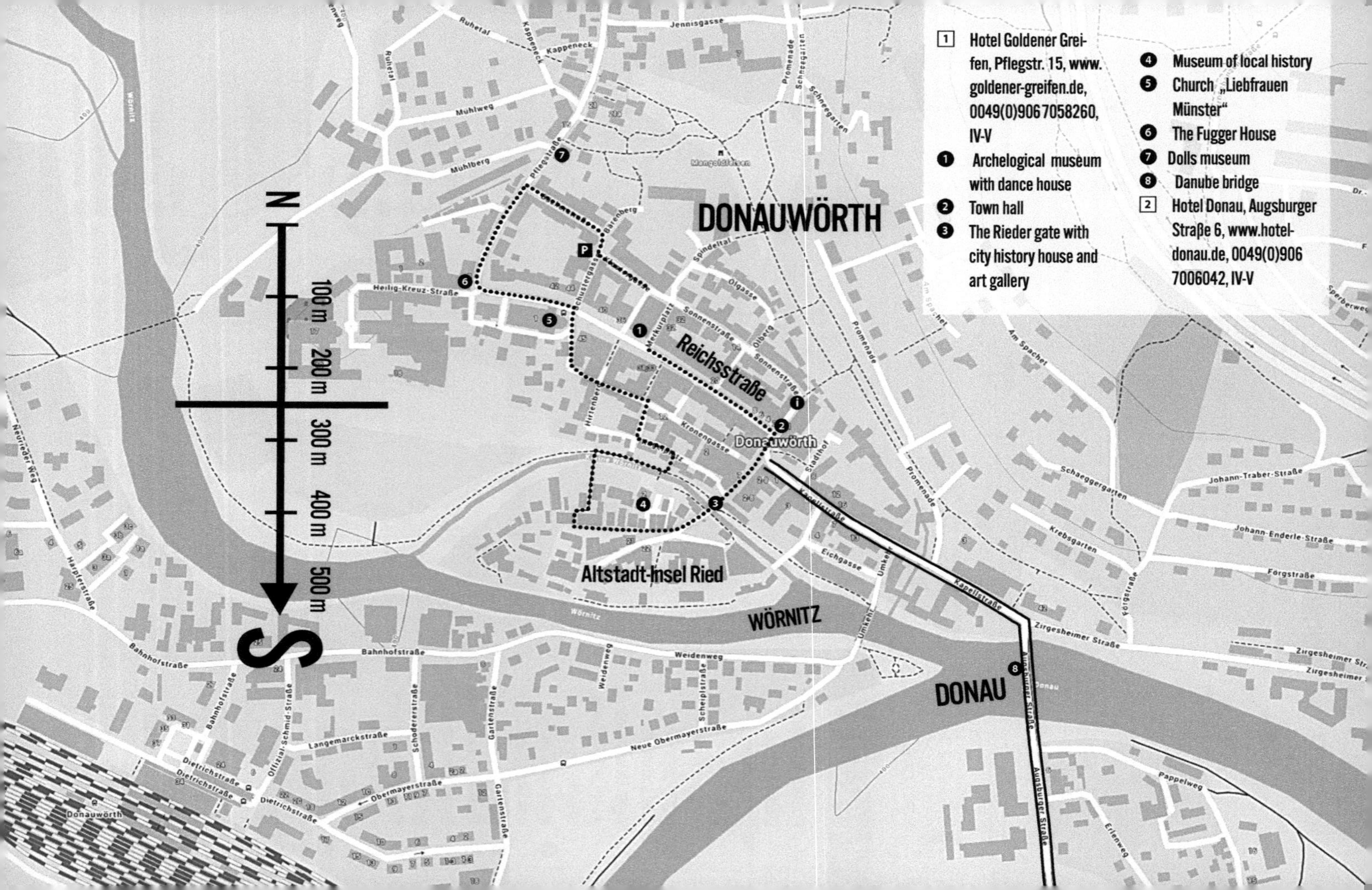

1 Hotel Goldener Greifen, Pflegstr. 15, www.goldener-greifen.de, 0049(0)9067058260, IV-V
1 Archelogical museum with dance house
2 Town hall
3 The Rieder gate with city history house and art gallery
4 Museum of local history
5 Church „Liebfrauen Münster“
6 The Fugger House
7 Dolls museum
8 Danube bridge
2 Hotel Donau, Augsburger Straße 6, www.hotel-donau.de, 0049(0)906 7006042, IV-V
DONAUWÖRTH
Reichsstraße
Altstadt-Insel Ried
WÖRNITZ
DONAU
N
S
100 m
200 m
300 m
400 m
500 m

Mouth of the Wörnitz into the Danube

View through the Ried Gate to the island of Ried. Photos (3): Lois Lammerhuber

The Imperial Road

Balloon Museum Gersthofen.

Monastery Holzen.

The site of the fort Submuntorium. Photo: Deininger

In Roman times, there were already settlements in the estuary region of the rivers Wörnitz, Schmutter and Lech and in the part of the Lechtal valley bordering Augsburg. The inconspicuous little hill between Mertingen and Druisheim was the site of Submuntorium-Burghöfe, a Roman fortress complex. Another military site is said to have stood in Langweid am Lech. The towns up to Drusheim are still part of the district of Donau-Ries. Beyond Drusheim, the district of Augsburg begins. Its largest towns are Meitingen, which gained market privileges in 1989, and Gersthofen, which became a town in 1969. The Roman road follows the Lech towards Augsburg. In some parts, it is still a road. In others, it is a dam on the ground. Most of it is covered by the national road number 2 today. The Roman road runs past the floodplains of the Lech river, which separates the district of Augsburg from the Wittelsbacher Land.

From the Danube to Augsburg

Several showcases at the town hall of Asbach-Bäumenheim document the Roman history of the area. The Roman road on which we leave the town follows the historical route precisely. The DON 28 district road, which takes our route to Mertingen, later replaced the Via Claudia Augusta as a connection between the Danube and Augsburg. Our route follows it for long stretches because it leads through several pretty town centers. Back then, traffic was not an issue. Mertingen has an active museum association. At the Sölde, a rural house at Mardostraße 10, you can find out about the residential culture of a farm in the 18th and 19th century. The Alte Schule museum behind the town hall at Fuggerstraße 3 showcases discoveries from Roman and pre-Roman times alongside exhibits about the Alemanni foundation (or rather, colonization) of the town. The Stadl museum at Hilaria-Lechner-Straße 13 houses a large collection of agricultural equipment, carriages, wheels and sleighs. ■ +49 (0)9078 9600 18, opens upon prior arrangement, www.museumsfreunde.mertingen.de. On a hill between Mertingen and Druisheim, you will find a notice board telling you about Submuntorium-Burghöfe and explain its function in a chain of fire signals. After a visit to the former Benedictine abbey of Holzen, which was founded in the 13th century and rebuilt in the late 17th century, continue to Nordendorf and Westendorf before stopping over in Ostendorf, where a pre-Christian stone has been fixed in the outer wall of St. Michael's Church. Between Waltershofen and Markt Meitingen, you pass a shopping center to your right. It was named after the Via Claudia Augusta. Just like the main road leading through the market town, it is right on the route of the old Roman road. A milestone marks the location near the Raiffeisenkasse bank. Before you enter Herbertshofen, you will find a notice board on the road. It contains information about the highly developed Roman land surveying system. A replica of a groma allows you to try your hand at it yourself. A power plant from 1907 near the Lech river before Langweid houses the Bavarian Lech Museum. ■ Lechwerkstraße 19, 86462 Langweid am Lech, +49 (0)821 328–1658, open every first Saturday of the month, 10 am–6 pm or upon prior arrangement. A few years ago, archaeologists discovered sections of the Via Claudia Augusta in Landweid. In the north of Gersthofen, the travel route crosses the old road twice. It leads downhill towards the town center on the upper edge of a slope running to the river. A small park contains a small Temple of Mercury. Merchants and travelers used to ask the god for safe passage. When you reach Gersthofen, consider visiting the balloon museum, which is dedicated to the history of balloon flight. ■ Bahnhofstraße 12, 86368 Gersthofen, +49 (0)821 2491 ext. 506, open on Wed, Fri: 1–5 pm, Thu: 10 am–7 pm, Sat, Sun, public holidays: 10 am–5 pm, www.ballonmuseum-gersthofen.de.

Regional cuisine like 2000 years ago

■ Gasthaus Alte Brauerei Mertingen, Hilaria-Lechner-Straße 21, 0049(0)9078 912 320
■ Restaurant Guava, Mertingen, Gewerbepark Ost 15 0049(0)163791 82 43

Overnight and camping possibilities in the maps and in the appendix

Questions and information about the subsection

■ Up to Mertingen: Hotline Ferienland Donau-Ries, 0049(0)90674 211
■ Beginning from Allmannshofen: Hotline Regio Augsburg Tourismus GmbH, 0049(0)821 50 2070
■ Hotline Via Claudia Augusta, 0043(0)664 27 63 555

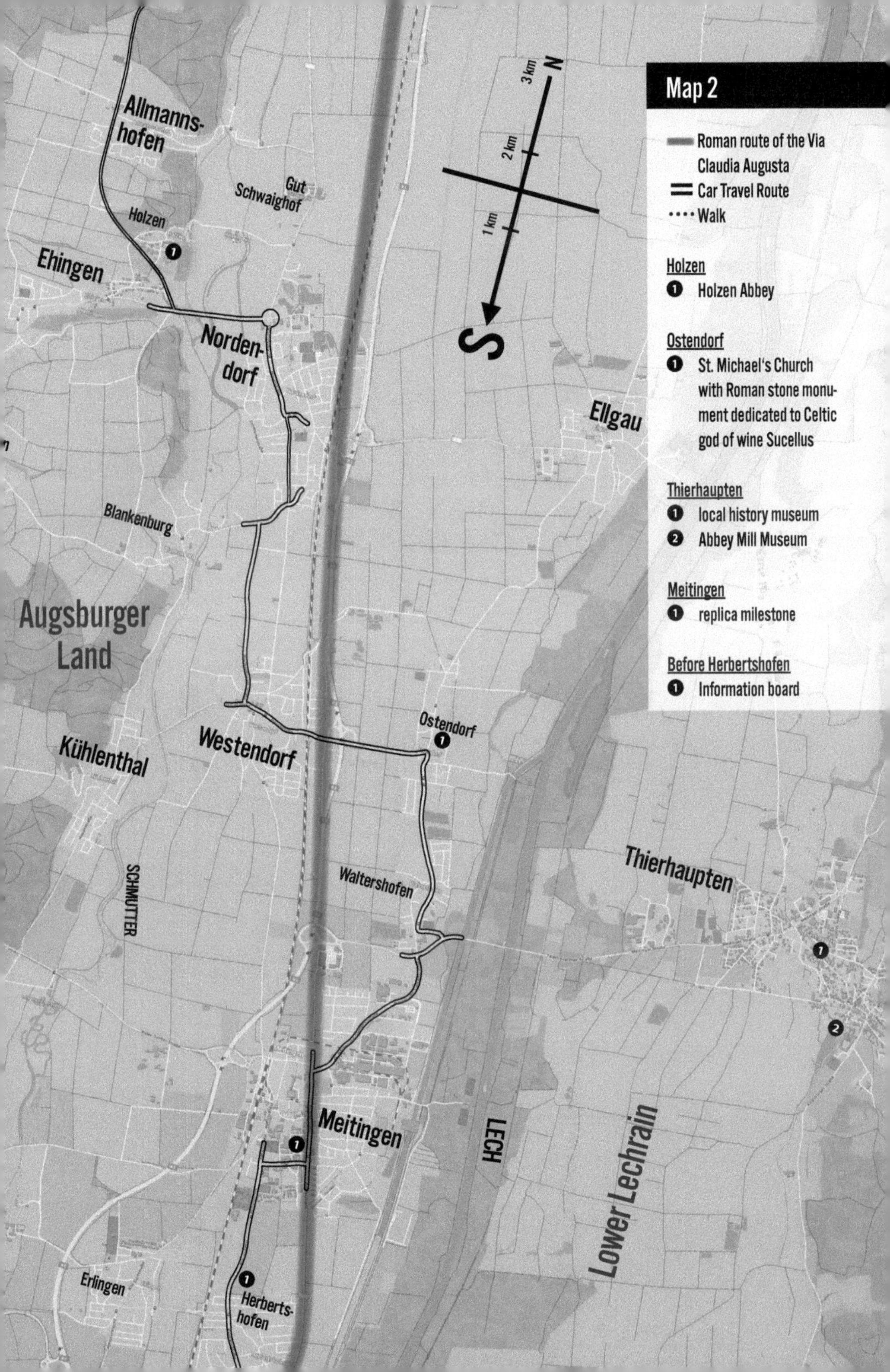

Map 2
Roman route of the Via Claudia Augusta
Car Travel Route
Walk
Holzen
1 Holzen Abbey
Ostendorf
1 St. Michael's Church with Roman stone monument dedicated to Celtic god of wine Sucellus
Thierhaupten
1 local history museum
2 Abbey Mill Museum
Meitingen
1 replica milestone
Before Herbertshofen
1 Information board
N
S
1 km
2 km
3 km
Allmannshofen
Holzen
Gut Schwaighof
Ehingen
Nordendorf
Ellgau
Blankenburg
Augsburger Land
Kühlenthal
Westendorf
Ostendorf
Waltershofen
Thierhaupten
SCHMUTTER
Meitingen
LECH
Lower Lechrain
Erlingen
Herbertshofen

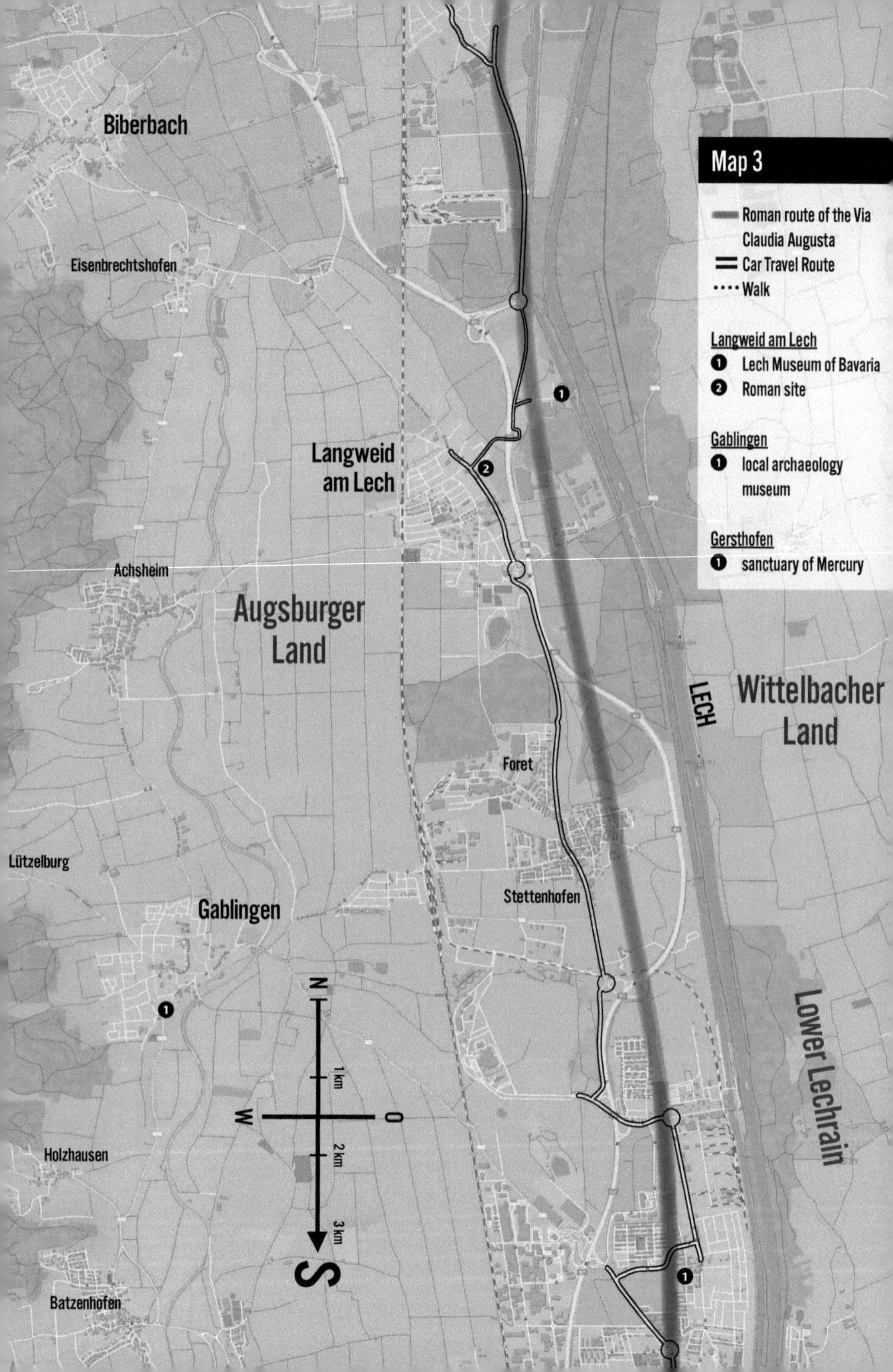
Map 3
Roman route of the Via Claudia Augusta
Car Travel Route
Walk
Langweid am Lech
1 Lech Museum of Bavaria
2 Roman site
Gablingen
1 local archaeology museum
Gersthofen
1 sanctuary of Mercury
Biberbach
Eisenbrechtshofen
Langweid am Lech
Achsheim
Augsburger Land
Wittelbacher Land
LECH
Foret
Lützelburg
Stettenhofen
Gablingen
Lower Lechrain
N
W
O
S
1 km
2 km
3 km
Holzhausen
Batzenhofen

03 Augsburg: the Roman provincial capital of Augusta Vindelicum (maps 4, 5)

After the Alpine Campaign in 15 B. C., Emperor Augustus' adoptive sons, Drusus and Tiberius, established a military camp in Oberhausen, a northern district. The camp was the foundation of Augusta Vindelicum, the later capital of the province of Rhaetia. Augsburg is probably Germany's second oldest city. It was most certainly one of the largest Roman towns north of the Alps. Spanning more than 25 ha, the settlement had up to 15,000 inhabitants in its heyday and offered them everything they would have expected from a Roman provincial capital: a temple, market hall, governor's palace, theater, spas ... All townhouses had running water. The Via Claudia Augusta passed the town to the west. In the central area between the town hall and the Mercury fountain, it is identical to the historical main road through the old town. Augsburg rose to even greater significance in the late Middle Ages and the beginning of the modern era, when the rich Fugger family established their global business empire from here. Later, the prince-bishops of Augsburg reigned over a vast expanse of land that stretched all the way to Tyrol.

An attractive route into the town center

Follow the old connecting road between Augsburg and Donauwörth (called Augsburger Straße until the border before becoming Donauwörther Straße) from Gersthofen to Augsburg. The northernmost part of the former Roman provincial capital is Oberhausen, where the Romans set up their first camp after the Alpine Campaign. Cross the Wertachbrücke bridge to the district between the two rivers, Wertach and Lech, where the city developed over the millennia. The route continues through the Fischertor gate, which used to be a part of the enceinte (wall) surrounding the city, and leads you through the oldest part of Augsburg. You will pass the birthplace of Leopold Mozart at Frauentorstraße 30 on the way. Have a good look at the cathedral from all sides, then head to the town hall square with its pedestrian zone. Just before the pedestrian zone begins, the road forks to the right, leading you to a parking garage at Ernst-Reuter-Platz.

2000 years of Augsburg

A guided tour in a taxi is the most comfortable way to travel through time: up to four people pay EUR 29 per hour. Augsburg's sights are all in close proximity to each other, however, so you can easily see them on foot. Head out from the parking lot and visit the former prince-bishops' residence (Fürstbischöfliche Residenz), whose inhabitants controlled the fate of the surrounding region up to Tyrol for a long time. Today, it is the seat of the Swabian regional government. From here, the route leads you around the cathedral and to the garden on Äußeres Pfaffengässchen, where you can catch an archaeological glimpse of Roman Augsburg. In 2014, the Fugger und Welser Erlebnismuseum opened in a Renaissance garden house, offering an interactive multimedia exhibition about the significance of Augsburg and the economical influence of its mercantile families on Europe and the world in the 16th century. After visiting the cathedral, have a look at the stone sculptures on the Roman wall on the southern cathedral square. On the opposite side of the street, at Peutingerstraße 11, you can see the house of the humanist Konrad Peutinger. The merchant, who collected Roman coins and stone monuments, is the father of Roman research in Augsburg. He also gave his name to the first world map of Roman roads, whose 12th-century copy he sought to publish. At the gate of his house, Roman and Jewish stone monuments have been fixed in the wall. The next stop on your route is the town hall, one of the most important secular Renaissance buildings north of the Alps. Alongside the Perlachturm tower, which offers wonderful views of the city, it is the symbol of Augsburg. The Goldener Saal inside the town hall is one of Germany's most significant cultural monuments from the Late Renaissance. Perched atop the monumental fountain, Emperor Augustus watches over the city he founded. On the stretch between the town hall and the Mercury fountain to the south, the Maximilianstraße is identical to the Roman road running past the city to the west. Head a little further west still to reach the Maximilianmuseum at Fuggerplatz 1. It is the storehouse of the city's art galleries and museums and contains three separate sections: sculptures, handicrafts, local history. Among its most fascinating treasures is a collection of sculptures from the Late Renaissance and goldworks from the era when the Fuggers' city was one of Central Europe's main centers of goldsmithing. But the greatest attraction of the museum is the Viermetzhof, its glass-covered inner courtyard. It showcases the restored figures of Augsburg's monumental fountains, the Augustus fountain, Hercules fountain and Mercury fountain. A little further along the road, at Zeugplatz 4, you can see the Baroque armory, which was also used as military barracks. Of course, the Fuggers also had their palace on Maximilanstraße (building 36). On the way back to the parking lot, you pass the Fuggerei, their social housing complex.

■ Leopold Mozart's birthplace, Frauentorstraße 30, 0049(0)821/502070, open Tue - Sun 10 am - 5 pm.
■ Perlachturm, Rathausplatz, open Good Friday to Nov. daily 10 am - 6 pm. In Advent Fri, Sat, Sun 1 - 7 pm.
■ Goldener Saal, Rathausplatz, open Mon - Sun 10 am - 6 pm. Fuggerei, Jakoberstraße 26, open April - Sept. 8 a.m. - 8 p.m., Oct. - March 9 a.m. - 6 p.m.
■ Maximilianmuseum, Fuggerpl. 1, 0049(0)821 324-4102, open Mon - Wed 7:30 a.m. - 4:30 p.m., Thurs 7:30 a.m. - 5:30 p.m., Fri 7:30 a.m. - 12:

Continuing your journey south

In the east, the travel route leads you past the center of the historical old town. It passes through another gate of the former enceinte, the Vogeltor, which used to guard the Jakobervorstadt district. Do not miss the archaeological site at Predigerberg. The Basilica of SS. Ulrich and Afra marks the end of Maximilianstraße. The route now takes you to Königsbrunn in a straight line, following Haunstetterstraße, which corresponds to the old Roman road. A little to the east, you will find the botanical gardens of the town. A Roman garden shows you many of the plants and growing methods that the Romans introduced to this area.

Special: Wittelsbacher Land

In the charming hill country between Augsburg, Ingolstadt and Munich lies the cradle of Altbaiern, the ancestral seat of the 800-year reign of the Bavarian royal house of the Wittelsbach. They were one of the most important high noble families in Europe and also provided kings in Hungary (1305), Sweden (1441 - 1448 and 1654 - 1720), Denmark and Norway (1440), Greece (1832 - 1862) and three times in the Roman-German Empire (1328/1400/1743), including two emperors. Their land is considered to be one of the castles and chateaux, some of which are still inhabited by noble families. The moated castle in Unterwittelbach is better known as „Sisi Castle". The later empress is said to have spent a lot of time there with her father Max and used it for riding exercises with her pony. Wittelbach's Friedberg Castle essentially dates back to the Renaissance and offers the ideal setting for the well-known castle concerts in the worth seeing, arcade-lined inner courtyard. Also worth seeing are the pilgrimage churches of the Maria Birnbaum monastery in Sielenbach, St. Leonhard in Inchenhofen, Herrgottsruh in Friedberg, Maria Kappel in Schmiechen and St. Afra im Felde as well as the town centers of Aichach and Friedberg. www.wittelsbacherland.de

Special: The rich Fuggers

In 1367, the weaver Hans Fugger moved from Graben im Lechfeld to the Free Imperial City of Augsburg and made a fortune trading cotton from Italy. One of his sons, Jakob, and his descendants turned it into a world-class business empire. They engaged in mining and traded in all kinds of goods throughout the then known world, from metals to spices to textiles and medicines. By the way, Hans Fugger already used the Via Claudia Augusta for cotton trade with Italy. It also connected the Fuggers with the profitable mining areas in the Alps. The family rose to the higher nobility and held high secular and ecclesiastical offices. The name Fugger became synonymous with wealth throughout Europe. The family even lent money to emperors and popes and made Charles V German king with 850,000 florins. In Augsburg, the Fugger City Palace at Maximilianstrasse 36 and the oldest social settlement, the „Fuggerei", bear witness to this period. There is also a Fuggerplatz. As of fall 2014, the Fugger-und-Welser-Erlebnismuseum also gives a vivid impression of the economic importance of Augsburg and its trading dynasties. Branches of the Fugger family still reside at the Fuggerschloss Babenhausen, Kirchheim Castle and Oberkirchberg Castle. The „Fuggerei" still provides housing for needy people today.
www.fugger.de

Overnight and camping possibilities in the maps and in the appendix

Questions and information about the subsection

■ Touristinfo Regio Augsburg Tourismus GmbH, Rathausplatz 1, 0049(0)821 502070
■ Via Claudia Augusta Hotline, 0043(0)664 27 63 555

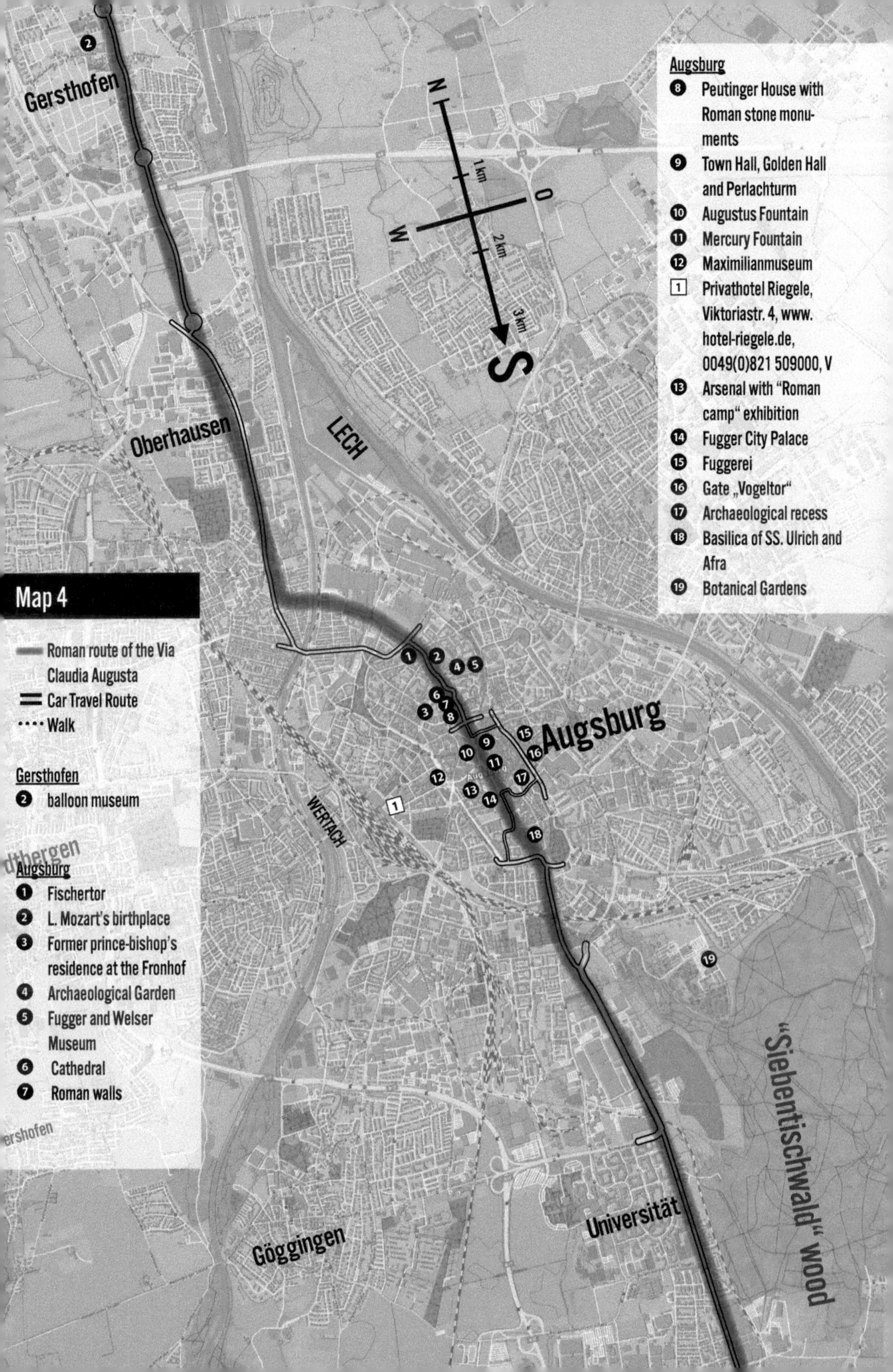

Map 4
Roman route of the Via Claudia Augusta
Car Travel Route
Walk
Gersthofen
2 balloon museum
Augsburg
1 Fischertor
2 L. Mozart's birthplace
3 Former prince-bishop's residence at the Fronhof
4 Archaeological Garden
5 Fugger and Welser Museum
6 Cathedral
7 Roman walls
Augsburg
8 Peutinger House with Roman stone monuments
9 Town Hall, Golden Hall and Perlachturm
10 Augustus Fountain
11 Mercury Fountain
12 Maximilianmuseum
1 Privathotel Riegele, Viktoriastr. 4, www. hotel-riegele.de, 0049(0)821 509000, V
13 Arsenal with "Roman camp" exhibition
14 Fugger City Palace
15 Fuggerei
16 Gate „Vogeltor"
17 Archaeological recess
18 Basilica of SS. Ulrich and Afra
19 Botanical Gardens
N
O
S
W
1 km
2 km
3 km
Gersthofen
Oberhausen
LECH
Augsburg
WERTACH
Göggingen
Universität
"Siebentischwald" wood

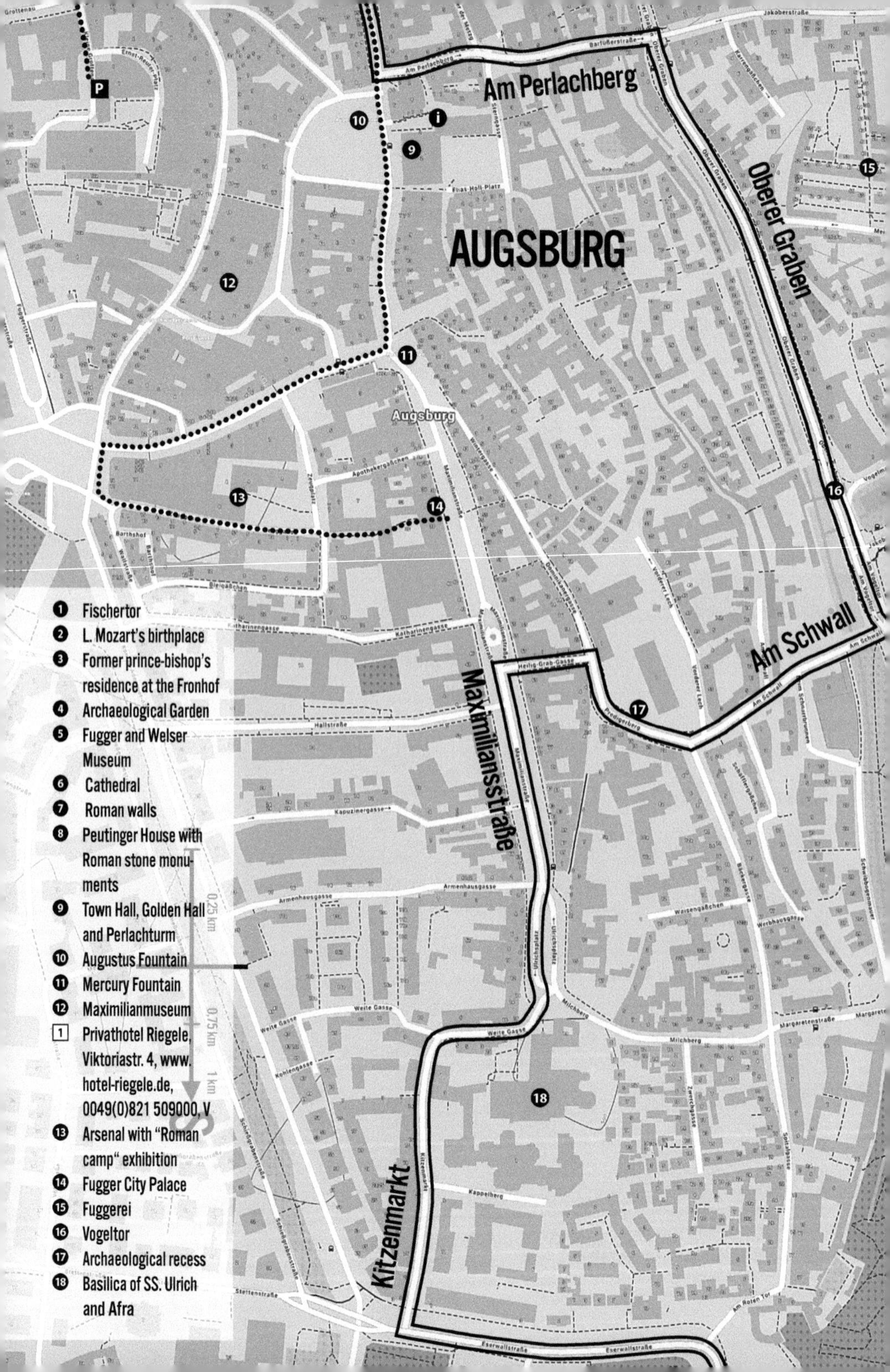
AUGSBURG
Am Perlachberg
Oberer Graben
Am Schwall
Maximiliansstraße
Kitzenmarkt
Augsburg
❶ Fischertor
❷ L. Mozart's birthplace
❸ Former prince-bishop's residence at the Fronhof
❹ Archaeological Garden
❺ Fugger and Welser Museum
❻ Cathedral
❼ Roman walls
❽ Peutinger House with Roman stone monuments
❾ Town Hall, Golden Hall and Perlachturm
❿ Augustus Fountain
⓫ Mercury Fountain
⓬ Maximilianmuseum
1 Privathotel Riegele, Viktoriastr. 4, www.hotel-riegele.de, 0049(0)821 509000, V
⓭ Arsenal with "Roman camp" exhibition
⓮ Fugger City Palace
⓯ Fuggerei
⓰ Vogeltor
⓱ Archaeological recess
⓲ Basilica of SS. Ulrich and Afra
0,25 km
0,75 km
1 km

Magnificent road in the footsteps of the Romans . Photo (4): Regio Augsburg Tourismus GmbH

Cyclists in the „Fuggerei

Golden hall

Roman wall south of the cathedral

At the town hall square. Photo: Christine Pemsl

The Lechfeld is a strikingly flat gravel plain that gained tragic fame after the Battle of Lechfeld against Hungary in 955. There were already settlements here in Roman times. Historians believe that the Roman road station Ad Novas, marked on the ancient road map Tabula Peutingeriana, was located in Igling. Another fortress from the Late Roman Empire is believed to have stood in Untermeitingen. In the south, Augsburg borders the relatively new town of Königsbrunn, where you can visit a Temple of Mithras. Recent settlement of the area only occurred in the early 19th century. Like the towns up to Obermeitingen, Königsbrunn is part of the district of Augsburg. It borders the district of Landsberg am Lech to the south. From the Lechfeld, you can clearly see long sections of the Roman road, which runs steadily towards the Alps. The hiking route takes you through picturesque towns along the old country road. Graben is the home town of Hans Fugger.

Where the king's fountains stand

On the order of the royal government of Swabia and Neuburg, two fountains were built on the long, straight road through Königsbrunn in 1833. The road largely follows the route of the old Roman road, and the fountains were intended to provide water to passersby and their animals. Three years later, the first settlers built their houses near the king's fountains. In 1967, Königsbrunn ('king's fountain') was granted town privileges. There is plenty to see here. The open-air Mercateum is the world's largest accessible globe that uses historical cartography. It shows a copy of the Tabula Peutingeriana, the first road map of Europe. It was produced by the Romans. There is an archaeological museum near the town hall. The Temple of Mithras at the municipal cemetery on Wertachstraβe is open to the public around the clock. Mithraism originated in Asia Minor and paved the way for Christianity. When the latter became the state religion in the fourth century, Mithraism came to be considered a competitor.

■ Archaeological museum, Markpl. 7, 86343 Königsbrunn, +49 (0)8231 606 260, open on every third Sunday of the month, 10 am–12 noon, guided tours from 10–11 am or upon prior agreement.

■ Mercateum, Königsallee 1, +49 (0)8231 919 573, open 1 May–31 October, every Sun and public holiday 2–7 pm, guided tours at 2:30 pm. Additional tours available upon agreement, www.mercateum.de

Continuing your journey through the Lechfeld region

Right after you cross the highway, you will see a gravel path on each side. It is called Via Claudia Augusta and, indeed, corresponds to the Roman route. Between Königsbrunn and Untermeitingen, you will find the longest intact and visible section of a Roman road in Germany. It measures 11 kilometers. The Via Claudia Augusta is particularly easy to spot as a grassy ridge in the northern new-build estate in Kleinaitingen and in a meadow, just north of a replicated milestone in Untermeitingen. In the town of Oberottmarshaushausen, the travel route takes a left and then continues in a straight line, following the old connecting road through a large, flat agricultural landscape and the attractive town centers of Kleinaitingen, Graben, Untermeitingen, Obermetingen, Hurlach and Unterigling. There used to be a ford near Untermeitingen until the 19th century. It was the only Lech crossing in the entire Lechfeld. The aristocratic Von Imhof family also shaped the development of the town. Their little palace houses the local library today. Both Schloss Igling castle and Schloss Hurlach castle are privately owned. The town hall of Igling occupies a particularly attractive, old building.

Overnight and camping possibilities in the maps and in the appendix

Questions and information about the subsection

■ Up to Untermeitingen: Hotline Regio Augsburg, 0049(0)821 50 2070

■ From Obermeitingen: Hotline Tourismusverband Ammersee-Lech, 0049(0)8191 128 247

■ Hotline Via Claudia Augusta, 0043(0)664 27 63 555

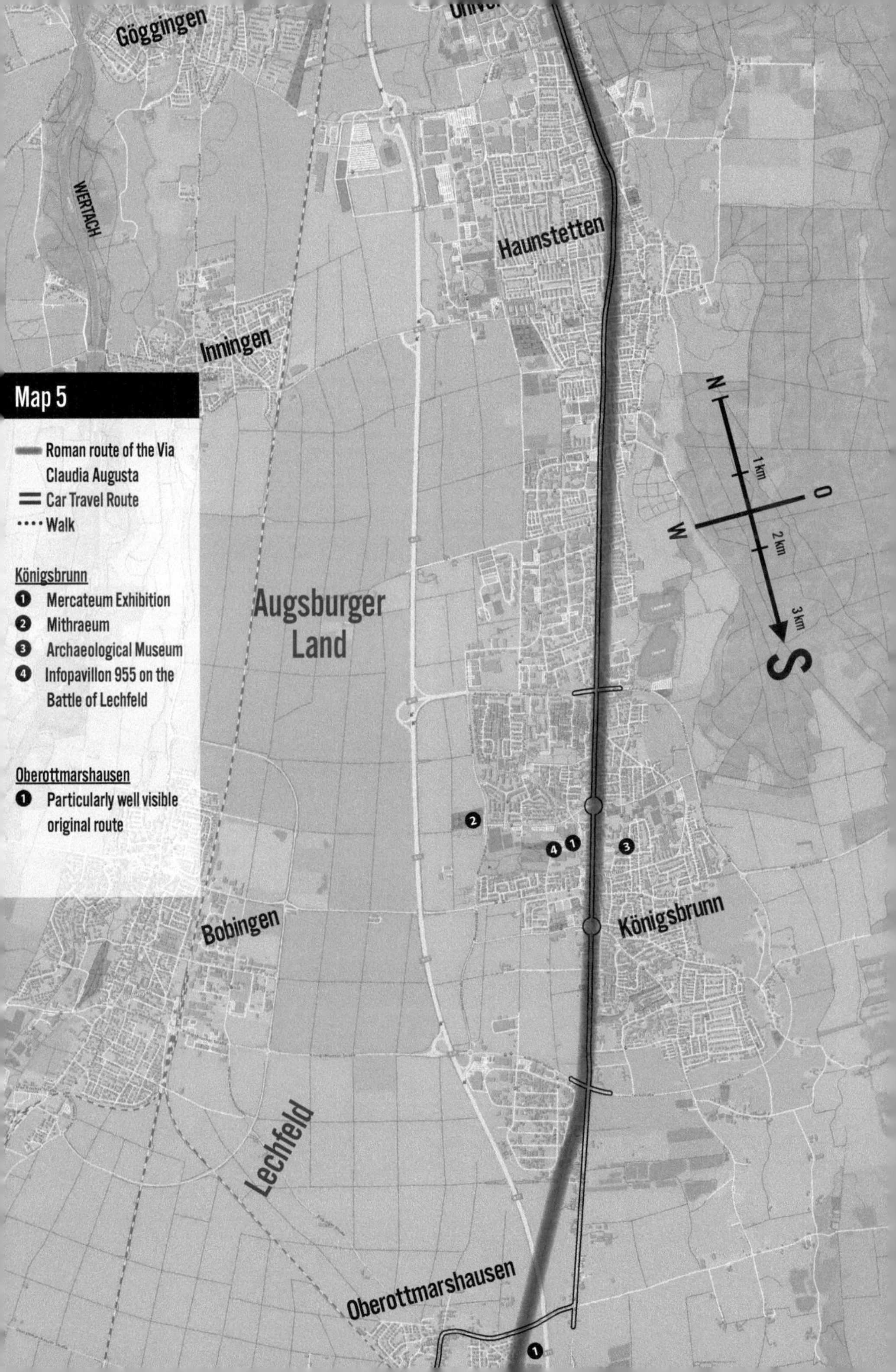
Map 5
Roman route of the Via Claudia Augusta
Car Travel Route
Walk
Königsbrunn
1 Mercateum Exhibition
2 Mithraeum
3 Archaeological Museum
4 Infopavillon 955 on the Battle of Lechfeld
Oberottmarshausen
1 Particularly well visible original route
Göggingen
WERTACH
Inningen
Haunstetten
Augsburger Land
Bobingen
Königsbrunn
Lechfeld
Oberottmarshausen
N
O
W
S
1 km
2 km
3 km

A walk-on globe with historical maps.

The mythrum at the cemetery of Königsbrunn. 2 Photo: Tschaikner

The old town of Landsberg behind the prominent Lech weir.

The main square with the lard tower, through which the salt road entered

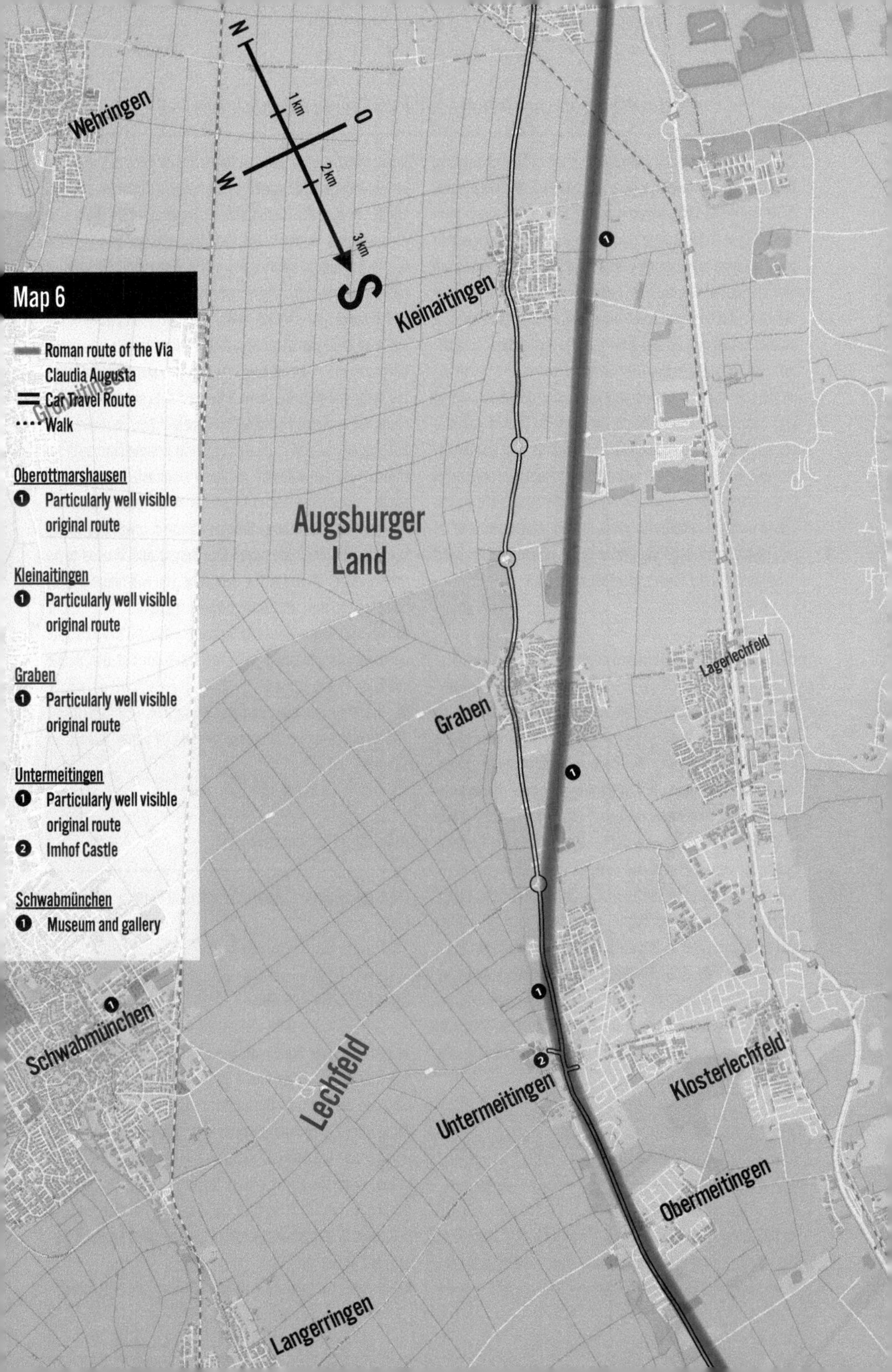

N
O
W
S
1 km
2 km
3 km
Map 6
Roman route of the Via Claudia Augusta
Car Travel Route
Walk
Oberottmarshausen
1 Particularly well visible original route
Kleinaitingen
1 Particularly well visible original route
Graben
1 Particularly well visible original route
Untermeitingen
1 Particularly well visible original route
2 Imhof Castle
Schwabmünchen
1 Museum and gallery
Wehringen
Kleinaitingen
Augsburger Land
Graben
Lagerlechfeld
Schwabmünchen
Lechfeld
Untermeitingen
Klosterlechfeld
Obermeitingen
Langerringen

The important salt road from Reichenhall to Munich crossed the Via Claudia Augusta here on its way to Switzerland. Duke Henry the Lion moved it a little way to the south from Kaufering in 1158. During that project, he had a bridge built and expanded the existing castle to protect it. The new complex was called the Castrum Landespurch. Nestled between the Lech and its high banks and overlooked by the castle, a settlement sprang up and grew rapidly. It would become the town of Landsberg in the 13th century. Today, the town to the west of the Lech is considerably larger, and its modern urban area dates back to the 19th century. The Via Claudia Augusta crossed some of the municipality westwards. Just like the river, it played an important role in the economic development of the town. The medieval old town is only accessible via the bridge over the Lech or its gates. It still retains some of its repeatedly expanded medieval walls. A recently redesigned main square is the town's greatest attraction.

Route to the medieval old town

The old town is located on the salt road rather than the Via Claudia Augusta. Before you catch your first glimpse of the old town behind the weir, you have an opportunity to explore the Mutterturm tower in the park by the river. Hubert von Herkomer built it in memory of his mother. It resembles a Norman keep. The renowned artist lived and worked in England, but he left his paintings and designs to his old home town. You can see them in the Herkomer Museum in the tower, which in itself is an extravagant example of an artist's living and working space in the 19th century. ■ Vorderer Anger 274, phone: +49 (0)8191 42 296, opening hours: upon arrangement by phone (closed on Sundays). You can leave your car by the river while you visit the Mutterturm, take photos of the weir, or meander through the old town. There is also the Schlossberg parking garage.

A walk through the old town

Most of the medieval main square of the town is reserved for pedestrians, as are the majority of its pretty alleyways. The striking tower is called Schöner Turm ('beautiful tower') or Schmalzturm. In the historical town hall, the ornate building across the road, you can find a tourist information office. The facade was designed by Dominikus Zimmermann, the builder of the Wieskirche church. He used to be the mayor of Landsberg. To get to the river, take the Salzgasse on the left of the tourist information office. The municipal utilities operate an outdoor swimming complex right next to the river, which makes for a lovely swim. The pretty alleyways of the old town take you all the way to the Sandauer Tor gate in the northern part of the old town. On your way there, you will pass the historical shoe museum, which exhibits shoes from eight centuries alongside a collection of celebrities' footwear. The Baroque-esque parish church of Maria Himmelfahrt with its three naves and splendid vestibule emphasizes the considerably larger influence of this town in the past. Head from the main square through the Schmalzturm tower and up the Lechberg to reach the paved Alte Bergstraße: it used to be the salt road. On top of the Lechberg, you will find the town museum and the Late Gothic Bayertor gate.

■ Von-Helfenstein-Gasse 426, phone: +49 (0)8191 128 360, open from April to January, Tue to Fri: 2–5 pm; Sat, Sun, public holidays: 11 am–5 pm.

■ Hist. shoe museum, Vorderer Anger 274, +49 (0)8191 42 296, opening hours: upon arrangement by phone (closed on Sundays).

Rejoining the Roman road

Cross the bridge and follow the salt road to rejoin the Roman road.

Special: Lake Ammer

Historically, they are connected by the Via Claudia Augusta and the Salt Road, the towns on the Lech, the city of Landsberg and the towns on the western shore of Lake Ammersee. Today, they are connected by an extensive cycling and hiking network and the common vacation region „Ammersee-Lech". In the region the guest relaxes together with the population and enjoys the advantages of the area. The third largest lake in Bavaria is surrounded by rolling hills, meadows, moors, forests and idyllic villages.

Ammersee offers plenty of variety in water sports activities -

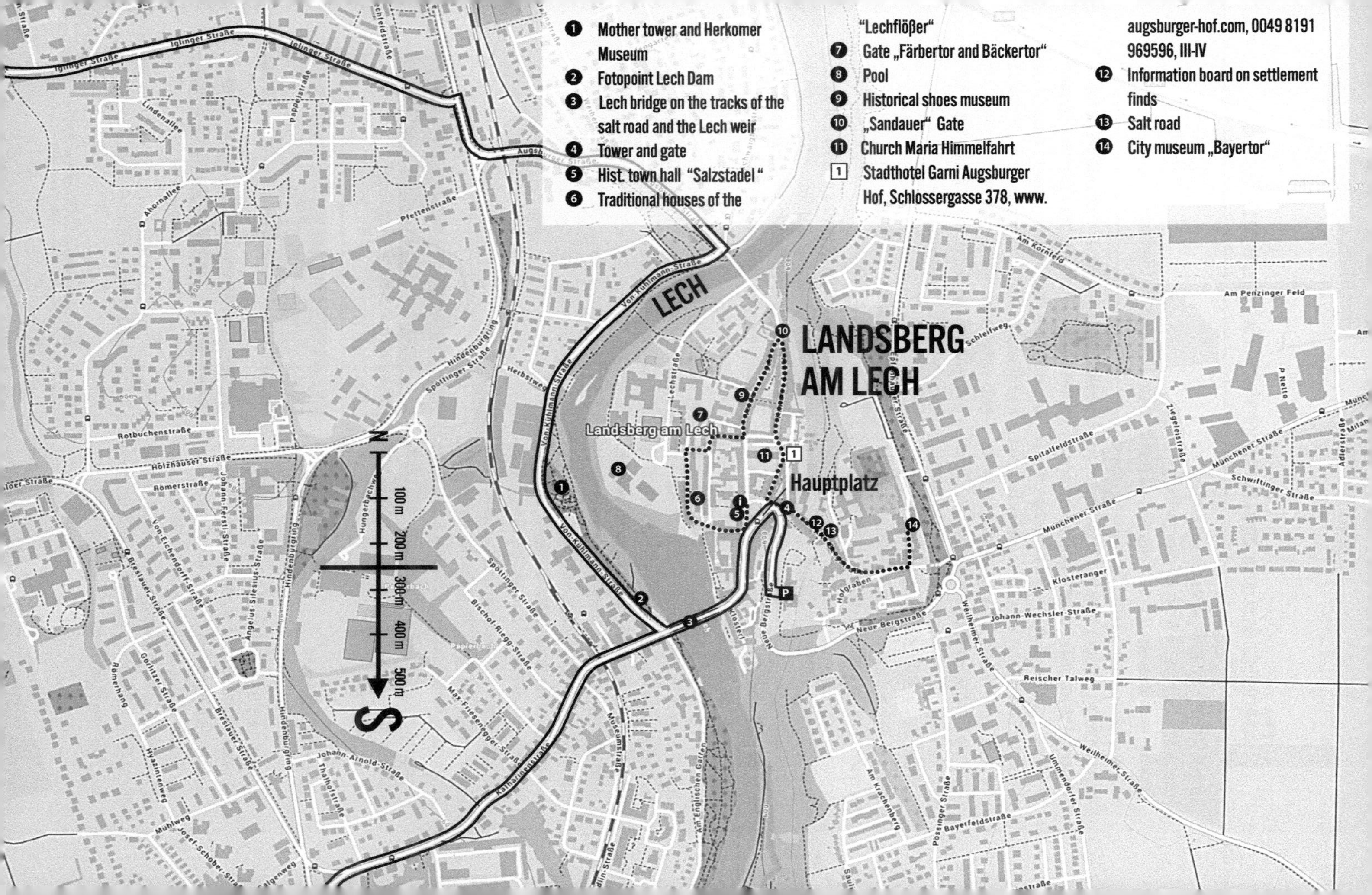

1 Mother tower and Herkomer Museum
2 Fotopoint Lech Dam
3 Lech bridge on the tracks of the salt road and the Lech weir
4 Tower and gate
5 Hist. town hall "Salzstadel"
6 Traditional houses of the "Lechflößer"
7 Gate „Färbertor and Bäckertor"
8 Pool
9 Historical shoes museum
10 „Sandauer" Gate
11 Church Maria Himmelfahrt
1 Stadthotel Garni Augsburger Hof, Schlossergasse 378, www.augsburger-hof.com, 0049 8191 969596, III-IV
12 Information board on settlement finds
13 Salt road
14 City museum „Bayertor"
LANDSBERG AM LECH
Hauptplatz
LECH
Landsberg am Lech
N
100 m
200 m
300 m
400 m
500 m
S

Between Landsberg and Schongau, the route leads crosses the Fuchstal valley to Epfach, the Roman Abodiacum before following the high banks of the Lech to Kinsau, Hohenfurch and Altenstadt, the mother parish of Schongau. Fuchstal is the valley of the Wiesbach river, a tributary of the Lech. It sits between the high banks of the Lech and a forested ridge to the west, next to the towns of Unterdießen, Asch, Leeder and Denklingen. 'Fuchs' is German for 'fox': the valley is said to be named for the brown color of its fields in fall. Just before Hohenfurch in the district of Weilheim-Schongau, you will climb the first hills since Donau-Ries. The villages in this section are particularly pretty and traditional. History enthusiasts will doubtlessly enjoy a visit to the site of the former Roman fortress of Abodiacum on the Lorenzberg, situated on a peninsula in the riverbend near Epfach.

The route from Landsberg to Epfach

Between Erpfting and Ellighofen, the travel route follows the original Roman road. In Ellinghofen, it forks off the old route to take you through the lovely villages of the Fuchstal valley. Unterdießen is overlooked by a castle built in 1589. In Oberdießen, you can visit the Malura Museum with paintings, drawings, watercolour works and collages by the Munich-born artist Oswald Malura: ■ 86944 Oberdießen, am Mühlweg 2, phone +49 (0)8243 3638. Asch has a particularly large number of old houses and a chestnut-lined avenue. Archaeologists have found that the parish church is the successor of a wooden church from the 9th century. The interior of St. Michael's church on a hill above Denklingen resembles the famous Wieskirche church in may ways. Near Denklingen, you rejoin the original route to head to Epfach, which occupies a peninsula in the Lech loop. The forest to the west of Denklingen offers an adventure path with a viewing platform on a Roman tower.

The Roman Abodiacum

A Roman fortress used to stand on the Lorenzberg hill. Today, the Lorenzkapelle chapel occupies the site. Visit the little Roman museum in Epfach for an impression of the old complex. This town has a particularly famous son: Claudius Paternus Clementianus served as the governor of North Africa. ■ Museum, Via Claudia 16, 86920 Epfach, +49 (0)8243 9601–0, open to the public 9 am–5 pm all year round.

From Abodiacum to Altenstadt

Between Epfach and Hohenfurch, the route follows the high bank of the Lech. You might want to take a detour to Kinsau on the way, which slopes down to the river on several terraces. Hohenfurch is located on the B17, the successor of the Via Claudia Augusta, which crosses under the travel route in the town center. The town is shaped by the River Schönach, and our route follows its course towards Schwabniederhofen.

The original parish of Schongau

Altenstadt is not only the predecessor settlement of the town of Schongau, which was later relocated. The Roman road also passed through the parish area. The proud town dedicated its own square to the Via Claudia Augusta with a replica of a piece of Roman road. A cross-section shows its construction from various layers of stone and gravel. In the village there is also one of the most beautiful sacral buildings on the Via Claudia Augusta, the Romanesque vaulted basilica.

Regional cuisine like 2000 years ago

■ Gasthof Janser, Altenstadt, Burgstraße 2, 0049(0)8861 22 17 26

Overnight and camping possibilities in the maps and in the appendix

Questions and information about the subsection

■ Up to Kinsau: Hotline Ammersee-Lech, 0049(0)8191 128 246

■ From Hohenfurch: Hotline Pfaffenwinkel, 0049(0)8861 211 3200

■ Hotline Via Claudia Augusta, 0043(0)664 27 63 55

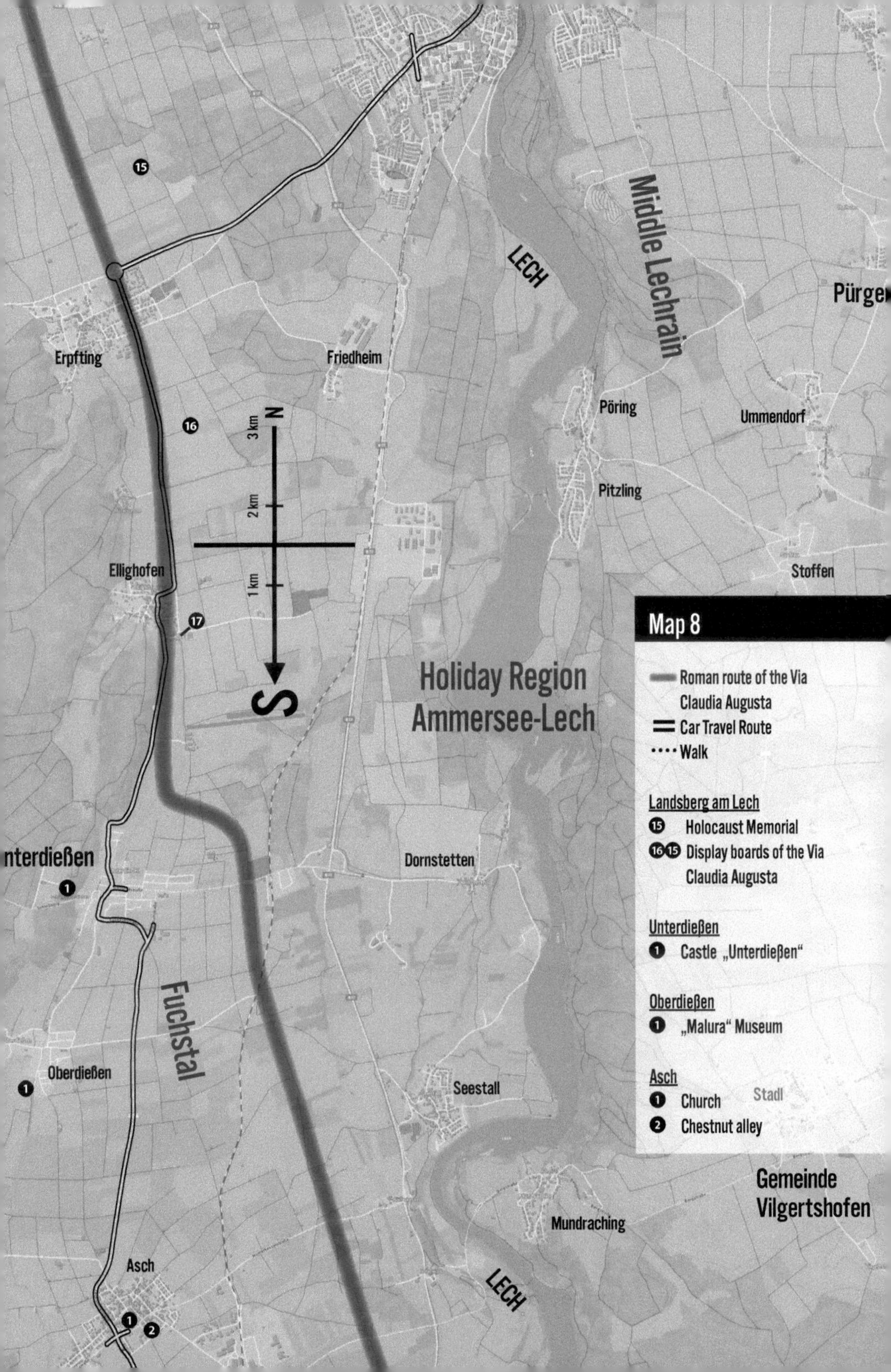
Map 8
Roman route of the Via Claudia Augusta
Car Travel Route
Walk
Landsberg am Lech
15 Holocaust Memorial
16 15 Display boards of the Via Claudia Augusta
Unterdießen
1 Castle „Unterdießen“
Oberdießen
1 „Malura“ Museum
Asch
1 Church
2 Chestnut alley
Stadl
Middle Lechrain
LECH
Pürge
Erpfting
Friedheim
Pöring
Ummendorf
Pitzling
Stoffen
Ellighofen
N
3 km
2 km
1 km
S
Holiday Region Ammersee-Lech
nterdießen
Dornstetten
Fuchstal
Oberdießen
Seestall
Gemeinde Vilgertshofen
Mundraching
LECH
Asch

The Romanesque vaulted basilica of Altenstadt. Photos (2): Tschaikner

The Lorenz Chapel on the Lorenzberg in front of the Lech steep bank

The old town of Schongau on the Lechumlaufberg mountain

Juggler photos (2): Tourist information Schongau

The Peitingen Villa Rustica

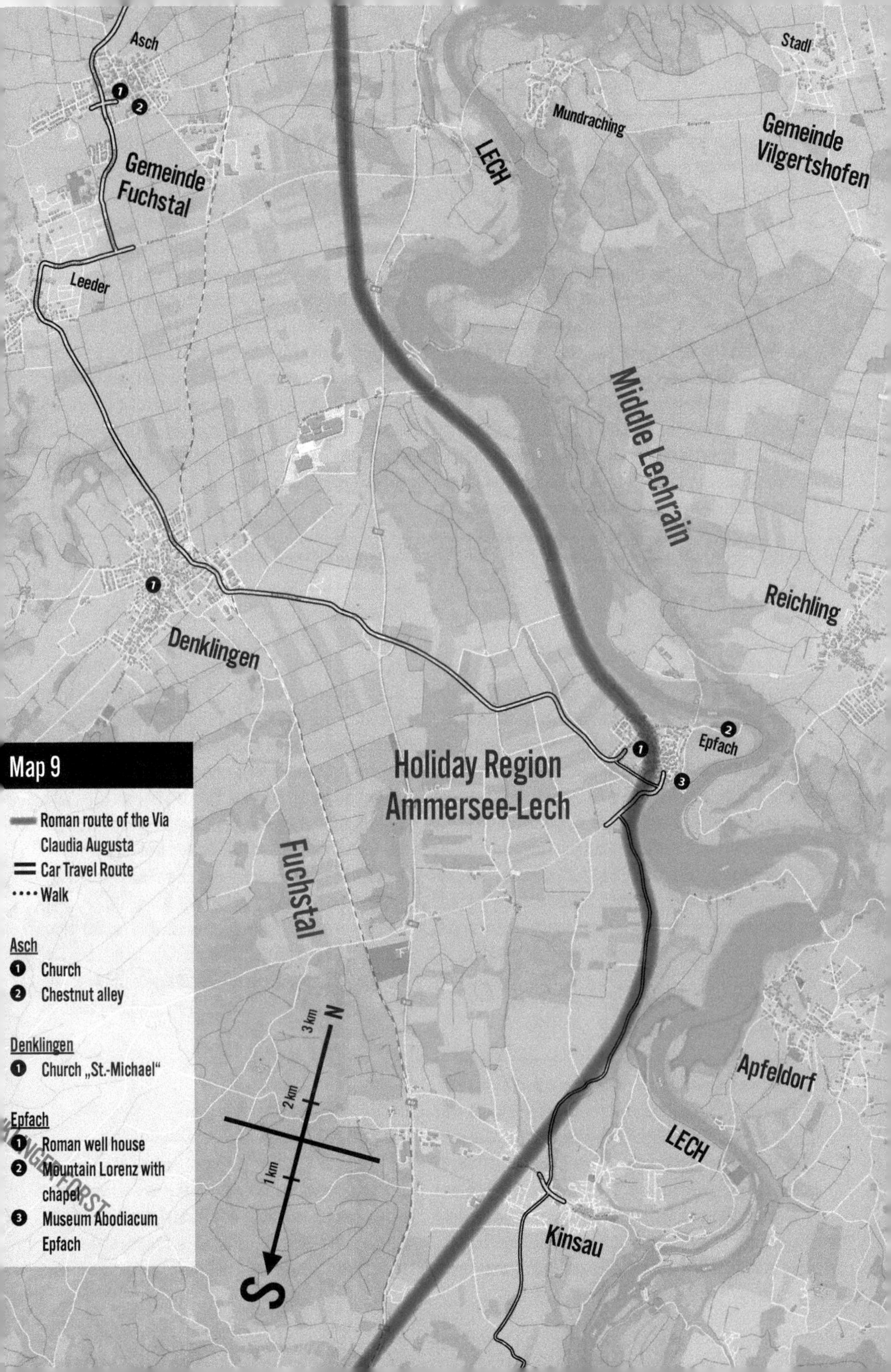

Asch
Stadl
Mundraching
Gemeinde Vilgertshofen
LECH
Gemeinde Fuchstal
Leeder
Middle Lechrain
Reichling
Denklingen
Epfach
Holiday Region Ammersee-Lech
Fuchstal
Apfeldorf
LECH
Kinsau
N
S
1 km
2 km
3 km
Map 9
Roman route of the Via Claudia Augusta
Car Travel Route
Walk
Asch
1 Church
2 Chestnut alley
Denklingen
1 Church „St.-Michael"
Epfach
1 Roman well house
2 Mountain Lorenz with chapel
3 Museum Abodiacum Epfach

During Roman times, another Roman road crossed the Alps via Garmisch and the Brennerpass. It was also called the Via Claudia, but it was not yet 'Augusta' (=imperial). In the Middle Ages, the roads that remained in use were dubbed the Upper Road and Lower Road. Their crossroads was an excellent spot to do business during Roman times and beyond. In Peiting to the east of the Lech, a Villa Rustica documents the outstanding domestic culture of the Romans. The town of Schongau, which was moved to the safer hill from its mother parish of Altenstadt in the 13th century, also flourished thanks to the nearby traffic hub. In 1331, the town was even granted the right to mint and issue its own coins. The old town has retained its entire town walls and can only be accessed through its gates. A large number of religious buildings also bear testimony to wealth of this region, which is called Pfaffenwinkel. Schongau and Peiting are considered its gateway. Wieskirche Pilgrimage Church is its best-known sacred building and a UNESCO World Heritage Site.

The route to Schongau

The old road from Altenstadt to Schongau first takes you down a dip, which used to be a part of the river. Millennia ago, the hill on which the old town stands used to be a meander cutoff of the Lech and almost completely surrounded by water. The Maxtor gate is the historical entrance to the old town. Our route takes us through the Münztor gate instead, which was created later to facilitate the flow of traffic. You can find an underground parking garage and a parking lot inside the walls. Save yourself the parking fee and park on the foot of the hill surrounded by the Lech: the walk across the Frauenberg and through the Frauentor gate will give you an impression of the old town walls.

A walk inside the town walls

If you want a particularly memorable experience of the town, take one of the guided tours on offer. They include a walk after dark and a tour for children. Alternatively, the old town is easily explored on your own. Walk through the Hl. Geist convent church and the courtyard of the former Carmelite monastery to get to an accessible section of the wall. Pass the former district court and continue to the Münzgebäude building at the eponymous Münztor gate. The Maxtor is one of the most beautiful gates in town. It also functions as the yard gate to Schloss Schongau, a little palace once owned by the Wittelsbach dynasty. Today, it houses the district administration. To find out more about the history of Schongau, visit the barrier-free town museum in the former St. Eramus hospital church. It offers a lot of information on coins, in particular, and its exhibits include Roman ones as well as ones minted in Schongau. Like the Frauentor, the gate of the Polizeidienerturm can only be entered on foot. The Gothic Ballenhaus used to facilitate trade on the salt road. Its location in the center of the square emphasizes the significance of the trade routes for Schongau. The Maria Himmelfahrt parish church is a successor of two old buildings, one Romanesque and one Gothic. ■ Stadtmuseum, Christophstr. 55-57, +49 (0)8861 254–605. Wed, Sat, Sun and public holidays, 2 pm–5 pm.

To the market town of Peiting

Like the old Roman road, our travel route leaves the old town of Schongau via the steep Lechberg. On the right side of the river, you will find Plantsch, a public waterpark and spa with indoor and outdoor pools and sauna facilities. There is also a lido on the Lechsee, just above the dam. This part of the deep, narrow Lechtal valley resembles a fjord. You can see some former inns near the bridge, where the old road towards Peiting crossed the river. A little way downriver, there is a fairytale forest with a petting zoo for children. Originally, the road ran across the hill between Schongau and Peiting. Today, it leads around it. The name of Peiting is probably derived from the Peutinger dynasty, who settled there as early as the sixth century. The center of the market town offers plenty of places to shop, eat and drink. Visit the museum in the Klösterle to find out about the history of the region and the locals' way of life. ■ Kapellenstraße 1, +49 (0)8861 6535, open Wednesdays, 2–5 pm, groups are asked to make a booking.

Peiting's Villa Rustica

The first traces of human settlement east of the Lech date back as far as the third century. A shelter on a former Roman country estate spanning several hectares contains a traditional bath house. The villa is a luxurious compound house built around an open court, a layout that is uncommon in Germany. It was inhabited between the mid-second until the fourth century. An inscribed lead tablet that was found here has captured the imagination of many visitors: it is believed to be a love spell. All around the shelter, there is a Roman herb garden with culinary and medical plants.

■ +49 (0)8861 6535, self-guided visits are welcome at any time (information panels available); guided tours upon prior arrangement.

Special: The Pfaffenwinkel

It would be difficult to find a region with a greater number and density of high-class monasteries and pilgrimage churches than the Pfaffenwinkel. The village priest Franz Sales Gailer coined the catchy name in the 18th century, referring to his own profession. Pfaffe (plural Pfaffen) is an old Bavarian term for priest. The Wessobrunn Prayer, one of the oldest poetic works in the German language, was discovered in the Wessobrunn monastery. The famous stucco-workers of the Wessobrunn School also came from the region. Two of their representatives, the brothers Dominikus and Johannes Baptist Zimmermann, helped an entire building to world fame with their artistic skills - the pilgrimage church of the flagellated Savior on the Wies. The world cultural heritage site „Wieskirche", as the sacred building is also called, is a first-class tourist magnet. A circuit that connects some of the most worth seeing sacred buildings and starts and ends at the Via Claudia Augusta: Gothic vault basilica in Altenstadt, Maria Himmelfahrt parish church in Schongau, Vilgertshofen pilgrimage church, Wessobrunn monastery, Bernried monastery, Polling monastery, Hohenpeißenberg pilgrimage church, Rottenbuch monastery, Ettal monastery, Wieskirche church and monastery in Steingaden, and the Georgskirche church on the Auerberg in Bernbeuren.

History(s):

The northernmost foothills of the last ice age, known as the Würm Ice Age, can be found towards Kinsau north of Hohenfurch. Torrential rivers emerged from the huge glaciers, taking huge amounts of debris with them and creating large gravel fields. With increasing warming, the glaciers receded further and further. The Lech and Ammer rivers emerged and were able to burrow deeper and deeper over time, creating veritable gorges. At the mountain, where since the Middle Ages the old town of Schongau is located, the Lech meets harder material and had to flow around it on the west side. About 5300 years ago, however, the torrential glacial river managed to break through and was able to continue flowing directly to the north on the eastern side of the mountain. In the east, an old water arm was initially preserved, which can still be seen in the terrain today and is called „Lazy Ditch". Thus, the mountain was once completely surrounded by water. One speaks of a former Lech circulating island.

Regional cuisine like 2000 years ago

■ Gasthof Zechenschenke, Peiting, Zechenstraße 2, 0049(0)8861 22 17 26

Overnight and camping possibilities in the maps and in the appendix

Questions and information about the subsection

■ Hotline Pfaffenwinkel, Tel. 0049(0)8861 211 3200
■ Touristinfo Schongau, Münzstraße 1, 0049(0)8861 214 181
■ Touristinfo Peiting, Ammergauer Straße 2, 0049(0)8861 6535
■ Hotline Via Claudia Augusta, 0043(0)664 27 63 555

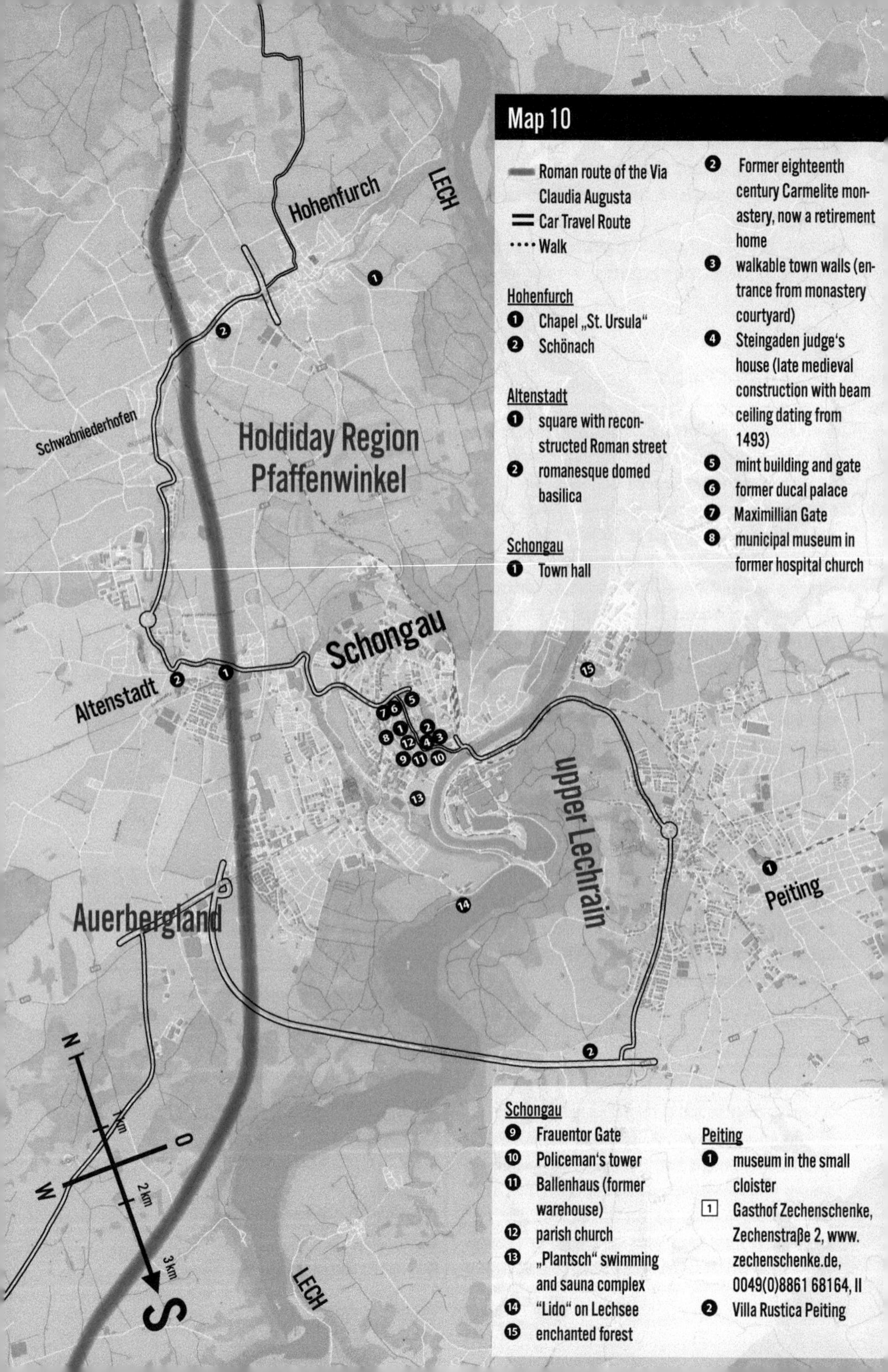
Map 10
Roman route of the Via Claudia Augusta
Car Travel Route
Walk
Hohenfurch
1 Chapel „St. Ursula“
2 Schönach
Altenstadt
1 square with reconstructed Roman street
2 romanesque domed basilica
Schongau
1 Town hall
2 Former eighteenth century Carmelite monastery, now a retirement home
3 walkable town walls (entrance from monastery courtyard)
4 Steingaden judge‘s house (late medieval construction with beam ceiling dating from 1493)
5 mint building and gate
6 former ducal palace
7 Maximillian Gate
8 municipal museum in former hospital church
Schongau
9 Frauentor Gate
10 Policeman‘s tower
11 Ballenhaus (former warehouse)
12 parish church
13 „Plantsch“ swimming and sauna complex
14 “Lido“ on Lechsee
15 enchanted forest
Peiting
1 museum in the small cloister
1 Gasthof Zechenschenke, Zechenstraße 2, www.zechenschenke.de, 0049(0)8861 68164, II
2 Villa Rustica Peiting
Hohenfurch
LECH
Schwabniederhofen
Holdiday Region Pfaffenwinkel
Schongau
Altenstadt
upper Lechrain
Peiting
Auerbergland
LECH
N
O
W
S
1 km
2 km
3 km

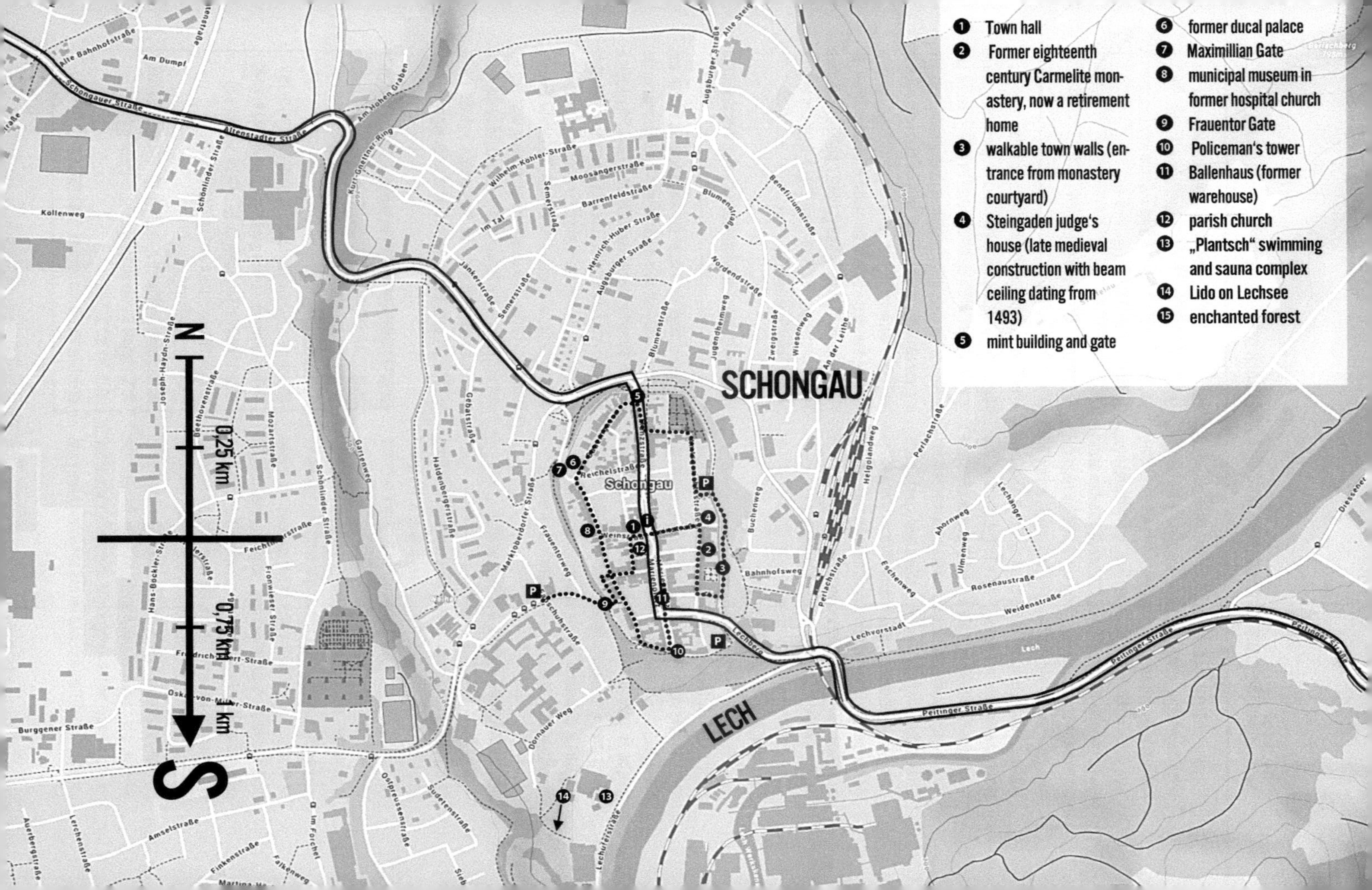

1 Town hall
2 Former eighteenth century Carmelite monastery, now a retirement home
3 walkable town walls (entrance from monastery courtyard)
4 Steingaden judge's house (late medieval construction with beam ceiling dating from 1493)
5 mint building and gate
6 former ducal palace
7 Maximillian Gate
8 municipal museum in former hospital church
9 Frauentor Gate
10 Policeman's tower
11 Ballenhaus (former warehouse)
12 parish church
13 „Plantsch“ swimming and sauna complex
14 Lido on Lechsee
15 enchanted forest
SCHONGAU
Schongau
LECH
Lech
N
S
0,25 km
0,75 km
1 km
Schongauer Straße
Altenstadter Straße
Peitinger Straße
Augsburger Straße
Lechberg
Bahnhofsweg
Frauentorweg
Reichelstraße
Am Hohen Graben
Kurt-Gnettner-Ring
Gartenweg
Schonlinder Straße
Haldenbergerstraße
Marktoberdorfer Straße
Lechvorstadt
Perlachstraße
Helgolandweg
Buchenweg
Blumenstraße
Jugendheimweg
Nordendstraße
Zweigstraße
Wiesenweg
An der Leithe
Benefiziumstraße
Semerstraße
Jankerstraße
Gebatstraße
Im Tal
Moosangerstraße
Barrenfeldstraße
Heinrich-Huber Straße
Wilhelm-Köhler-Straße
Mozartstraße
Beethovenstraße
Joseph-Haydn-Straße
Hans-Böckler-Straße
Fronwieser Straße
Friedrich-Ebert-Straße
Oskar-von-Miller-Straße
Burggener Straße
Lerchenstraße
Auerbergstraße
Amselstraße
Finkenstraße
Falkenweg
Im Forchet
Ostpreussenstraße
Sudetenstraße
Dornauer Weg
Lechuferstraße
Eschenweg
Ahornweg
Ulmenweg
Lechanger
Rosenaustraße
Weidenstraße
Köllenweg
Am Dumpf
Alte Bahnhofstraße
Alte Steig

08 The Auerbergland: lands around a foothill that has seen settlements for millennia (maps 10 - 12)

The municipalities in the Alpine foothills around the Auerberg initiated the initiative to revive the entire length of the Via Claudia Augusta. In this region, the Auerbergland, there are particularly many visible sections of the old Roman road. Its inhabitants have come up with many interesting ways of drawing attention to this important part of their heritage. There are quite a few historical highlights here: the site of millennia-old settlements around the Auerberg, the rafters' village of Lechbruck am See, the Bavarian Via Claudia Augusta info center, and the Forggensee boat tour that follows the Roman road are well worth your time. Verdant hills and forests punctuated by lakes and set against a spectacular Alpine backdrop make the region a nature lover's paradise. Its pretty holiday destinations have retained their authentic village atmosphere. The Roman road mostly followed the Lech through the Auerbergland. Some parts crossed the river in the area where it was dammed to create the Forggensee lake.

The listed farmhouses of Burggen

The route initially takes you from Schongau towards Marktoberdorf, then forks onto a little road that leads to Burggen over picturesque hills covered in forests and meadows. In the town, the road bends twice. The listed St.-Anna-Straβe on the right-hand side is lined with typical, regional farmhouses. The Schwarzkreuzstraβe opposite offers an observation point with lovely views of the Litzauer Lechschleife, a picturesque river loop.

Bernbeuren, the Auerberg and its museum

On the way to Bernbeuren, you will pass the beautiful natural area of Haslacher See lake. You can take a swim in the lake if you like. At the first major intersection in the town, our route turns right and then takes the next left. The Auerberg Museum is on the left. It entertainingly recounts the history of settlement on the Auerberg. The Celts already settled on this hill for its strategically favorable location. In Roman times, there used to be a craftsmen's settlement here, which produced catapult parts among other things. Researchers assume that it is the city of Damasia mentioned by Strabo. The road onto the Auerberg forks to the right after passing the museum. Alternatively, an adventure path leads through the Feuersteinschlucht gorge to the peak. It is a two-hour walk from the museum. On top of the hill, the platform on the Georgskirche church offers wonderful, panoramic views. The panoramic inn has an in-house bakery and makes for a lovely break. ■ Auerbergmuseum, Mühlenstraβe 9, +49 (0)8860 210, open from mid-April to mid-October: Sat 3–5 pm, Sun and public holidays 2–5 pm and upon prior arrangement by telephone. www.auerbergmuseum.de

The rafters' village of Lechbruch

After Lechbruck am See, the Allgäu starts. Follow the signs to Füssen. In Bavaria, the entire Via Claudia Augusta runs parallel to the Lech river, which the Romans used for transportation, too. Lechbruck has dedicated a museum to its long tradition of rafting; you can find it in the buildings opposite the tourist information office. Between 15 June and 30 September, you can book a rafting tour on the Lech at the tourist information office. ■ Flöβermuseum, Waidach 8, +49 (0)8862 / 987830, open from April to September: Thu, 5:30–7 pm, Sun: 4–6 pm and by prior booking, www.floesser-lechbruck.de

Via Claudia Augusta Information Center, Rosshaupten

Continue through the hills of the Allgäu towards Füssen and Rosshaupten. Do not miss the Sameister-Kapelle chapel on the way. The Schmutterweiher lake on the other side of the road is a swimming spot. Follow the B16 and take the exit to the village of Rosshaupten. Besides the museum, the Pfannerhaus at the central intersection also houses the Bavarian Via Claudia Augusta Information Center. Head east from the museum to see an art park dedicated to the Roman road. It is operated by the Rosshaupten artists' association. ■ Museum, Hauptstraβe 1, +49 (0)8367 364, open every day from 9 am–6 pm during the season.

Questions and information about the subsection

■ Up to Bernbeuren: Ferienreg. Pfaffenwinkel, 0049(0)8861 211 3200

■ Touristinfo Bernbeuren, Markpl. 4, 0049(0)8860 910 10

■ From Lechbruck: Ferienreg. Ostallgäu, 0049(0)8342 911 506

■ Lechbruck am See, Flöβerstr. 1, 0049(0)8862 987 830

■ Touristinfo Lechbruck am See, Flöβerstraβe 1, 0049(0)8862 987 830

■ Touristinfo Rosshaupten, Hauptstr. 10, 0049(0)8367 364

■ Touristinfo Rieden am Forggensee, Lindenweg 4, 0049(0)8362 370 25

■ Hotline Via Claudia Augusta, 0043(0)664 27 63 555

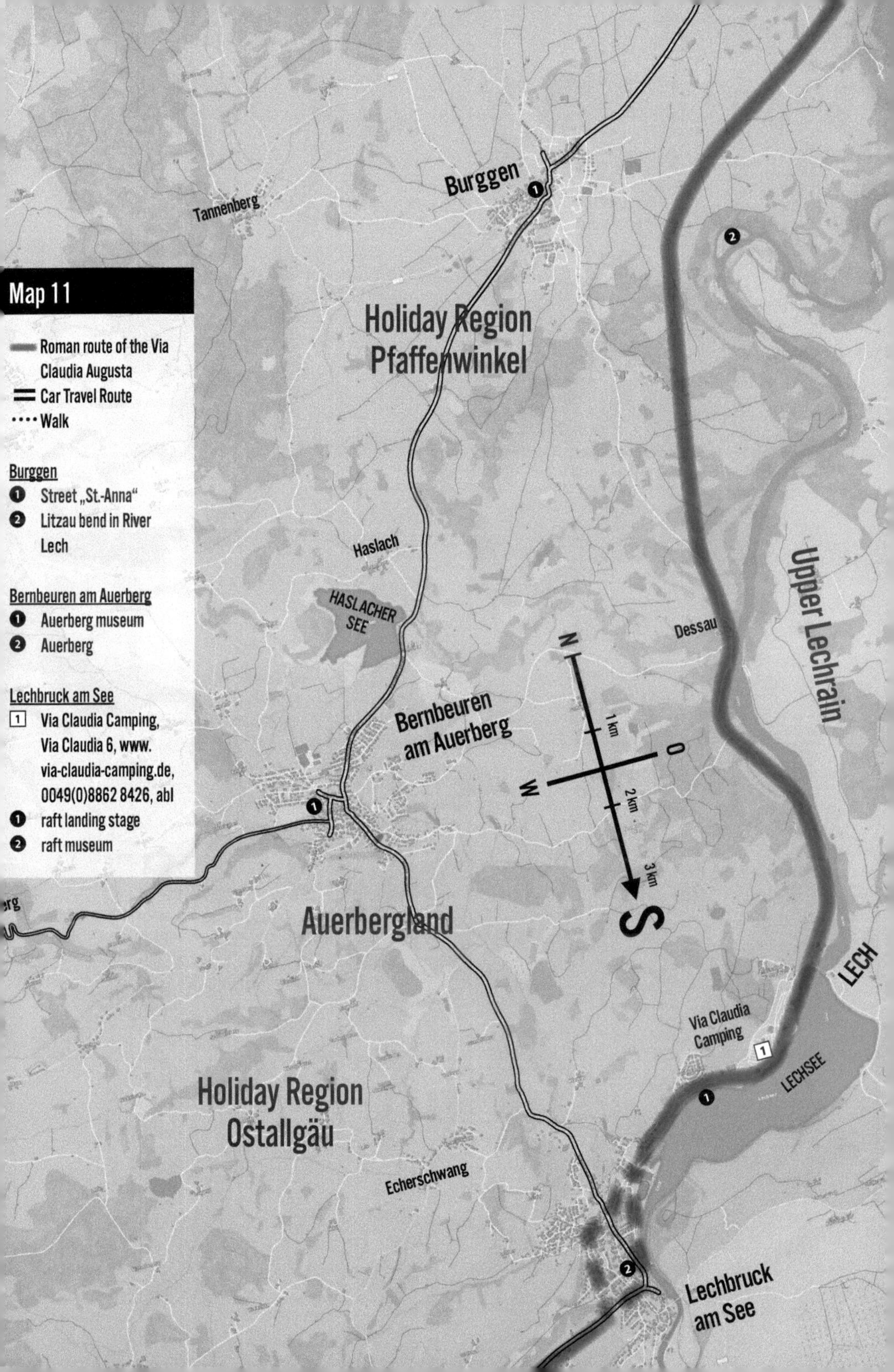
Map 11
Roman route of the Via Claudia Augusta
Car Travel Route
Walk
Burggen
❶ Street „St.-Anna“
❷ Litzau bend in River Lech
Bernbeuren am Auerberg
❶ Auerberg museum
❷ Auerberg
Lechbruck am See
1 Via Claudia Camping, Via Claudia 6, www.via-claudia-camping.de, 0049(0)8862 8426, abl
❶ raft landing stage
❷ raft museum
Burggen
Tannenberg
Holiday Region Pfaffenwinkel
Haslach
HASLACHER SEE
Dessau
Upper Lechrain
N
O
W
S
1 km
2 km
3 km
Bernbeuren am Auerberg
Auerbergland
LECH
Via Claudia Camping
LECHSEE
Holiday Region Ostallgäu
Echerschwang
Lechbruck am See

Haslach Lake and Auerberg

Farmhouse of the listed St. Anna Street. Photo: Bruno Faller

Church of St. George on the Auerberg

Raft for rafting in rafting village

Village museum „Pfannerhaus“. Photo: Reinhard Walk

Roman resting place at the Forggensee in Rieden

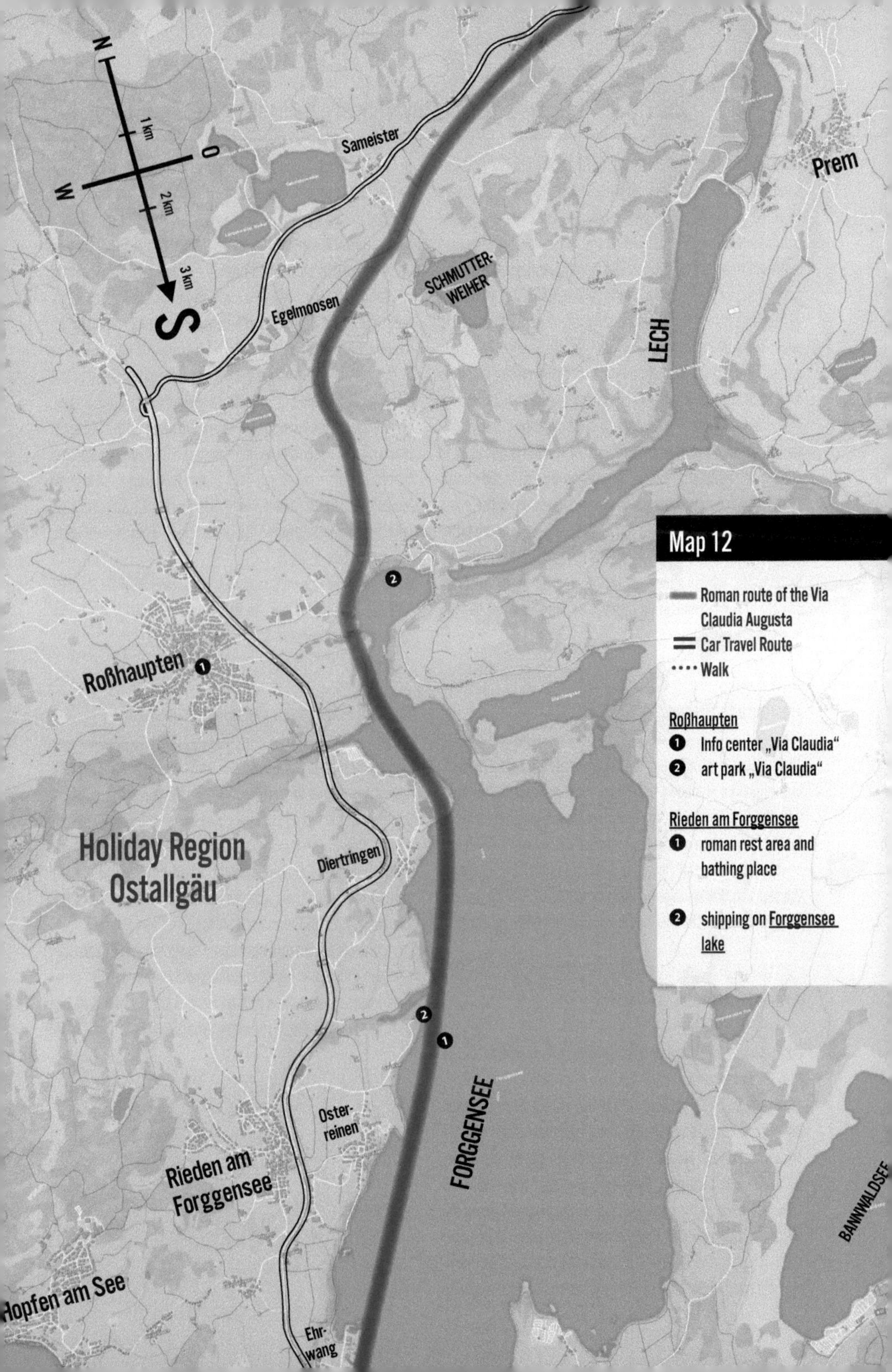
N
O
S
W
1 km
2 km
3 km
Sameister
Prem
Egelmoosen
SCHMUTTER-
WEIHER
LECH
Roßhaupten
Holiday Region
Ostallgäu
Diertringen
FORGGENSEE
Oster-
reinen
Rieden am
Forggensee
Hopfen am See
Ehr-
wang
BANNWALDSEE
Map 12
Roman route of the Via Claudia Augusta
Car Travel Route
Walk
Roßhaupten
1 Info center „Via Claudia“
2 art park „Via Claudia“
Rieden am Forggensee
1 roman rest area and bathing place
2 shipping on Forggensee lake

09 Füssen & Schwangau: the royal beauty of Allgäu (map 13)

The beautiful stretch of land where the Lech exits the Alps has been inhabited since Roman times. A Roman fortress used to stand on the Füssen's castle hill. The Via Claudia Augusta passed beneath it. The Reichenstraße, the modern promenade in the old town, corresponds exactly to the route of the Roman road. At the valley station of the Tegelberg Cable Car, remnants of a private spa from a Villa Rustica grant us a glimpse into upper-class domestic life during the Roman Empire. The foundation of medieval Füssen and its long violin-making tradition date back to Saint Magnus of Füssen, who settled here as a religious hermit in the 8th century. In the 9th century, a Benedictine monastery was founded on the spot where his cell used to stand and named after him: St. Mang's Abbey. Later, the people of Wittelsbach and Ludwig II of Bavaria discovered the spectacular natural landscape of the Alpine foothills, and the latter decided to build his fairytale castles here. You are standing in Schwangau, where guests of the Königliche Kristall-Therme spa get to unwind and let themselves be pampered just like the Romans used to do.

The route to Füssen

The Augsburgerstraße runs to the center of Füssen in a perfectly straight line. It follows the Roman road, as does its continuation, the Reichenstraße. At the Kaiser-Maximilian-Platz with its tourist information office, it becomes a pedestrian area that is a lovely place to walk and rest. To explore the old town, follow the signs to "Parkgarage im Sparkassenhaus (P5)" before you reach the center. The tourist information office is next door.

A walk through the old town

Opposite the exit of the parking garage at Hotel Hirsch, a little alley leads to the quiet part of the old town. Walk along Drehergasse, Brotmarkt and Lechhalde to the river. Before you reach the river, you will pass the Church of the Holy Spirit with its attractive Rococo facade. The Benedictine St. Mang's Abbey is right on the riverbank. After its foundation, the town grew around it. Head to the opposite bank of the Lech and enjoy the so-called 'Magnus view' (Magnusblick) of the abbey and the old town. It is one of Füssen's most beautiful vistas. Cross the inner courtyard of St. Mang's Abbey to reach the local museum of Füssen, which recounts the history of the town and its tradition of lute and violin manufacture. Head to Magnusplatz to the north of the abbey, look at the Baroque St. Mang's Church, then take the little alley up to the High Castle of Füssen. On your way up to the castle, you will be treated to many splendid views of the former summer residence of the prince-bishops of Augsburg. It is one of Bavaria's best-preserved castle complexes. Its inside is decorated with Late-Gothic illusionistic paintings. The Gothic ceiling of the knights' hall and the branch gallery of the Bavarian State Painting Collections are particularly impressive. Walk a few steps from the northeastern wing of the abbey to reach the town fountain on Reichenstraße. The pedestrian zone that begins here takes you back to Kaiser-Maximilian-Platz. ■ Museum der Stadt Füssen, Lechhalde 3, +49 (0)8362 903 143, open from April to October: Tue–Sun, 11 am–5 pm; November to March: Fri–Sun, 1–4 pm.

■ Galerien im Hohen Schloss, Magnusplatz 10, +49 (0)8362 940 162, open from April to October: Tue–Sun, 11 am–5 pm; November to March: Fri–Sun, 1–4 pm.

Through Schwangau and Hohenschwangau

At the entrance to the pedestrian zone, where the Via Claudia Augusta is closed to traffic nowadays, the travel route leaves the town to the left and crosses the Lech on the König-Ludwig-Brücke bridge. The river marks the boundary between Füssen and Schwangau. Continue straight ahead through the district of Horn to reach Schwangau. As you enter the town, pass the Königliche Kristall-Therme spa on the left. Pass the tourist information office and turn right to see the remnants of a bath in a Roman villa at the Tegelbergbahn cable car parking lot. Now, head to the royal castles of Maximilian II and Ludwig II of Bavaria, the kings of the Wittelsbach dynasty.

The bathing house of the Roman villa

During the construction of the Tegelbergbahn cable car, the remnants of a bath from a Roman country manor were discovered. It was heated by a sophisticated firing system. Protected by a shelter, it gives you an authentic impression of Roman bathing culture.

■ 0049 (0)8362 8198-0, open daily 9 am–5 pm, guided tours available upon request.

The route to Tyrol

From Hohenschwangau, head back to the König-Ludwig-Brücke bridge via Alterschrofen. Take the Tiroler Straße on the left just before you reach the bridge. It follows the Lech along the old town of Füssen towards Tyrol.

Special: The royal castles

The castles of Maximilian II and Ludwig II can be experienced from the Schwangau district of Hohenschwangau.

Hohenschwangau Castle: The ruins of the medieval Schwanstein Castle were rebuilt into Hohenschwangau Castle in neo-Gothic style between 1833 and 1837 by the Bavarian Crown Prince Maximilian, later King Maximilian II and the father of Ludwig II. The Bavarian royal family used the castle primarily as a summer residence. Ludwig II and his younger brother Otto spent large parts of their childhood and youth here. The interiors were decorated in the spirit of Romanticism with murals depicting themes from the medieval world of legends. Also worth seeing are the Schwansee Park south of Hohenschwangau and the Alpsee lake. If you're lucky, you'll meet the swans there, with whom King Ludwig had a special relationship.

Neuschwanstein Castle: High above the rushing Pöllat River, Ludwig II created a synthesis of the arts from 1869 until his death in 1886 that still bears no comparison today. The breathtaking location and fairy-tale interior design captivate visitors from all over the world every day. Ludwig II had the castle built in the style of a medieval knight's castle of the 12th/13th century. Due to his early death, however, it could not be completed. Thus, the originally planned keep is missing. Inside, only the first floor, the 3rd and 4th floors have been completed. The interiors are decorated with scenes from medieval German sagas.

■ Ticket Center Hohenschwangau, Alpseestr. 12, +49 (0)8362 930 830, open April-Sept. 8 a.m.-5 p.m. and Oct.-March 9 a.m.-3 p.m., www.ticket-center-hohenschwangau.de.

■ Museum of the Bavarian Kings: Located directly on Alpsee Lake, this museum uses state-of-the-art museum technology to tell the story of the Wittelsbach dynasty, especially Maximilian II and Ludwig II, and their castles.

Alpseestraße 27, +49 (0)8362 930 830, open April - Sept. 9 a.m. -7 p.m., Oct. - Mar. 10 a.m. - 6 p.m., the museum is barrier-free.

Regional cuisine like 2000 years ago

■ Hotel Restaurant Hirsch, Füssen, Kaiser-Maximilian-Platz 7, 0049(0)8362 93 980

■ Ruchti's Hotel & Restaurant, Füssen / Bad Faulenbach, Alatseestraße 38, 0049(0)8362 910 10

Overnight and camping possibilities in the maps and in the appendix

Questions and information about the subsection

■ Touristinfo Füssen Tourimus und Marketing, Kaiser-Maximilian-Platz 1, 0049(0)8362 93 850

■ Touristinfo Schwangau, Münchener Straße 2, 0049(0)8362 81 980

■ Hotline Via Claudia Augusta , 0043(0)664 27 63 555

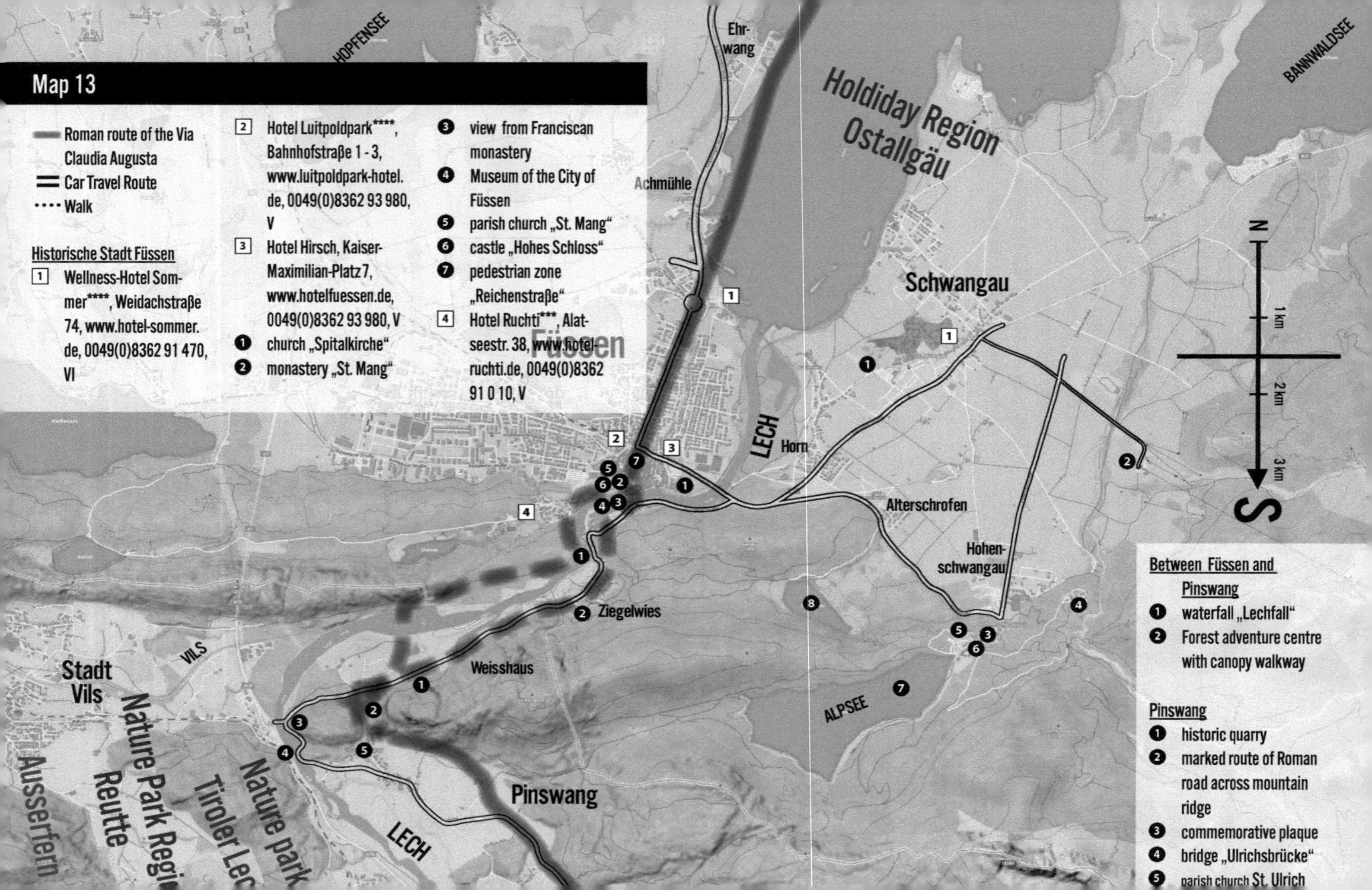
Map 13
Roman route of the Via Claudia Augusta
Car Travel Route
Walk
Historische Stadt Füssen
1 Wellness-Hotel Sommer****, Weidachstraße 74, www.hotel-sommer.de, 0049(0)8362 91 470, VI
2 Hotel Luitpoldpark****, Bahnhofstraße 1 - 3, www.luitpoldpark-hotel.de, 0049(0)8362 93 980, V
3 Hotel Hirsch, Kaiser-Maximilian-Platz 7, www.hotelfuessen.de, 0049(0)8362 93 980, V
❶ church „Spitalkirche“
❷ monastery „St. Mang“
❸ view from Franciscan monastery
❹ Museum of the City of Füssen
❺ parish church „St. Mang“
❻ castle „Hohes Schloss“
❼ pedestrian zone „Reichenstraße“
4 Hotel Ruchti***, Alatseestr. 38, www.hotel-ruchti.de, 0049(0)8362 91 0 10, V
Between Füssen and Pinswang
❶ waterfall „Lechfall“
❷ Forest adventure centre with canopy walkway
Pinswang
❶ historic quarry
❷ marked route of Roman road across mountain ridge
❸ commemorative plaque
❹ bridge „Ulrichsbrücke“
❺ parish church St. Ulrich
HOPFENSEE
BANNWALDSEE
Holdiday Region Ostallgäu
Ehr-wang
Achmühle
Schwangau
Füssen
LECH
Horn
Alterschrofen
Hohen-schwangau
Ziegelwies
Weisshaus
ALPSEE
VILS
Stadt Vils
Pinswang
Nature park Tiroler Lec
Nature Park Regi
Reutte
Ausserfern
N
S
1 km
2 km
3 km

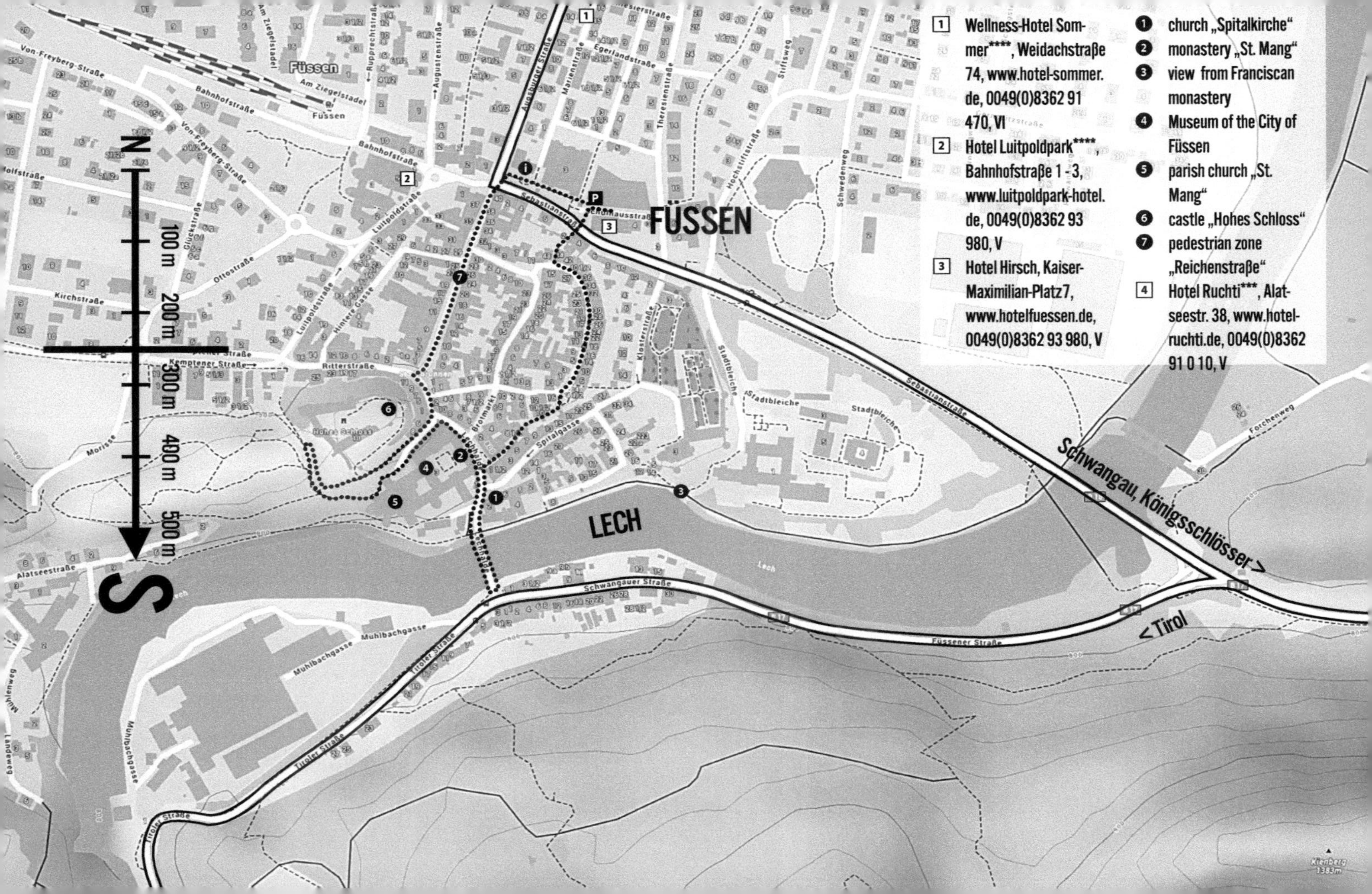

1 Wellness-Hotel Sommer****, Weidachstraße 74, www.hotel-sommer.de, 0049(0)8362 91 470, VI
2 Hotel Luitpoldpark****, Bahnhofstraße 1 - 3, www.luitpoldpark-hotel.de, 0049(0)8362 93 980, V
3 Hotel Hirsch, Kaiser-Maximilian-Platz7, www.hotelfuessen.de, 0049(0)8362 93 980, V
4 Hotel Ruchti***, Alatseestr. 38, www.hotel-ruchti.de, 0049(0)8362 91 0 10, V
1 church „Spitalkirche“
2 monastery „St. Mang“
3 view from Franciscan monastery
4 Museum of the City of Füssen
5 parish church „St. Mang“
6 castle „Hohes Schloss“
7 pedestrian zone „Reichenstraße“
FÜSSEN
LECH
Schwangau, Königsschlösser >
<Tirol
N
S
100 m
200 m
300 m
400 m
500 m

Füssen with the High Castle. Photo: Füssen Tourism and Marketing / www.guenterstandl.de

St. Mang Monastery. Reichenstrasse. Photos: Tschaikner

Reichenstrasse in the footsteps of the Roman road

Crystal spa

Remains of a Roman bathhouse in Schwangau. Photo: Peter Schäffer

10 The Lech river: at the gateway to Tyrol and the Alps (maps 13, 14)

The first mountain ridges at the border between Germany and Austria form a gate, which the Via Claudia Augusta crossed into the Alps and the Reutte nature reserve region in Tyrol. This is where the only untouched section of the Lech in the northern Alps begins. The realm of the 'last wild one', as the nature park exhibition dubs the river, is dominated by extensive gravel banks and wetlands that cover the entire valley in some sections. Since time immemorial, the river has determined where settlements and roads could be built. Large parts of the valley have always been prone to flooding, so the Roman route of the Via Claudia Augusta crossed two plateaus between Füssen and the valley basin of Reutte: the mountain ridge between the Stiglberg and Kratzer and the Kniepass.

Car route from Füssen to Reutte

First we go around the old town of Füssen. From the south of the bridge, which crosses the Lech about where the Roman road crossed the river, you have a great view of the historic center. Then the route crosses the Austrian border on the picturesque old country road, lined with trees on the right and left. Then the route leads through the picturesque Unter- and Oberpinswang, before it goes over the Kniepass to Pflach.

additional details about some sights

On a bridge above the Lech Falls, you can watch the river thundering out of the Alps. From there on, the Lech was and still is floatable.

The Füssen Forest Experience Center makes the forest habitat, between the wild river and the steep slopes of the Allgäu mountain forest, come alive in its original form - with an exhibition and adventure trails. A special highlight is the 480 m long and 21 high treetop path. ■ Tiroler Str. 10, Füssen, 0043(0)8362 93875-50, open May 1 - Oct. 31, daily 10 a.m. - 5 p.m., Nov. 1 - April 30, Tues. - Thurs. 10 a.m. - 4 p.m. and Fri. 10 a.m. - 1 p.m., two adventure trails can be walked at any time. www.walderlebniszentrum.eu

Even the Romans quarried yellow marble in the historic quarry near Weißhaus. A sarcophagus exhibited in Kempten, for example, was made of this marble.

On the inside of a road bend, a memorial plaque reminds of the new construction of the road in 1772 - 1784, around the Stiglberg. Until the new construction, the Roman road over the ridge was the main road.

From the 18 m high bird watching tower at the Lechauen you have a great view of the interesting habitats. Display boards explain what the visitor sees. A bird discovery trail around a stillwater also begins at the tower. In the floodplain forest and on the nearby banks of the Lech, the fauna and flora can be experienced up close.

History(s)

Because parts of the valley were completely flooded again and again, the Roman route of the Via Claudia Augusta already led from Füssen to the Reuten basin over 2 hills - over the mountain ridge between Stiglberg and Kratzer and over the Kniepass.

The medieval or modern successor road of the Via Claudia Augusta is known as the „Salt Road". In contrast to the first European single market in Roman times, without tolls and customs duties, the salt road was governed by the very protectionist Rodfuhr system. Local hauliers had the exclusive right to transport certain goods on short distances between the defeat places, where the goods had to be reloaded. Noblemen or merchants who repaired the roads charged tolls. The princes collected customs duties.

Regional cuisine like 2000 years ago

■ Gasthof Guthof Zum Schluxen
6600 Unterpinswang 23, 0043(0)5677 8903

Overnight and camping possibilities in the appendix and in the maps

Questions and information about the subsection

■ Hotline Via Claudia Augusta, 0043(0)664 27 63 555
■ Touristinfo Naturparkregion Reutte, Untermarkt 34, 6600 Reutte, 0043(0)5672 62 336
■ Via Claudia Augusta Info, 0043(0)664 27 63 555

Map 14

Roman route of the Via Claudia Augusta
Car Travel Route
Walk

Pflach

1. "Kniepass" pass
2. listed railway bridge
3. birdwatching tower

Reutte, Breitenwang

1. deanery parish church
2. salt barn
3. Museum of Local History „Grünes Haus"
4. historic inn „Zum Mohren"

[1] Gasthof Hotel Zum Mohren****, Untermarkt 26, www.hotel-mohren.at, 0043(0)5672 62 345, V

5. house with typical façade paintings „Zeilerhaus"
6. district commission in former granary and local authority in historic inn
7. fontain "Via-Claudia-Augusta-Brunnen"
8. historic inns

Lechaschau

1. bridge where the salt road once crossed the Lech river

[1] Hotel Romantik Krone, Wängler Str. 6, www.romantik-krone.at, 0043(0)5672 62 354, IV-V

2. lake „Frauensee"

Ehenbichl at the foot of Ehrenberg

[1] Wander-Hotel Maximilian, Reuttenerstr. 1, www.hotelmaximilian.at, 0043(0)5672 62 585, V

Ehrenberg

1. world of castles "Ehrenberg" visitors' centre Klause 1, www.ehrenberg.at, 0043(0)5672 62007
2. "Ehrenberg" customs station with "On the Knight's Trail" adventure museum
3. "The Last Wild River" nature exhibition of Tiroler Lech Nature Park
4. castle ruins „Ehrenberg"
5. baroque adventure fortress with panoramic view over Lech Valley
6. „highline179" one of the world's longest suspension bridges for pedestrians
7. „Fortress Claudia"
8. medieval banqueting hall „Ehrenberg Arena"

[1] Hotel-Gasthof Klause der Burgenwelt Ehrenberg, Klause 2-5, www.ehrenberg.at, 0043(0)5672 62213, II-V

9. restaurant in the translocated Lermoos salt barn
10. historic barracks

Heiterwang am See

1. start of the new Heiterwang bypass
2. old main road in the footsteps of the Romans
3. ate medieval main through-road
4. lake with excursion boat

Ehrenberg Castle Ruin

Lech Falls south of Füssen

Treetop trail in the Füssen Forest Adventure Center

Deanery parish church Breitenwang

former inns along the road

Museum of local history in the Green House in Reutte

Experience exhibition „On the trail of the knight

Lechauen, seen from the bird watching tower in Pflach

11 Central Außerfern: the market of Reutte and Breitenwang (map 14)

In the valley basin of Reutte, the Via Claudia Augusta led through Breitenwang towards Ehrenberg. It is believed that the town had a Roman road station just before the ascent. Around 1464, when the salt road from Hall in Tirol to the region around Lake Constance was relatively new, the Roman road was moved to Reutte, and the market town developed into a regional center. Many Roman buildings have survived to this day. Characteristic architectural artworks adorn the facades of the houses in Reutte; many of them were painted by the Zeiler family of artists. The fortress complex of Ehrenberg is located to the south of Reutte. Its four towering fortresses used to constitute a barrage against Bavaria. The complex even had outer baileys between Pflach and Pinswang/Musau, where the border used to be. Vils was a walled Bavarian town.

To Breitenwang

A little side road takes you to Breitenwang. (The Roman road is buried underneath this road.) It is very likely that there used to be a Roman road station underneath today's deanery parish church. From the tourist information office at Untermarkt and Obermarkt, head through Reutte. After you pass the roundabout, the road through the center corresponds to the salt road between Hall in Tirol and the Lake Constance area. Follow the Fernpass national road for a while and pass the Ehrenberger Klause customs station on the way.

Breitenwang, spiritual capital of the Ausserfern region

Records from 1278 already mention 'Ruhi propre Breitwanch' (Reutte near Breitenwang). They show that the town used to be even more significant than today's district capital of Reutte. Breitenwang is probably the oldest settlement in the Tyrolean Ausserfern region, and it remains its spiritual center to this day. The local deanery parish church is dedicated to Saint Peter, which suggests Late-Roman roots. Historians also believe that the Roman road station was on the church grounds. The funeral chapel of the parish church, now dedicated to Saint Peter and Saint Paul, houses a famous stucco Danse Macabre by Thomas Seitz. Open daily, 8 am–5 pm.

The center of the market town of Reutte

Reutte as it was shaped by the salt road begins at Untermarkt, where you will find the salt depot and the Museum im Grünen Haus on the right side of the little street. Old inns, town houses and craftsmen's houses line the Obermarkt, too. The building that houses the central district authority today used to be the granary. The Via Claudia Augusta Fountain at Isserplatz emphasizes the importance of the Roman road to the town. ■ Museum im Grünen Haus 6600 Reutte, Untermarkt 25, +43 (0)5672 72 304. open Tue–Sat, 1–5 pm and upon arrangement, www.museum-reutte.at

Special: Burgenwelt Ehrenberg

The four fortresses that make up the Ehrenberg castle ensemble and the walls that separate them used to form a continuous complex. All travelers had to pass the gate of the Klause fortifications above which Ehrenberg Castle thrones. Fort Claudia on the eastern hill and the Baroque Schlosskopf fortress complete the ensemble. Today, the interactive exhibition 'Dem Ritter auf der Spur' ('on the knight's tracks') can be found inside the Klause. A new building next door houses the nature park exhibition 'Der letzte Wilde' ('the last wild one'). Schlosskopf fortress is the highest of the four, and its ruins have been turned into a staged Baroque construction site. It offers spectacular views of the Lechtal valley. Heading past Ehrenberg fortress and a wheelchair-accessible hornwork, cross one of the world's longest pedestrian suspension bridges, Highline 179, to reach Fort Claudia.

Special: Nature Park Tiroler Lech

The last wild river in the northern Alpine region is still allowed to shape its course under its own power. In its wide riverbed it stages itself again and again anew. Branches of the river branch and unite. Stones from its side valleys are continuously deposited by the river to form mighty gravel banks. What is really constant is the constant change. Vast floodplain forests, clear spring lakes and the mountain world of the Allgäu and Lechtal Alps make the nature park one of the most beautiful and pristine alpine landscapes. River floodplains are the „jungles" of Central Europe. 1116 or one third of all plants native to Tyrol grow in the nature park. Of these, one third or 392 species are classified as very valuable or endangered. The new nature exhibition „Der letzte Wilde" (The Last Wild One) in the Ehrenberg Castle World makes it possible to experience the nature park and its special features with all the senses in nine themed islands. ■ Klause 1, +43 (0)5672 62007 open daily from 10 am - 5 pm. Closed from mid Nov. to 25 Dec. 2014 inclusive. www.naturpark-tiroler-lech.at

History(s)

The Roman road Via Claudia Augusta continued to be used in the Middle Ages. Although it was hardly maintained
the well-built „ancient alpine highway" withstood traffic for a long time. Over time, however, there were more and more problems with the deteriorating roads. Especially in the Alps, traveling was not without danger. Travel speeds, as they were known in ancient times, were no longer conceivable. In some places there were roads that were no longer usable. In order to revive trade, sovereigns and merchants began towards the end of the Middle Ages to repair the old transport links or to build new roads.
new roads. Of course, the counties and regional merchants had fewer means at their disposal for this than the Europe-wide Roman Empire with its central tax sovereignty. The new roads were therefore as simple and inexpensive as possible. At the beginning of modern times the
road over the Fernpass was improved and rebuilt in sections. In the ascent from the Reutten basin to the Ehrenberger Klause, remains of a substitute road can be seen, on which the traffic could continue while the new „salt road" was built. The traffic was obviously still or again considerable. The map shows the course of the Roman road. The gravel road up to Ehrenberg, corresponds to the salt road. Halfway up, the Roman road can also be discovered crossing the gravel road.

Regional cuisine like 2000 years ago

■ Hotel Gasthof Mohren, Reutte, Untermarkt 26, 0043(0)5672 62345.
■ Hotel-Restaurant Maximilian, Ehenbichl bei Reutte, 0043(0)5672 62 885.
■ Landgasthof Klause, Burgenwelt Ehrenberg, 0043(0)5672 62 213.

Overnight and camping possibilities in the appendix and in the maps

Questions and information about the subsection

■ Touristinfo Naturparkregion Reutte, Untermarkt 34, 0043(0)5672 62 336
■ Hotline Via Claudia Augusta, 0043(0) 664 27 63 555

Map 15

Roman route of the Via Claudia Augusta
= Car Travel Route
···· Walk

Heiterwang am See

- ❹ lake with excursion boat
- [1] Hotel Fischer am See, Fischer am See 1, www.fischeramsee.at, 0043(0)5672 5674 51 16, V

Bichlbach

- [1] Gasthof Sonne & Pension Tyrol, Gipfl 13-64, www.feineler.com, 0043(0)5674 5282, II
- ❶ guild church „ St. Joseph“
- ❷ Sports & leisure park with swimming lake and minigolf course
- ❸ village street on old Roman road
- ❹ Guildhall Museum Bichlbach, Wahl 31, www.zunftmuseum.at, 0043(0)5674 5205
- ❺ zoo and petting zoo
- ❻ mountain for a long time mowed to the top „Mähberg“

Berwang

- ❶ “Bärenarena Berwang“ with open-air swimming pool and miniature golf course
- ❷ museum of local history
- ❸ Rotlech gorge and waterfall

Berwang

- ❹ “Stadlbräu“ Austria‘s highest brewery with brewery tour

Wengle + Lähn

- ❶ main through-road on old Roman road
- ❷ village street on route of Roman road
- ❸ village reconstructed at new location after an avalanche

Lermoos

- [1] Hotel Garni Lärchenhof****, Gries 16, www.laerchenhof-lermoos.at, 0043(0)5673 2197, IV-V
- ❶ open-air pool
- ❷ observation platform Tuftlalm with view of three settlements and moorland
- [2] Haus Olympia & Restaurant Bauernstube, Innsbrucker-Straße 4, www.zoller-lermoos.at, 0043(0)5673 3131, III
- ❸ parish church
- [3] Pension Garni Bartlhof, Schladgasse 1, www.bartlhof.at, 0043(0)5673 2894, III
- ❹ panoramic view from “tree trunk road“
- ❺ “Drei Mohren Museum“: museum about the history of Lermoos

12 Zwischentoren: living by the road, living off the road (maps 14 und 15)

From Heiterwang onwards, the landscape becomes more alpine. You can easily tell that it is covered in snow for longer stretches of the spring. This may be a blessing for holidaymakers, but it has always brought hard work and meager harvests to the farmers of the region. The area between the two gates of Ehrenberg and Fernstein is called 'Zwischentoren' (literally: between gates). Its people have depended on the road for a long time. Many operated small farms to grow their own food while also offering haulage and other services to passersby to make a living. The slopes of the mountains were mowed up to the peaks in order to feed the local animals and those of travelers. Between Heiterwang and Bichlbach , you can still see these slopes today. When the road over the Arlberg Pass and, later, the Arlberg railway were built, the road suddenly lost its status as an important thoroughfare, plunging the people of the road into bitter poverty. Many were forced to leave their home region to seek manual work elsewhere. The children who left the Alps for Swabia came to be known as 'Swabian children'.

The route from Ehrenberg to Leermoos

Just like the Roman route and the salt road, our route runs through the gate of the Klause Ehrenberg fortress. For many centuries, this was the only way of crossing the reservoir, where carters had to pay a toll. Today, those in a rush can bypass Ehrenberg and its neighbouring town of Heiterwang. The new bypass is not the first of its kind. The Roman road crossed the town in a straight line; the salt road curved through the center; the old national road, which was still in use until a few years ago, was straight again. Travelers who want to see the best parts of the town should follow the long curve of the old road through the center: it is lined with historical houses. Before you reach the Maria Himmelfahrt parish church, which has some discernible Gothic elements, consider a detour to the Heiterwanger See lake. Bichlbach at the entrance of the Berwang high valley and Namlos used to be the guild center of Ausserfern. Austria's only guild church and the Bichlbach guild museum are here. Another worthwhile detour takes you from the national road to the pretty villages of Wengle and Lähn. Lähn owes its name to a catastrophic avalanche, during which it was flattened and rebuilt elsewhere. 'Lähn' is a Tyrolean word for 'avalanche'.

The guild church and guild museum in Bichlbach

The members of the guild brotherhood of St. Joseph zu Bichlbach were known as skilled craftsmen. After the old road faded into insignificance, they left their home region in droves. Before that migration, however, they used to meet at the St. Joseph guild church, and you can still see many examples of their craftsmanship there. The Bichlbach guild museum in the old Mesnerhaus building near the parish church is dedicated to the guilds and the esteemed carpenters, masons, painters and sculptors of the Ausserfern region. Volunteers spent many hours renovating the building, and it remains a cultural and social hotspot to this day. Besides the museum, it houses the library and tourist information office.

■ Wahl 31a, Bichlbach, +43 (0)5674 5205, open Mon–Fri, 8 am–12 noon and Tue 7:30 pm–10 pm. www.zunftmuseum.at

Heiterwanger See, a historical fishing ground

It was thanks to its many fish that Heiterwang was first mentioned in official records in 1288. Maximilian I, Holy Roman Emperor, himself liked to fish and hunt in the area. The Heiterwanger See lake was originally 68 cm higher than it is today. A canal now connects it to the Plansee lake in the municipality of Reutte/ Breitenwang. Both lakes have high-quality water that is not just appreciated by their fish. Thanks to their excellent underwater visibility and depth of 60–77 meters, the lakes are highly popular among divers, too. You can experience them above water, too: one of Austria's highest-altitude commercial boating lines crosses them regularly. ■ Fischer am See 1, 6611 Heiterwang, +43 (0)5674 5116, departure times: 10:10 am, 11:00 am, 1:10 pm, 2:00 pm, 3:10 pm, 4:00 pm. www.fischeramsee.at

Overnight and camping possibilities in the appendix and in the maps

Questions and information about the subsection

■ **Touristinfo 6611 Heiterwang am See**
Oberdorf 4, 0043(0)5673 20000–700
■ **Touristinfo 6621 Bichlbach**
Wahl 31a, 0043(0)5673 20000–500
■ **Hotline Via Claudia Augusta 0043(0)664 27 63 555**

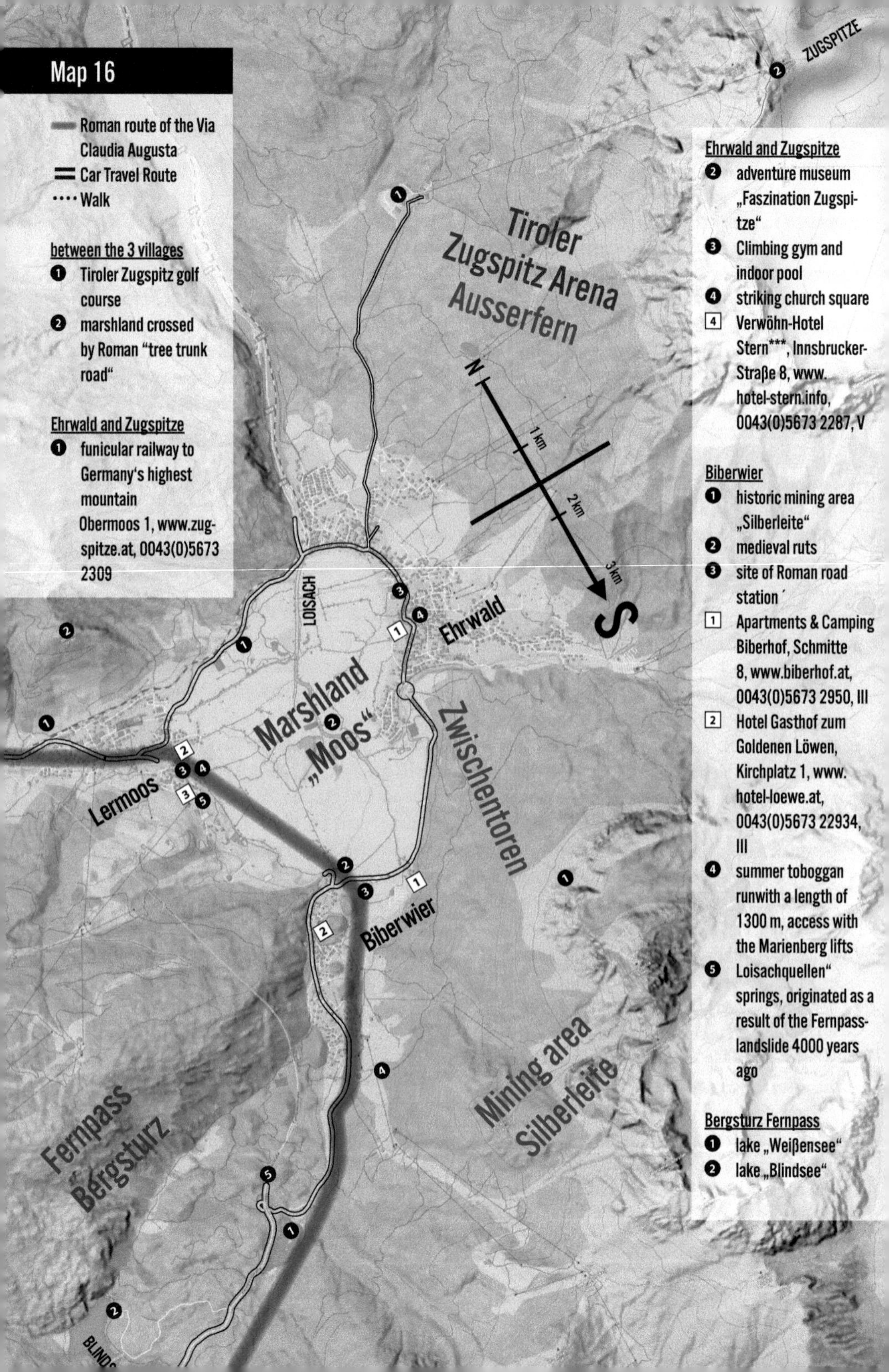
Map 16
Roman route of the Via Claudia Augusta
Car Travel Route
Walk
between the 3 villages
❶ Tiroler Zugspitz golf course
❷ marshland crossed by Roman "tree trunk road"
Ehrwald and Zugspitze
❶ funicular railway to Germany's highest mountain Obermoos 1, www.zugspitze.at, 0043(0)5673 2309
Ehrwald and Zugspitze
❷ adventure museum „Faszination Zugspitze“
❸ Climbing gym and indoor pool
❹ striking church square
4 Verwöhn-Hotel Stern***, Innsbrucker-Straße 8, www.hotel-stern.info, 0043(0)5673 2287, V
Biberwier
❶ historic mining area „Silberleite“
❷ medieval ruts
❸ site of Roman road station´
1 Apartments & Camping Biberhof, Schmitte 8, www.biberhof.at, 0043(0)5673 2950, III
2 Hotel Gasthof zum Goldenen Löwen, Kirchplatz 1, www.hotel-loewe.at, 0043(0)5673 22934, III
❹ summer toboggan runwith a length of 1300 m, access with the Marienberg lifts
❺ Loisachquellen“ springs, originated as a result of the Fernpass-landslide 4000 years ago
Bergsturz Fernpass
❶ lake „Weißensee“
❷ lake „Blindsee“
ZUGSPITZE
Tiroler Zugspitz Arena Ausserfern
N
1 km
2 km
3 km
S
LOISACH
Ehrwald
Marshland „Moos“
Zwischentoren
Lermoos
Biberwier
Mining area Silberleite
Fernpass Bergsturz

13 The natural region on the Tyrolean side of the Zugspitze (map16)

Once you enter Lermoos, you will know exactly why the region is called the Tyrolean Zugspitz Arena. The picturesque Moos wetland, which used to carry the Via Claudia Augusta on thousands of logs, is the ring of the arena. The quirky holiday destinations of Ehrwald, Lermoos and Biberwier sit on the box seats surrounding it. The spectacular mountains surrounding Lermoos are the stands. Among them towers the Zugspitze, Germany's highest mountain. Since 1926, the Tyrolean Zugspitze Cable Car has transported passengers from Ehrwald to the summit. After the old road paled into insignificance, the construction of the cable car became a symbol of a new, brighter economic future for Zwischentoren in the tourism industry.

Crossing the nature park on the foot of the Zugspitze

The Fernpass national road crosses the Lermooser Tunnel today, bypassing the towns on the way to head straight to the Fernpass. Our route leaves the national road at the Lermoos exit and follows the old Roman road through the nature park. To take you past all three holiday destinations, it runs past the Moos wetlands through Lermoos, Ehrwald and Biberwier rather than bypassing Ehrwald like the historical roads did.

Lermoos, a town sustained by its road

The road has brought economic activity to the Ausserfern's most important tourist destination for centuries. Lermoos is one of the oldest towns in this district. The earliest records mentioning 'Larinmoos' ('larch moss') date to 1020. At the time of the salt road, there was an interim warehouse above the St. Catherine parish church. Travelers unloaded their carriages here, and the goods were transferred to the local wagoners' vehicles. Below the church, at the entrance to the wetlands, a transparent panorama panel shows you the location of the Roman log road. If you want to find it yourself, all you need to do is jump through the swamp! Most of the ground is soft. The solid parts are where the road is buried.

Barrel staves made in Ehrwald

Multiple graves from Roman times provide evidence of early human settlement in the area. At the time of the salt road, many Ehrwald locals made a living producing staves for the Hall salt barrels. In the 19th century, the region's largest municipality was a center of comb, pipe and pipe stem manufacture. When the Tyrolean Zugspitze Cable Car was built, a new economic boom began. The large churchyard is one of Ehrwald's most characteristic features. Ehrwald is also known as a village of artists. Ludwig Ganghofer, the conductor Clemens Krauss, his wife, the opera singer Viorica Ursuleac, and the painter Rudolf Schramm-Zittau spent parts of their lives here. You can see their gravestones at the cemetery alongside that of Heinrich von Srbik, historian and minister of education. The cemetery also houses many of the artful burial crosses designed by the blacksmith Franz Guem, famous throughout Tyrol.

The mining town of Biberwier

The last Roman rest station before the Fernpass used to stand on the meadow to the northeast of the village. There are wheel tracks in the rocks underneath the first bend towards Lermoos, which were left there later. As the old log road could no longer be maintained, the salt road snaked along the hill. The smallest of the three towns in the valley basin was also the most important mining town in the entire Ausserfern: sulfidic copper ores were mined from the Silberleithe mountain above Biberwier, which the locals of Schwaz used to extract silver from the rocks. There was an active mining industry here until 1921.

Special: Roman beating road through the moss

In 46 AD Claudius had the only imperial road across the Alps built. Thousands of pioneers and slaves were busy with it. One of their masterpieces was the dead-straight thrashing road through the moor between Lermoos and Biberwier. With pioneer axes they felled thousands of trees for the substructure that would support the road on the soft ground. On top of this, the gravel was heaped up with baskets. The road ditches were also dug only with spades. Mosquitoes in the summer, wet, ice-cold feet in the fall - despite the prevailing pioneering spirit, the soldiers must have condemned Claudius and his master builders more than once. After all, the road could have gone along the slope - as it does today! But the Roman road-building philosophy was straight ahead without compromise. The ongoing maintenance was the responsibility of the population - a great burden, especially when the road was not generally renovated for more than 100 years due to lack of military priority. It is understandable that people were not exactly in favor of Rome at the time. A masterpiece was also achieved by the archaeologists, who from 1992 to 1995 - struggling with the groundwater like the Romans - uncovered and explored layer after layer of the unique bog road, which was 1.8 meters high in total. In order to preserve it in the bog, the original road had to be filled in again. But perhaps it will be possible to reconstruct a piece of it.

Special: Zugspitze – see the Roman road from an altitude of 2962 meters

At the Tiroler Zugspitz Arena, the Via Claudia Augusta meets the foot of Germany's highest mountain. Its high altitude gives you spectacular views in all directions. Besides the mountains themselves, you can see the Bavarian Alpine Foreland which the Roman road used to cross, the historical route through the valley basin underneath the striking summit, and the Fernpass. The Tyrolean Zugspitze Cable Car, whose construction in the 1930s marked a milestone of Tyrol's development into a tourist destination and brought new hope of economic growth to the region, takes you to the summit in a matter of minutes. There are observation platforms and restaurants on the German and Austrian side, and the Faszination Zugspitze Museum illustrates the history of the cable car among other topics. ■ Tyrolean Zugspitze Cable Car valley station, Obermoos 1, 6632 Ehrwald, +43 (0)5673 2309, operating hours: 24 May–2 November, 8:40 am–4:40 pm, www.zugspitze.at

Regional cuisine like 2000 years ago

■ Restaurant Bauernstube
6631 Lermoos, Innsbrucker Str. 4, 0043(0)5673 3131
■ Gasthof Panorama
6632 Ehrwald, Ebne 32, 0043(0)5673 3393
■ Hotel Gasthof Löwe
6633 Biberwier, Kirchplatz 1, 0043(0)5673 2293

Overnight and camping possibilities in the appendix and in the maps

Questions and information about the subsection

■ Touristinfo 6631 Lermoos
Unterdorf 15, 0043(0)5673 20000–300
■ Touristinfo 6632 Ehrwald
Kirchplatz 1, 0043(0)5673 20000–200
■ Touristinfo 6633 Biberwier
Fernpaßstr. 27, 0043(0)5673 20000–600
■ Hotline Via Claudia Augusta 0043(0)664 27 63 555

Bike route between Heiterwang and Bichlbach

Refreshment at the Lussbach. Photo: Anton Vorauer.

In the guild museum

The „Moos“ between Lermoos, Ehrwald and Biberwier. On the right the Zugspitze

The particularly spacious church square of Ehrwald

Roman road station and beating road. Photos: Pöll

14 The Fernpass landslide site: old paths through stunning nature (map 17)

The Fernpass is the site of a landslide which blocked passage through the area about 4000 years ago. Nature arduously reclaimed the landscape over time. Even today, the topsoil is still thin, and the vegetation reflects that: despite the relatively low altitude of the pass (1216 meters today, 1260 in Roman times), you will spot high-alpine plants here. Paths and roads from the pre-Roman and Roman era, the early modern period, the 19th century and today criss-cross the fascinating landscape. Plans for a tunnel are being discussed. The Roman Via Claudia Augusta ran from Biberwier to the old top of the Fernpass in a straight line. Its route is mostly identical with that of the power line in this area. From the highest point of the pass, the road steadily descended down the slope to the Samerangersee lake. In the late Middle Ages, the Fernpass road was rerouted to cross the top of the Fernpass we know today.

Route across the Fernpass

On the old country road, our route follows that of the Via Claudia Augusta to the Weißensee lake. It continues on the Fernpass national road, while the Roman road runs to the higher, old top of the Fernpass in a straight line. In Roman times, most people traveled on foot. Inclines were no problem for them. What counted was the shortest route. Across all of Tyrol, the Roman road only had four curves. Between 1540 and 1543, the burgrave of Ehrenberg had a new road built. It crosses the national road on the current pass plateau today. Information panels tell visitors about the fascinating nature around them. Down the hill from the pass plateau, you can see a path on the left-hand side, about halfway to a bend in the road. The path corresponds to the Roman road. The old top of the Fernpass towers high above the bend.

Seven emerald lakes

There are seven lakes around the Fernpass, and they have more to offer than their brilliant color alone. The Blindsee is a popular Alpine swimming destination. Just before the bend in the national road, a little path takes you to a paid parking lot near the shore of the lake. If the barrier is closed, the parking lot is full. You can park at the Weißensee instead; the Blindsee is only a brief hike away. The Fernsteinsee is best enjoyed during a boat trip or a walk around the lake.

The landslide site

On the top of the pass, interested travelers can walk down the gravel path from the early modern period (today's Via Claudia Augusta cycling and hiking route) to see the assumed Afrigal landslide site. It is covered in the largest number of mountain pines in the eastern Alps. Information panels explain the special nature of the area.

Schloss Fernstein castle ensemble

Next to the Fernsteinsee lake, there are various important buildings: Schloss Fernstein castle, a hotel and restaurant, a rest stop, a chapel, and a little farm that belongs to the castle. You can walk around the entire Fernsteinsee. Cross the bridge on the southeastern shore of the lake to get to an island with a small, private palace. Sigismund, Archduke of Austria, had it built for his wife, Eleanor of Scotland.

Regional cuisine like 2000 years ago

■ Hotel Restaurant Schloss Fernstein
6465 Nassereith, Fernstein, 0043(0)5265 5210

Overnight and camping possibilities in the appendix and in the maps

Questions and information about the subsection

■ Touristinfo 6633 Biberwier
Fernpaßstr. 27, 0043(0)5673 20000–600
■ Touristinfo 6465 Nassereith
Postplatz 28, Tel. 0043(0)5412 6910–41
■ Via Claudia Augusta Info 0043(0)664 27 63 555

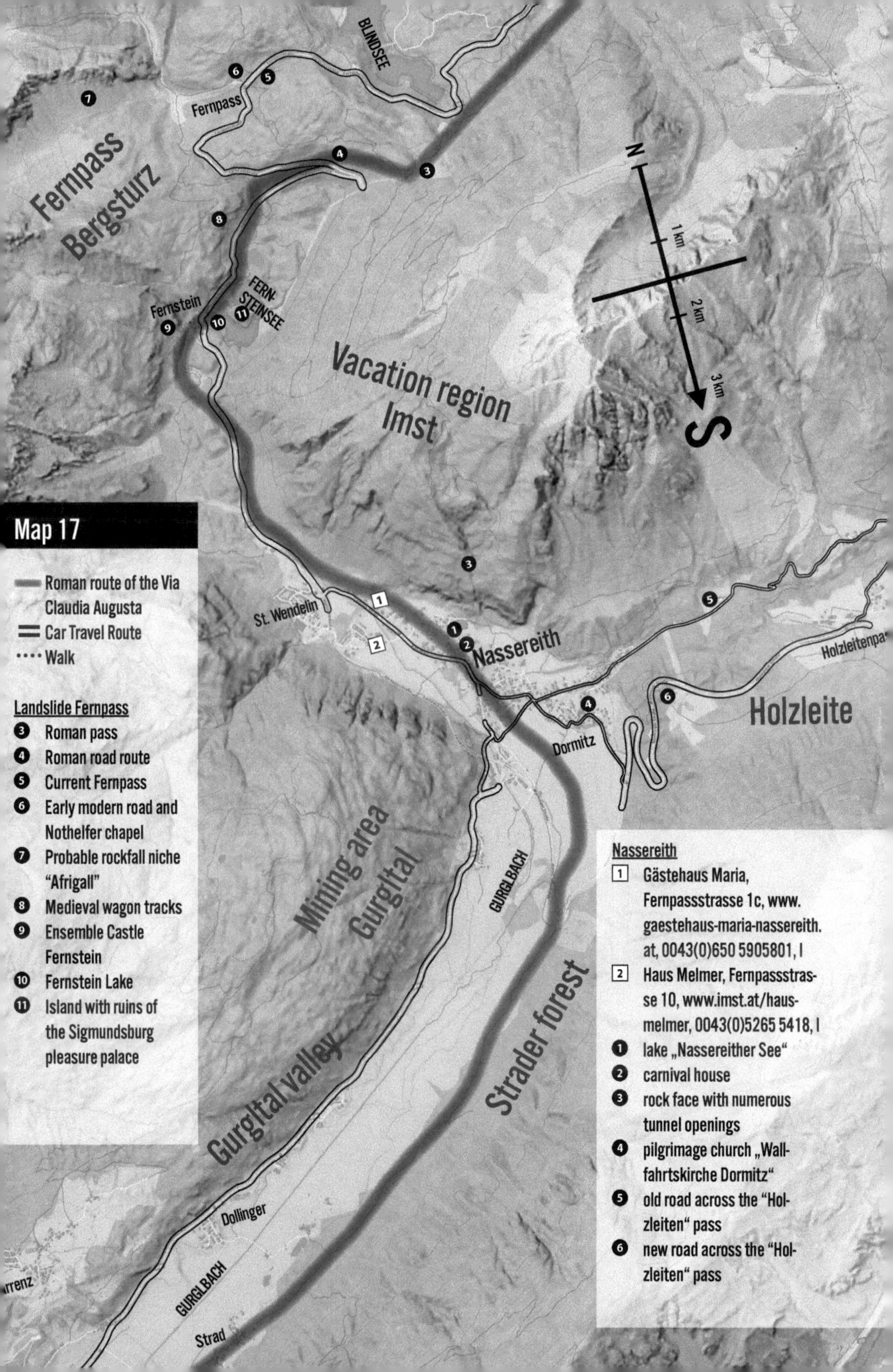

BLINDSEE
Fernpass
Fernpass Bergsturz
N
1 km
2 km
3 km
S
FERN-STEINSEE
Fernstein
Vacation region Imst
Map 17
Roman route of the Via Claudia Augusta
Car Travel Route
Walk
Landslide Fernpass
3 Roman pass
4 Roman road route
5 Current Fernpass
6 Early modern road and Nothelfer chapel
7 Probable rockfall niche "Afrigall"
8 Medieval wagon tracks
9 Ensemble Castle Fernstein
10 Fernstein Lake
11 Island with ruins of the Sigmundsburg pleasure palace
St. Wendelin
Nassereith
Holzleitenpa
Holzleite
Dormitz
Mining area Gurgltal
GURGLBACH
Strader forest
Gurgltal valley
Dollinger
GURGLBACH
Strad
Nassereith
1 Gästehaus Maria, Fernpassstrasse 1c, www.gaestehaus-maria-nassereith.at, 0043(0)650 5905801, I
2 Haus Melmer, Fernpassstrasse 10, www.imst.at/haus-melmer, 0043(0)5265 5418, I
1 lake „Nassereither See“
2 carnival house
3 rock face with numerous tunnel openings
4 pilgrimage church „Wallfahrtskirche Dormitz“
5 old road across the “Holzleiten“ pass
6 new road across the “Holzleiten“ pass

Lake Fernstein with the Fernpass road and the ensemble Schloss Hotel Fernstein. Photo Fernstein Castle

Fernpass with Blindsee

Early modern Fernpass road

Nassereith carnival house

Miners' world Gurgltal

View from Dormitz into the Gurgl valley

15 The Gurgltal valley, a center of mining history and Carnival traditions (maps 17, 18)

The Gurgltal valley is an idyllic landscape that is popular with local and foreign leisure-seekers alike. Humans settled in the picturesque valley at a very early stage. Historians believe that the shrine in the village of Dollinger-Lager on the northern slopes between Nassereith and Tarrenz was in use between the Hallstatt period and the Roman age. From Fernstein, the Roman road ran to the parish church of Nassereith in a straight line before nestling into the southern side of the valley, avoiding the sunny side, which was prone to rockfall. It only crossed the valley between Strad and Tarrenz and continued towards Imst along the sunny slopes. Nassereith was already a traffic hub in prehistorical times and during the Roman Empire: this is where the roads through the Gurgltal valley and across the Mieminger Plateau met. Archaeologists have proven that a Roman settlement existed in Dormitz, a little way away from the Roman Via Claudia Augusta. Roman roadside guesthouse in the Strader Wald forest It is also believed that a Roman road station stood in the Dormitz area. The section between the Fernpass and Imst used to be one of Tyrol's most important mining areas. Visit the Knappenwelt Gurgltal, an authentically reconstructed mining village in Tarrenz, to learn more about this aspect of the history of this region. The locals predominantly mined galena, which they used to produce silver from the ores found in Schwaz, and zinc. Imst, the district capital, was also the seat of the mining court, whose jurisdiction covered a large area stretching to the Ausserfern, Reschenpass and Vorarlberg. The Via Claudia Augusta was also used as a transportation route for the mining sector. And the three towns of the Gurgltal valley – Nassereith, Tarrenz and Imst – share another important tradition: the Carnival.

The route from Fernstein to Imst

The expansive village center surrounding the Nazarene parish church and the splendid Postplatz square date back to the heyday of Nassereith, a mining town at the intersection of the roads towards Innsbruck, Imst and the Fernpass. Like many towns, Nassereith first developed along the road that succeeded the Via Claudia Augusta. Our travel route follows the old road up the Holzleitensattel saddle towards Innsbruck, before joining the new road to head back down the pass. About halfway down, it forks towards Dormitz with its pilgrimage church of St. Nicholas. A Roman road station is believed to have stood here. On the way to Imst, the route crosses Tarrenz, which has many old inns, some of which are still in business. Besides the business brought by the road and the mining industry, Tarrenz used to be a nail-forging town. The local carnival tradition is all about witches.

Fasnachtshaus Nassereith

The Fasnachtshaus museum offers a very interesting film and life-sized puppets dressed in the costumes of the famous "Schellerlaufen" carnival. It also functions as the carnival club house, so you can see all the masks here. ■ Sachsengasse 81a, +43 (0)680 3131184, www.fasnacht-nassereith.at.

Knappenwelt Gurgltal and the Healer of Tarrenz

The Knappenwelt is an adventure village expertly developed and run by the locals. It consists of reconstructed buildings, ore-mining facilities, and an adit. There is even a miners' sleeping hall where travelers can spend the night. The nearby exhibition about the healer of the Gurgltal valley is worth visiting, too. She was burned at the stake as a witch. ■ Tschirgant 1, +43 (0)5412 63023, open 1 May to 31 October: Tue–Sun, 10 am–5 pm or upon arrangement.

The beer museum of Schloss Starkenberg castle (Tarrenz)

Once upon a time, the Starkenberg knights resided at this castle. For the past 200 years, it has also been the source of one of Tyrol's delicious beers. The Starkenberger Bier-Mythos museum is located in this 700-year-old castle. It even contains a beer swimming pool! ■ Griesegg 1, +43 (0)5412 66 201–0, www.starkenberg.at

Regional cuisine like 2000 years ago

■ **Hotel Restaurant Schloss Fernstein**
6465 Nassereith, Fernstein, 0043(0)5265 5210

Overnight and camping possibilities in the appendix and in the maps

Questions and information about the subsection

■ **Touristinfo 6633 Biberwier**
Fernpaßstr. 27, 0043(0)5673 20000–600
■ **Touristinfo 6465 Nassereith**
Postplatz 28, Tel. 0043(0)5412 6910–41
■ **Via Claudia Augusta Info 0043(0)664 27 63 555**

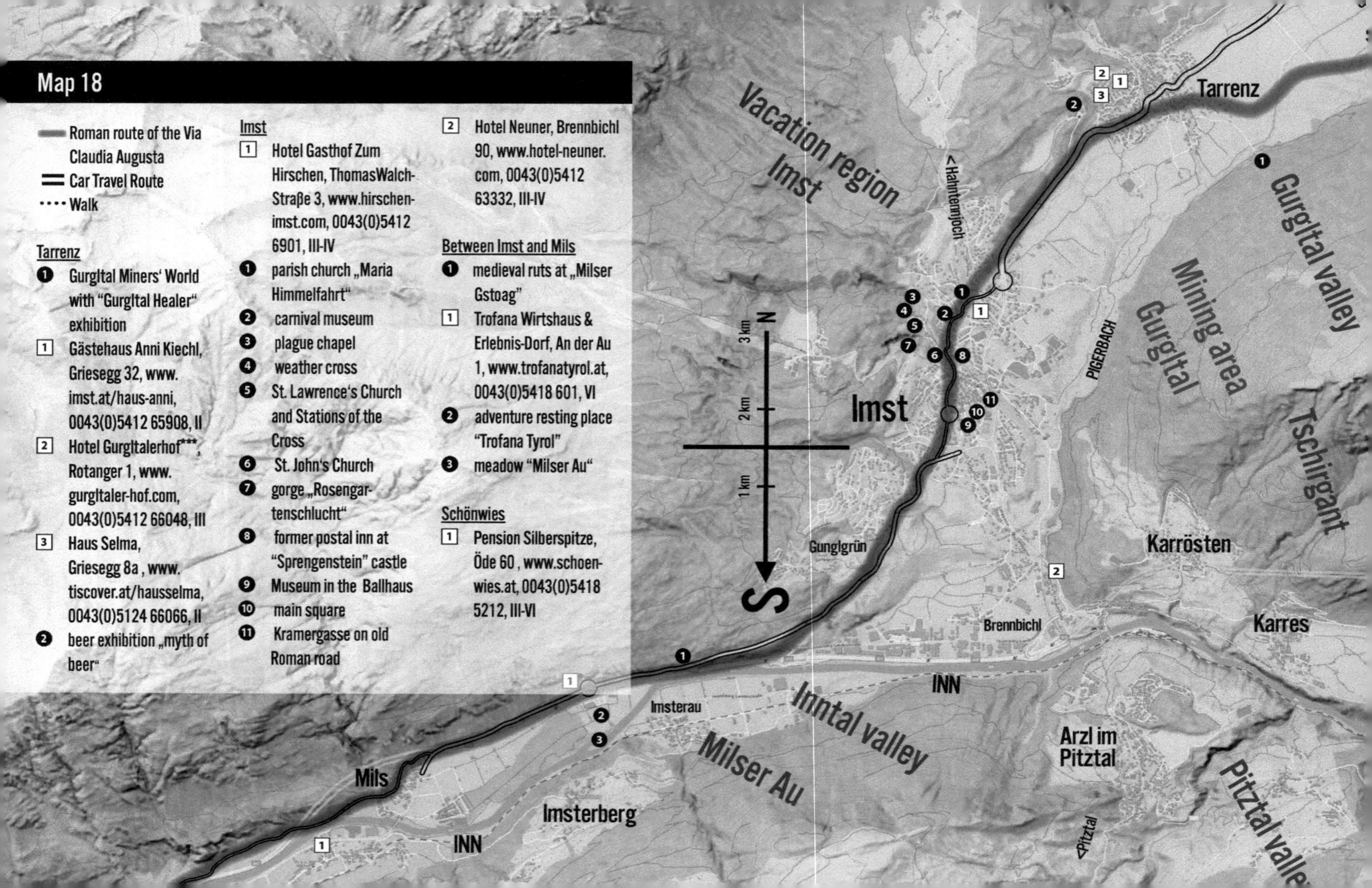

Map 18
Roman route of the Via Claudia Augusta
Car Travel Route
Walk
Tarrenz
1 Gurgltal Miners' World with "Gurgltal Healer" exhibition
[1] Gästehaus Anni Kiechl, Griesegg 32, www.imst.at/haus-anni, 0043(0)5412 65908, II
[2] Hotel Gurgltalerhof***, Rotanger 1, www.gurgltaler-hof.com, 0043(0)5412 66048, III
[3] Haus Selma, Griesegg 8a , www.tiscover.at/hausselma, 0043(0)5124 66066, II
2 beer exhibition „myth of beer"
Imst
[1] Hotel Gasthof Zum Hirschen, ThomasWalch-Straße 3, www.hirschen-imst.com, 0043(0)5412 6901, III-IV
[2] Hotel Neuner, Brennbichl 90, www.hotel-neuner.com, 0043(0)5412 63332, III-IV
1 parish church „Maria Himmelfahrt"
2 carnival museum
3 plague chapel
4 weather cross
5 St. Lawrence's Church and Stations of the Cross
6 St. John's Church
7 gorge „Rosengartenschlucht"
8 former postal inn at "Sprengenstein" castle
9 Museum in the Ballhaus
10 main square
11 Kramergasse on old Roman road
Between Imst and Mils
1 medieval ruts at „Milser Gstoag"
[1] Trofana Wirtshaus & Erlebnis-Dorf, An der Au 1, www.trofanatyrol.at, 0043(0)5418 601, VI
2 adventure resting place "Trofana Tyrol"
3 meadow "Milser Au"
Schönwies
[1] Pension Silberspitze, Öde 60 , www.schoenwies.at, 0043(0)5418 5212, III-VI
Tarrenz
Vacation region Imst
< Hahntennjoch
Gurgltal valley
Mining area Gurgltal
PIGERBACH
Tschirgant
Imst
N
3 km
2 km
1 km
S
Gunglgrün
Karrösten
Brennbichl
Karres
INN
Imsterau
Inntal valley
Milser Au
Arzl im Pitztal
<Pitztal
Pitztal valle
Mils
Imsterberg
INN

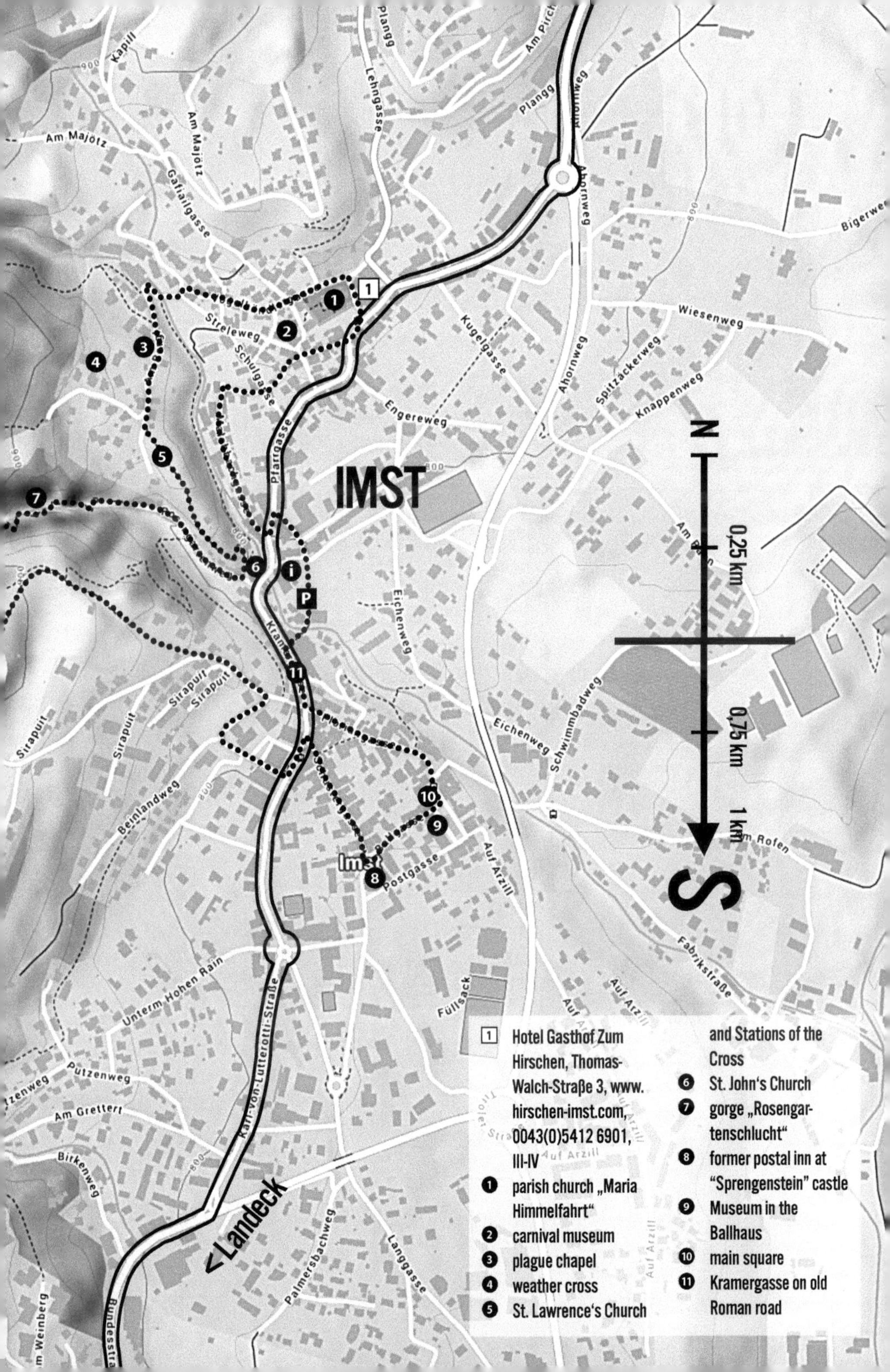
IMST
<Landeck
N
0,25 km
0,75 km
1 km
S
Pfarrgasse
Kramergasse
Schulgasse
Streleweg
Kugelgasse
Engereweg
Eichenweg
Ahornweg
Wiesenweg
Spitzäckerweg
Knappenweg
Schwimmbadweg
Lehngasse
Plangg
Am Pirchl
Am Majötz
Gafiallgasse
Kapill
Bigerweg
Sirapuit
Beinlandweg
Unterm Hohen Rain
Putzenweg
Am Grettert
Birkenweg
Karl-von-Lutterotti-Straße
Postgasse
Auf Arzill
Füllsack
Fabrikstraße
Am Rofen
Palmersbachweg
Langgasse
Trojet Straße
Am Weinberg
Bundesstraße
1 Hotel Gasthof Zum Hirschen, Thomas-Walch-Straße 3, www.hirschen-imst.com, 0043(0)5412 6901, III-IV
1 parish church „Maria Himmelfahrt“
2 carnival museum
3 plague chapel
4 weather cross
5 St. Lawrence‘s Church and Stations of the Cross
6 St. John‘s Church
7 gorge „Rosengartenschlucht“
8 former postal inn at “Sprengenstein” castle
9 Museum in the Ballhaus
10 main square
11 Kramergasse on old Roman road

Imst on the sunny slope.

The Rosengarten Gorge. Photo: Imst Tourism / Martin Lugger

The oldest piece of Imst, the Laurentius church

Imst Schemenlaufen World Heritage Site

historical Kramergasse

16 Oppidum Humiste: the Rhaetian and Roman roots of Imst (map 18)

Records from the 7th century mention an 'Oppidum Humiste'. This almost certainly refers to Imst, which also used to be a road station on the Via Claudia Augusta. The term 'Oppidum' even suggests a fortified settlement from pre-Roman times. It is likely that the district capital was inhabited permanently from Rhaetian times through the Roman Empire until the 7th century. The Laurentiuskirche church on the striking Bergl hill above the town center dates back to the 5th century A. D. and shows that the settlement was already quite large back then. It was probably the largest settlement between Füssen and Meran/Merano. Roman Imst is buried under the old town, however, and what little remains of its is difficult to study. Later, the current district capital of Imst became the seat of the central mining authority and the home of the bird trading profession, which inspired the popular operetta 'The Bird Seller'. The people of Imst are particularly proud of their traditional Carnival, which takes place every four years. Have a look at the museum dedicated to it.

The route to Imst

Between Tarrenz and Imst, the old Roman road is a little way above the modern road. It leaves the slope in the city to head straight for the parish church. Afterwards, it crosses the city approximately underneath the old main road, which our travel route also follows. There are very little parking options in the center, so it makes sense to leave your car at the large parking lot while you take a walk.

A walk through Imst

The first few steps of your walk through town take you past multiple fountains. Imst is known for its many fountains, and there is even a guidebook dedicated to them. The Maria Himmelfahrt parish church has the tallest steeple in all of Tyrol at 84.5 meters. Viewed from the spacious cemetery, the late-Gothic architecture truly comes into its own. The exterior of the church was reconstructed in the Gothic style in 1909 and 1912. One of the gothic frescoes on the outer wall depicts a mining scene from 1478 in memory of the glory days when Imst was the seat of the central mining authority. The foundation of the church was laid in 1462. Later, the miners helped to build the long structure that remains to this day. The inside of the church retained its Baroque design. Walk through the cemetery to the Mesnerhaus building, which houses the carnival museum (Haus der Fasnacht) today. The walk also takes you through some of the old alleyways of Imst's Oberstadt district. The Vogelhändlergasse ('bird sellers' road') is named after the famous bird sellers of Imst. During the great fire of Imst in 1822, all but 14 of the town's 220 houses were destroyed. On the way to the Bergl hill, you will pass the Pestkapelle chapel, named after the great plague, and the nearby Laurentiuskirche church. During its restoration, remnants of an apsed church from the late Roman era were found. From the Bergl hill, you have a lovely view of the town center and the old Roman road. It leads straight from the parish church to the foot of the hill. From there, it is virtually identical to the Kramergasse. Walk down the Bergl hill on the processional walkway to get to the Johanneskirche church. The Schutzengelbrunnen (guardian angel's fountain) next to the church marks the entrance of the Rosengartenschlucht gorge. The road continues along steep paths, bridges and walkways up to the Blue Grotto. If you don't have time for the whole walk, continue along the Kramergasse. The Hotel Post inside Schloss Sprengenstein castle, the Ballhaus ('bale house'), and the main square show that the road used to run through the Unterstadt district a little way to the south. Opposite the Postgasthof inn, you can still see the stables that were once used for the change of horses. They were turned into a garage later. From the end of the Middle Ages on, goods transported along the old road were bundled into bales, stored and loaded at the Ballhaus ('bale house'). Today, it houses the Museum im Ballhaus, which documents the history and culture of the town. ■ Ballgasse 1, +43 (0)5412 6980 – 0, open on Tue, Thu, Fri 2–6 pm, Sat 9 am–12 noon, closed on public holidays, www.kultur-imst.at

The exhibition at the Haus der Fasnacht

The Haus der Fasnacht is the meeting point of all carnival enthusiasts who participate in the grand 'Schemenlaufen' carnival every four years. Two years before each event, the boys of the town celebrate their own carnival, the 'Buabe-Fasnacht'. Only the boys and men of Imst are allowed to participate. The women sow the costumes. There are strict rules to the carnival dance, and some of them have been in place for centuries. The carnival processions of Imst are famous far beyond the town itself, and their magical spectacle draws in visitors from near and far. With its mythical atmosphere, this centuries-old performance captivates its spectators. In 2010, UNESCO has added the Schemenlaufen of Imst to the Representative List of the Intangible Cultural Heritage of Humanity. A spectacular ensemble of hundreds of mask-wearers celebrates the triumph of spring over winter. The central characters of the Schemenlaufen are called Roller and Scheller. The youthful Roller dances ahead of the Scheller, an elderly man with an impressive moustache. Sackner, Spritzer and Kübelemajen are the guardians of the procession and guide the main characters through the crowds. After the grand entrance of the two most elegant figures of the carnival, countless others join them. On Monday, the day after the Schemenlaufen, all participants come together for another procession through Imst. They are in costumes but without masks, and the elegant party continues in a slightly more uninhibited manner. The Haus der Fasnacht is a clubhouse and an archive of costumes and masks, which you can see at its exhibition. Countless masks and a highly impressive film allow you to immerse yourself in the carnival tradition even while the event is not happening. ■ 6460 Imst, Streleweg 6, +43 (0)5412 6910–0, open on Fri, 4–7 pm, and upon arrangement, www.fasnacht.at.

Excursion: follow the Romans out of Imst

As you exit the historical Kramergasse, take a right towards Hoch-Imst, where you can take a ride on the Alpine Coaster, the world's longest alpine rollercoaster. ■ Imster Bergbahnen, Hoch-Imst 19, +43 (0)5412 66322, www.imster-bergbahnen.at. From here, the historical Roman route is largely identical with the national road towards Landeck. Above the road lies the Sonnberg settlement, the home of the first SOS Children's Village. Hermann Gmeiner's vision of giving children a new home soon conquered the whole world. There are SOS Children's Villages in 130 countries today. ■ Sonnberg, 6460 Imst, +43 (0)5412 66234–0, www.sos-kinderdorf.at

Special: Climbing in the footsteps of miners

The Romans probably already mined for ore along the Via Claudia Augusta. Later, the area between Fernpass and Imst was a mining stronghold. In order to reach the treasures in the steep mountain face behind Nassereith, the miners climbed up to the mouth holes via extensive systems of steep tracks and ladders, which attentive observers can still recognize today. In addition to the climbing gardens and routes on this wall, there are numerous other climbing paradises along the Roman Road. Whether bouldering, sport climbing, alpine multi-pitch tours or family-friendly climbing gardens and via ferrata - from two-hour pastimes to alpine tours lasting several days. From bizarre ice formations and waterfalls in winter to idyllically situated climbing gardens and bouldering crags in summer. Most routes are very well secured. Inexperienced climbers can rely on well-trained, experienced climbing guides. For less enjoyable days, there are numerous indoor climbing gyms as well as adventurous alternative programs. All topos and info on access, protection, etc. can be found at www.climbers-paradise.com

Special: Imst, a region of springs

If there is anything that the Imst holiday region has more than enough of, it is water. Smart policymakers knew how to make the many springs useful. There are many artistically designed fountains in Imst; most of them have been here for a long time. In the past, most households used to get their cooking and washing water from their nearest well. Large items of laundry were washed here, and potatoes were cleaned in the small basins. Cows drank from the large basin, while their owners enjoyed a little gossip. This made the wells social spots, too. Those with the right to use the wells organized in groups to ensure that the wells were kept clean and functional. Some of those groups are still active today; one of their tasks is to decorate the fountains for processions. The saints that adorn the fountains often lent their names to the squares on which they stand, too.
Discover all the fountains of the upper and lower circle with the guidebook from Imst-Tourismus (browse or download at ■ www.imst.at).

Regional cuisine like 2000 years ago

Here could be an inn that has at least one dish on the menu continuously as it was 2000 years ago.

Overnight and camping possibilities in the appendix and in the maps

Questions and information about the subsection

■ Touristinfo Imst, Johannespl. 4, 0043(0)5412 6910-0
■ Via Claudia Augusta Info 0043(0)664 27 63 555

Kronburg Castle on a rocky spur, high above the Inn Valley. Photo: Anton Vorauer

Medieval wagon tracks at the „Milser Gstoag". Photo: Tschaikner

The Milser Au. Photo: Imst Tourism / Wenzler

Mils near Imst

17 In Roman footsteps: from Imst to the district of Landeck (maps 18, 19)

The Inntal valley between Imst and Landeck offers pleasant villages, one of the few remaining floodplains of the Inn, and Kronburg castle throning high above the valley on a rock. You will also be treated to spectacular views of the surrounding mountains. Do not forget to look back at the Tschirgant between the Inntal and Gurgltal valleys. Around the halfway mark between Imst and Landeck lies Mils with the motorway service area and 'adventure village' of Trofana Tyrol. It offers all services which an old Roman road station would have offered to travelers along the Via Claudia Augusta – and then some.

The route from Imst to Landeck

The road to Imst clings to the sunny slope as it crosses the hill on the national road towards Landeck. In the beginning, the old Roman road is underneath the current road. A little later, near the hill, it is slightly above it; at the slope, it is underneath it. When you head back into the valley, keep your eyes open to spot the wheel tracks next to the guardrails. A little further down the road, take the turn towards Mils. Cross the town in a straight line and take the little road to Starkenbach. Up to here, the route has been following the Via Claudia Augusta almost completely. At Starkenbach, the Roman road first crossed the Starkenbach stream, then the Inn river. After you cross the bridge across the stream, you will see a building that used to be an inn on the old road. On the opposite bank of the Inn, facing the mouth of the stream, stands the head of a bridge that existed until the 19th century. Our travel route now follows the left side of the river to Zams.

The ruins and pilgrimage church of Kronburg

Kronburg castle sits on a promontory high above the Inntal valley. You can reach it on foot from the eponymous pilgrimage church. To visit it, leave the route before Mils and cross the Inn river to Schönwies. At the end of the road through town, take a left towards Kronburg castle.

A road station just like in Roman times

The Romans built road stations at regular intervals along the Via Claudia Augusta. Travelers on official duty stopped their for room and board. There were facilities to park your carriages and keep your horses overnight, and most road stations also had a small bath house and a temple. Imst, Landeck and Nauders all had such a road station or 'mansio'. As demand from private travelers increased, similar stops sprung up for them, too. Archaeologists discovered one in the forest between Nassereith and Tarrenz. According to them, the themed service station 'Trofana Tyrol' authentically mirrors the function of those ancient establishments. Designed in the style of a Tyrolean mountain village, it is a place for travelers to eat, drink and sleep. The 'Hitte-Hatte-Au' section outside has a pond, a Kneipp station and a large children's playground. Even a chapel has been built here. The glass-covered marketplace selling Tyrolean delicacies at the center of Trofana Tyrol has become a popular meeting spot for locals. Its Cafeteria Tirolino is open around the clock. ■ An der Au 1, 5493 Mils bei Imst, +43 (0)5418 601–0. www.trofanatyrol.at.

Adventure on the river - Even the Romans „rafted“

With the growth of the cities in the foothills of the Alps in the 12th century, the demand for wood increased and the rivers from the Alps were used to bring in large quantities of wood. The Inn was one of the most used rivers. It is very likely that the Romans also used its power to transport heavy loads. The untamed river courses were of course always a challenge and an adventure. Today, the Inn River is navigated by inflatable boats from Imst through the Imst Gorge to Roppen. With experienced boat guides and all safety precautions a low risk, but an unforgettable adventure on the traces of history and with great impressions of the gorge landscape.

■ 0049(0) (0)821 343 464-0, www.lemmingtours.com

Regional cuisine like 2000 years ago

■ Erlebnisdorf „Trofana Tyrol“, 6493 Mils bei Imst, An der Au 1, 0043(0)5493 601

Questions and information about the subsection

■ Touristinfo Imst, Johannespl. 4, 0043(0)5412 6910-0
■ Touristinfo TirolWest, 6511 Zams, Malserstr. 10 0043(0)5442 65 600
■ Via Claudia Augusta Info 0043(0)664 27 63 555

Map 19

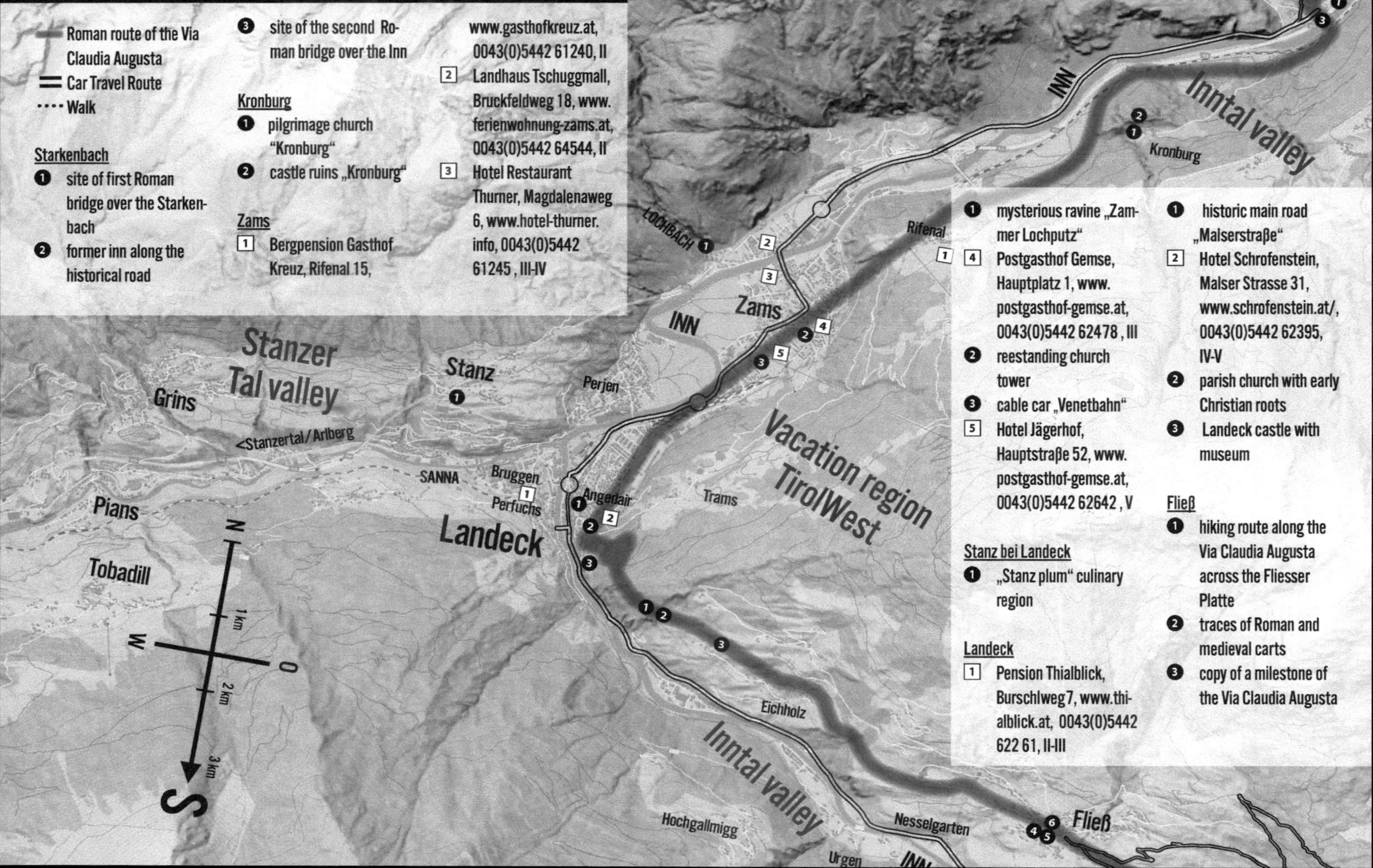

Roman route of the Via Claudia Augusta
Car Travel Route
Walk
Starkenbach
1 site of first Roman bridge over the Starkenbach
2 former inn along the historical road
3 site of the second Roman bridge over the Inn
Kronburg
1 pilgrimage church “Kronburg“
2 castle ruins „Kronburg“
Zams
[1] Bergpension Gasthof Kreuz, Rifenal 15, www.gasthofkreuz.at, 0043(0)5442 61240, II
[2] Landhaus Tschuggmall, Bruckfeldweg 18, www.ferienwohnung-zams.at, 0043(0)5442 64544, II
[3] Hotel Restaurant Thurner, Magdalenaweg 6, www.hotel-thurner.info, 0043(0)5442 61245 , III-IV
1 mysterious ravine „Zammer Lochputz“
[4] Postgasthof Gemse, Hauptplatz 1, www.postgasthof-gemse.at, 0043(0)5442 62478 , III
2 reestanding church tower
3 cable car „Venetbahn“
[5] Hotel Jägerhof, Hauptstraße 52, www.postgasthof-gemse.at, 0043(0)5442 62642 , V
Stanz bei Landeck
1 „Stanz plum“ culinary region
Landeck
[1] Pension Thialblick, Burschlweg 7, www.thialblick.at, 0043(0)5442 622 61, II-III
1 historic main road „Malserstraße“
[2] Hotel Schrofenstein, Malser Strasse 31, www.schrofenstein.at/, 0043(0)5442 62395, IV-V
2 parish church with early Christian roots
3 Landeck castle with museum
Fließ
1 hiking route along the Via Claudia Augusta across the Fliesser Platte
2 traces of Roman and medieval carts
3 copy of a milestone of the Via Claudia Augusta
Inntal valley
INN
Kronburg
LOCHBACH
Rifenal
Zams
INN
Stanzer Tal valley
Stanz
Perjen
Grins
<Stanzertal / Arlberg
SANNA
Bruggen
Perfuchs
Angedair
Pians
Landeck
Trams
Vacation region TirolWest
Tobadill
N
W
O
S
1 km
2 km
3 km
Eichholz
Inntal valley
Hochgallmigg
Nesselgarten
Fließ
Urgen
INN

The sunny slopes around Landeck have been the site of human settlement since pre-Roman and Roman times. Many archaeological finds have proven that: in Fließ, Stanz, Grins and near Kronburg castle. As was recently determined, the parish church of Landeck dates back to early Christianity, suggesting a sizable Roman settlement. Archaeologists already assumed that a Roman road station stood in today's district capital, as the Roman road leads from the slopes into the valley here. Landeck is surrounded by multiple fortress complexes. Schloss Landeck castle, the former seat of the court, is the most significant and the best preserved of them. The Arlberg railway was a major catalyst for the development of the town. The sunny slopes of the valley are favorable for agriculture as well as human settlement. Do not miss your chance to sample the excellent produce of this culinary region.

Route through Zams, Landeck and Fließ

Just before you reach Zams, the national road crosses the Inn river. Ahead of the bridge, the Zammer Lochputz gorge is on your right. The route takes you through Zams, where you pass the striking, free-standing steeple. The valley station of the Venetbergbahn cable car is on the road to Landeck. Enter Landeck and take a half left at the roundabout to enter Malserstraße, the historical main street of the town. There are several shops and restaurants here. Further up, you will see Schloss Landeck castle and the parish church. The road continues south in a straight line, passing Urgen and Nesselgarten on its way to Neuer Zoll, a district of Fließ. Here, it forks towards Fließ, where you can find the Via Claudia Augusta Documentation Center of Tyrol. Just before the town center, a little road on the left leads to the visitor center of the Kaunergrat Nature Park. Continue on this road to get to the entrance to the Kaunertal valley and Prutz.

The Lochputz – Tyrol's mystical gorge

A popular destination for day trippers, this gorge gives you dizzying and breath-taking views of one of Tyrol's wildest waters. Do not miss this unique experience. ■ 6511 Zams, Lötz 38, +43 (0)5442 65 600, Opening hours: 1 May to 30 September: every day 9:30 am–5:30 pm, 1 October to 31 October: every day 10 am–5 pm. 25 December to 25 February. Every Wednesday in July and August, a guided tour 8 pm–9:30 pm. www.zammer-lochputz.at.

A bird's-eye view of the Via Claudia Augusta

Let the Venet cable car take you from 780 m to 2,208 m in just eight minutes. The Venet is a natural and culinary paradise. Enjoy a spectacular, panoramic view of the surrounding mountainscapes, hike along the 'Tiroler Edle' route and sample some chocolate on the way, take in a few more incredible vistas from the 'Path of the Prospect' route, or pick one of the many restaurants to eat, drink and be merry, ■ 6511 Zams, Hauptstraße 38, +43 (0)5442 62 663. 6 June to 28 September and 2–5 October, 8:30am–5 pm, www.venet.at

Schloss Landeck castle and the parish church

Located in a 13th-century castle, this unusual local museum allows you to immerse yourself in the history of our ancestors as they fight for their survival. Travel through time and enjoy the stories retold at Schloss Landeck castle. ■ 6500 Landeck, Schlossweg 2, +43 (0)5442 63 202, opening hours: 13 April to 26 October, every day 10 am–5 pm.

A little hike and a leisurely walk

A two-hour hike takes you from Schloss Landeck castle to the village of Fließ, treating you to spectacular views as you cross the slope. In Fließ, head to the Via Claudia Augusta Documentation Center and the archaeological museum. The route leads you across the dry slopes of Fließ, a fascinating habitat that is home to thousands of butterfly species. On the Fließer Platte plateau, you can still see wheel tracks left in the rock surface during various epochs. The small walking path on the sunny slope between Stanz and Grinz is called 'Grüß-Gott-Weg', named for a local greeting that is exchanged very frequently on this busy route. This region is a center of schnapps production, and you will pass plenty of distilleries processing the famous Stanzer plums into tasty spirits. The sunny slope has been a site of human settlement for millennia, and it offers beautiful views of the valley.

The museum of Flieβ and the Via Claudia Augusta Documentation Center

In Flieβ, you will find the Via Claudia Augusta Documentation Center of Tyrol, which showcases discoveries from the imperial Roman road, a copy of the entire Roman road map Tabula Peutingeriana, and an entertaining film in which a Roman tells his lover about his trip along the Via Claudia Augusta. The archaeological museum on the other side of the road houses the town's most significant archaeological discoveries from the Bronze Age and the Iron Age. ■ Via Claudia Augusta Documentation Center and Museum Flieβ, 6521 Flieβ No. 89, 0043 (0)5449 200 65, opening hours: May to October, Tue–Sun, 10 am–12 noon and 3–5 pm. www.museum.fliess. at High above Flieβ, at the historical crossing of the Piller mountain into the Pitztal valley, there is an old sacrificial site for burnt offerings. Nearby, the dizzying 'Gache Blick' viewpoint gives you sweeping views of the steep gorge to the Oberes Gericht and the visitor center of the Kaunergrat nature park, which offers a nature exhibition and a restaurant with a panorama terrace. ■ 6521 Flieβ, Gachen Blick 100, +43 (0)5449 6304, Restaurant Gachenblick +43 (0)664 4408552

Special: A paradise for gourmets - among plums, spirits and chocolate

The leisure region TirolWest is an incredible destination for foodies. No matter what your palate craves, it certainly won't go without. Home-made fruit spirits from the Stanzer Zwetschke culinary region. Fresh, regional farm products from the Landecker Frischemarkt. A cornucopia of sprouts from Tonis Sprossengarten. Fresh Tiroggl bread from Landeck. Sophisticated chocolate delicacies from Tyrol. Treat yourself! The expansive orchards in Grins and Stanz are not only some of Europe's highest-altitude fruit plantations, they also grow some of Tyrol's tastiest fruit. After all, the famous Stanzer Zwetschke (plums) are processed into the region's best-known spirits – and for a good reason. These high-proof, high-quality schnapps delicacies have earned the region the title of 'Austria's culinary capital'. Enjoy a little glass after dinner and savor the pleasant warmth of these fine, fruity delights. ■ Genussregion TirolWest +43 (0)5442 65 600.

Special: Kaunergrat, the nature park spanning a whole mountain range

The nature park stretches from the upper Inntal valley to the Ötztal Alps. It includes the Pitztal valley, the Kaunertal valley, and the municipality of Flieβ. Its countless hiking trails grant you passage through a stunningly beautiful landscape with a rich flora and fauna. The park covers all altitudes, soaring from the Inn floodplains at 750 meters all the way to the magnificent three-thousand-meter giants of the Ötztal alps. As the largest stretch of unspoilt nature in all of Tyrol, it is home to 1,200 ibexes and 1,100 butterfly species. Between the sacrificial site on the Piller Sattel mountain pass and the 'Gachen Blick' viewpoint, you will find the visitor center of the nature park. It houses a multimedia exhibition titled '3000 m VERTIKAL' and a panorama restaurant with breathtaking views.

■ 6521 Flieβ, Gachblick 100, +43 (0)5449 6304, open June to September: Mon–Sun, 10 am–6 pm, October to May: Mon–Sun, 10 am–5pm (Sat: ticket machine), www.kaunergrat.at.

Regional cuisine like 2000 years ago

■ Postgasthof Gemse
6511 Zams, Hauptplatz 1, 0043(0)5442 62478
■ Hotel Restaurant Thurner
6511 Zams, Magdalenaweg 6, 0043(0)5442 61245
■ Hotel Restaurant Jägerhof
6511 Zams, Hauptstraβe 52, 0043(0)5442 62 642
■ Hotel Enzian
6500 Landeck, Adamhofgasse 6, 0043(0)5442 62066
■ Hotel Restaurant Schrofenstein
6500 Landeck, Malserstraβe 31, 0043(0)5442 62395

Overnight and camping possibilities in the appendix and in the maps

Questions and information about the subsection

■ Touristinfo TirolWest, 6500 Landeck, Malserstr. 10
0043(0)5442 65 600
■ Hotline Via Claudia Augusta 0043(0)664 27 63 55

Landeck Castle. Photo (2): Albin Niederstrasser

Archaeological Museum Flow

High class noble distilleries

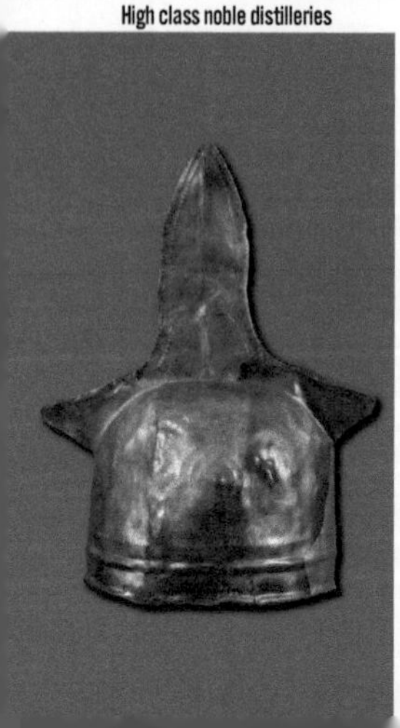

Zammer perforated plaster. Photo: TirolWest / guenterstandl.de

The Upper Court: from the Pontlatzbrücke bridge to Altfinstermünz (maps 20, 21)

The Oberes Gericht ('upper court') is an area stretching from Landeck to Nauders. Its name is based on the seat of the court, which used to be at Schloss Laudegg castle above Prutz before moving to Schloss Siegmundsried castle in the 17th century. This is one of the Via Claudia Augusta's best-preserved sections. It illustrates well how important the road was for the development of settlements. Many sections of the old country road, which has been replaced by the parallel B180 since, correspond to the Roman road. It passes picturesque towns and hamlets, castles and fortresses, manors and inns, farms and churches and a few old bridges. The most impressive bridge is that at Altfinstermünz, which used to be a customs station erected by the Romans where the Roman road crossed the Inn river.

Crossing the Oberes Gericht to Altfinstermünz

From the 'Gache Blick', our route takes us to Kauns at the entrance of the Kaunertal valley. From here, you can either head straight through the valley to get to Prutz or take a detour to the Kaunertal Glacier. If you choose the latter option, you will see the lovingly renovated Berneck castle a few hundred meters down the road. It used to guard the road across the Piller into the Pitztal valley. Today, it is privately owned, but guided tours are available from July to September, Sat and Sun, 10–11 am, ■ +43 (0)5472)6332. Also visit the Sauerbrunnquelle, a public spring on the bank of the Inn opposite of Prutz. Its water helps alleviate stomach and intestinal illness. The healing powers of the water have been known for 800 years, and princes, bishops, abbots and other important personalities took advantage of them up until the 20th century. To this day, the water is bottled and sold in some restaurants. On your way to the spring, you will cross the listed Prutzer bridge across the Inn river. Far above it, Burg Laudegg castle thrones on a rock. The residential tower dates back to the 13th century and is privately owned today. Our route takes us further along the old national road. Up to Pfunds, it largely corresponds to the Roman road. A swimming lake between Prutz and Ried beckons you to take a dip: with an island and a waterslide, it is a great place to relax or have a blast. The town of Ried im Oberinntal is characterized by Schloss Siegmundsried castle. Built in the late 15th century, it was named after Sigismund, Archduke of Austria. Guided tours of the castle are available regularly; call ■ +43 (0)50 225 100. At a bend in St. Christina, the route passes an old forge. In Steinbrücken, murals that are rare for this region can be viewed at an old farm. Observant travelers will spot a stone bridge on the bank of the Inn opposite Tösens. It leads to a side road towards Serfaus and has been dubbed "Roman bridge" by the locals. It is one of the three oldest medieval arch bridges in Tyrol. The next bridge over the Inn, located a little way down the road, is also listed. The Via Claudia Augusta now leads you past a string of picturesque hamlets called Tschuppbach, Schönegg, Stein, Lafairs und Birkach. In the past, carriages followed the old road to the Tschuppbach and Traube inns in Pfunds-Stuben.

Picturesque town of Pfunds, straddling the Inn river

The two districts of Pfunds, Pfunds-Dorf and Pfunds-Stuben, on the right and left side of the Inn river have many houses with Gothic architectural elements. They are characterized by external stone staircases and Romanesque or Gothic archways. There is a local-heritage museum at the church square in Pfunds-Dorf. Our route continues through the gate in the 11th-century tower and crosses the river to Pfunds-Stuben. On Dorfstraße, pay attention to the Liebfrauenkirche church, which houses an altar by the southern German master sculptor Jörg Lederer alongside lovely frescoes. The Richterhof building has three memorial panels on its gabled facade. ■ Museum, Dorf 103, +43 (0)5474 5229, guided tours available in summer: Sun 10 am–12 noon and 1:30–4 pm, Wed 1:30–3:30 pm

The historical customs station of Altfinstermünz

Before crossing the Kajetansbrücke bridge to Nauders, make sure you take a detour to the historical customs station of Altfinstermünz. Expect a 25-minute walk from the well-signposted parking lot just below Engadinerstraße. As remote as Altfinstermünz appears to be today, it used to be an important traffic hub that was easily accessible from several directions. Apart from the Via Claudia Augusta, which led to the Reschenpass, there was a road to the Unterengadin. Between the 9th and 11th century, Altfinstermünz used to be a toll station and the seat of the court for the Unterengadin region, Nauders and Pfunds. Its name was first mentioned in records from 1159. It translates to "threateningly towering rock". The fortification structures, such as the bridge tower and Schloss Siegmundseck, were built in 1472 to keep out invaders from the Engadin. They first had to hold their own during the Swabian War in 1499. The imposing, five-storey gate tower with machicolations and a fighting platform dates to the early 16th century. From 1652, Finstermünz formed the border between Tyrol and Grisons. In 1779, the customs office was moved to Martinsbruck, and the ensemble was bought by private investors. Until 1855, all southbound traffic had to squeeze through the narrow gate in the bridge tower of the former customs station. Take a guided tour and view the accompanying documentary to learn about its function and history. ■ +43 (0)5474 200 43 or 0043 (0)664 39 59 471, open 1 June to 15 October. 11 am–5 pm, closed Mondays. Guided tours, snacks and drinks available upon request from Easter until November. www.altfinstermuenz.com.

Special: Prutzer Sauerbrunn

In prehistory and early history, people had a close relationship with nature. Springs with special water were among the special places where they drew strength. In order to find such places, people paid attention to the springs where animals liked to drink and stay, especially when they were sick. People tasted, listened to their bodies and observed the effect on others. Mysticism and religion also played an important role. In ancient times, for the first time, people had the means to scientifically investigate ingredients and effects. Perhaps it was already known then that the water of the "Prutzer Sauerbrunnen" contains important minerals such as iron, calcium, magnesium as well as sulfur, and even a little natural carbonic acid, which makes it sparkling and fresh. With the fall of the Roman Empire, much knowledge was lost, replaced in the Middle Ages by feeling and faith. The Prutz people noticed the extraordinary taste of the water. They also observed that it was good for them - especially for problems with digestive organs. Since then, many come to get from the water - an impulse for early tourism. Today we know a lot and some people even think they know everything. What sometimes falls a little short is the ability to observe constantly and patiently, to listen, to feel and also simply to believe. If we do not know or understand something, it does not mean that it does not exist. With that in mind, "Bless you!"

Special: highlights to the right and left of the valley and the road

Once you reach the Oberes Gericht, there are countless trips waiting for you on the left and right side of the Inntal valley and the Roman road. The Kaunertaler Glacier Road is one of the most beautiful panoramic roads in the Alps. It passes the Gepatsch Reservoir on its way to the Weißseeferner glacier (2750 m). From the mountain village of Fendels, take the cable car to reach a hiking paradise with spectacular vistas. Walk along the Radurschlklamm gorge, where you can see an old mill and sawmill, or drive from Pfunds to the Tschey high valley, a spot as romantic and unspoilt as it gets. From the Kajetansbrücke, head to Spiss, the highest-altitude municipality in Austria (1628 m). Above and to the west of Nauders lie the Schwarzer See and Grüner See lakes. Both are lovely natural monuments. To the east, there is a cable car that takes you to the Alpine waterpark Goldwasser, a fun and educational place to spend an afternoon with all the family. www.nauders.com, www.tiroler-oberland.com, www.kaunertal.com

Regional cuisine like 2000 years ago

■ Hotel Gasthof Kreuz
6542 Pfunds-Stuben 3, 0043(0)5474 5218

Overnight and camping possibilities in the appendix and in the maps

Questions and information about the subsection

■ Touristinfo Prutz-Faggen
6522 Prutz, Hintergasse 2, 0043(0)50 225 500
■ Touristinfo Ried im Oberinntal
6531 Ried, Kirchplatz 48, 0043(0)50 225 100
■ Touristinfo Pfunds-Stuben
6542 Pfunds, Stubener Str. 40, 0043(0)50 225 300
■ Hotline Via Claudia Augusta 0043(0)664 27 63 555

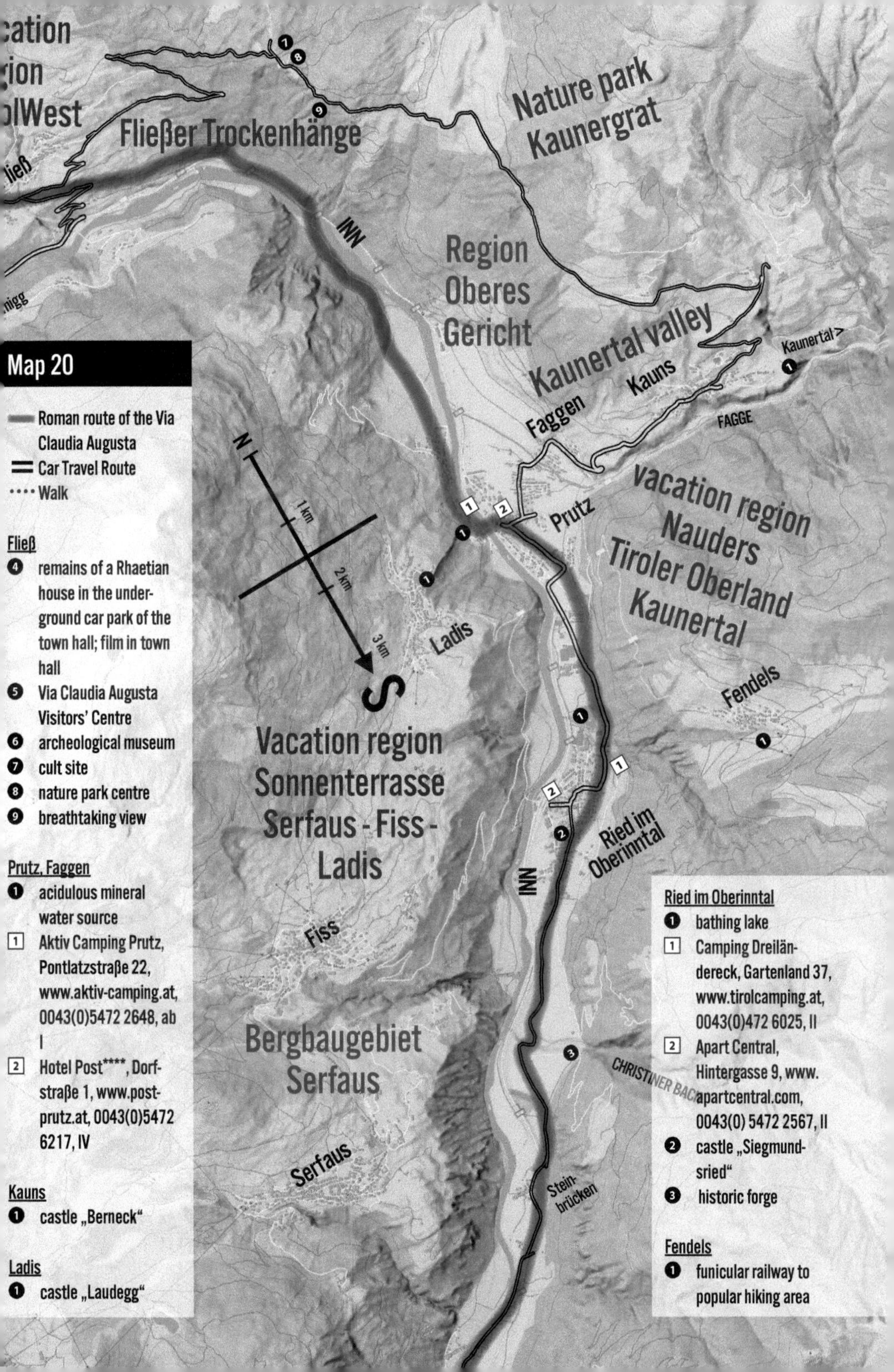

Map 20
Roman route of the Via Claudia Augusta
Car Travel Route
Walk
Fließ
4 remains of a Rhaetian house in the underground car park of the town hall; film in town hall
5 Via Claudia Augusta Visitors' Centre
6 archeological museum
7 cult site
8 nature park centre
9 breathtaking view
Prutz, Faggen
1 acidulous mineral water source
[1] Aktiv Camping Prutz, Pontlatzstraße 22, www.aktiv-camping.at, 0043(0)5472 2648, ab I
[2] Hotel Post****, Dorfstraße 1, www.post-prutz.at, 0043(0)5472 6217, IV
Kauns
1 castle „Berneck"
Ladis
1 castle „Laudegg"
Ried im Oberinntal
1 bathing lake
[1] Camping Dreiländereck, Gartenland 37, www.tirolcamping.at, 0043(0)472 6025, II
[2] Apart Central, Hintergasse 9, www.apartcentral.com, 0043(0) 5472 2567, II
2 castle „Siegmundsried"
3 historic forge
Fendels
1 funicular railway to popular hiking area
Fließer Trockenhänge
Nature park Kaunergrat
INN
Region Oberes Gericht
Kaunertal valley
Kauns
Kaunertal >
Faggen
FAGGE
Prutz
vacation region Nauders Tiroler Oberland Kaunertal
N
1 km
2 km
3 km
S
Ladis
Fendels
Vacation region Sonnenterrasse Serfaus - Fiss - Ladis
Ried im Oberinntal
Fiss
Bergbaugebiet Serfaus
CHRISTINER BACH
Serfaus
Stein-brücken

Map 21

Roman route of the Via Claudia Augusta
Car Travel Route
Walk

Tösens

1. one of the oldest stone arch bridges of the Tyrol

[1] Gasthof Tschuppbach, Tschuppbach 1, www.urlaubambauernhof.at/tschuppbach, 0043(0)5477 443, III-IV

Pfunds

1. Museum "Pfunds"
2. bridge tower "Turmloch" and bridge across the Inn
3. church „Liebfrauenkirche"

[1] Hotel Gasthof Kreuz****, Stuben 43, www.hotelkreuz.at, 0043(0)5474 5218, V

[2] Pension St. Lukas***, Stuben 47, www.pensionstlukas.com, 0043(0) 5474 5476, III

[3] Hotel Tyrol, Stubenerstrasse 296, www.hoteltyrol-austria.at, 0043(0)5474 5247 , V-VI

4. jugde's residence
5. ravine "Radurschlklamm"
6. historic mill and saw mill
7. mountain valley "Tschey"
8. „Minifundus" park with miniatures of houses of Pfunds
9. historical mining area "Platzertal"

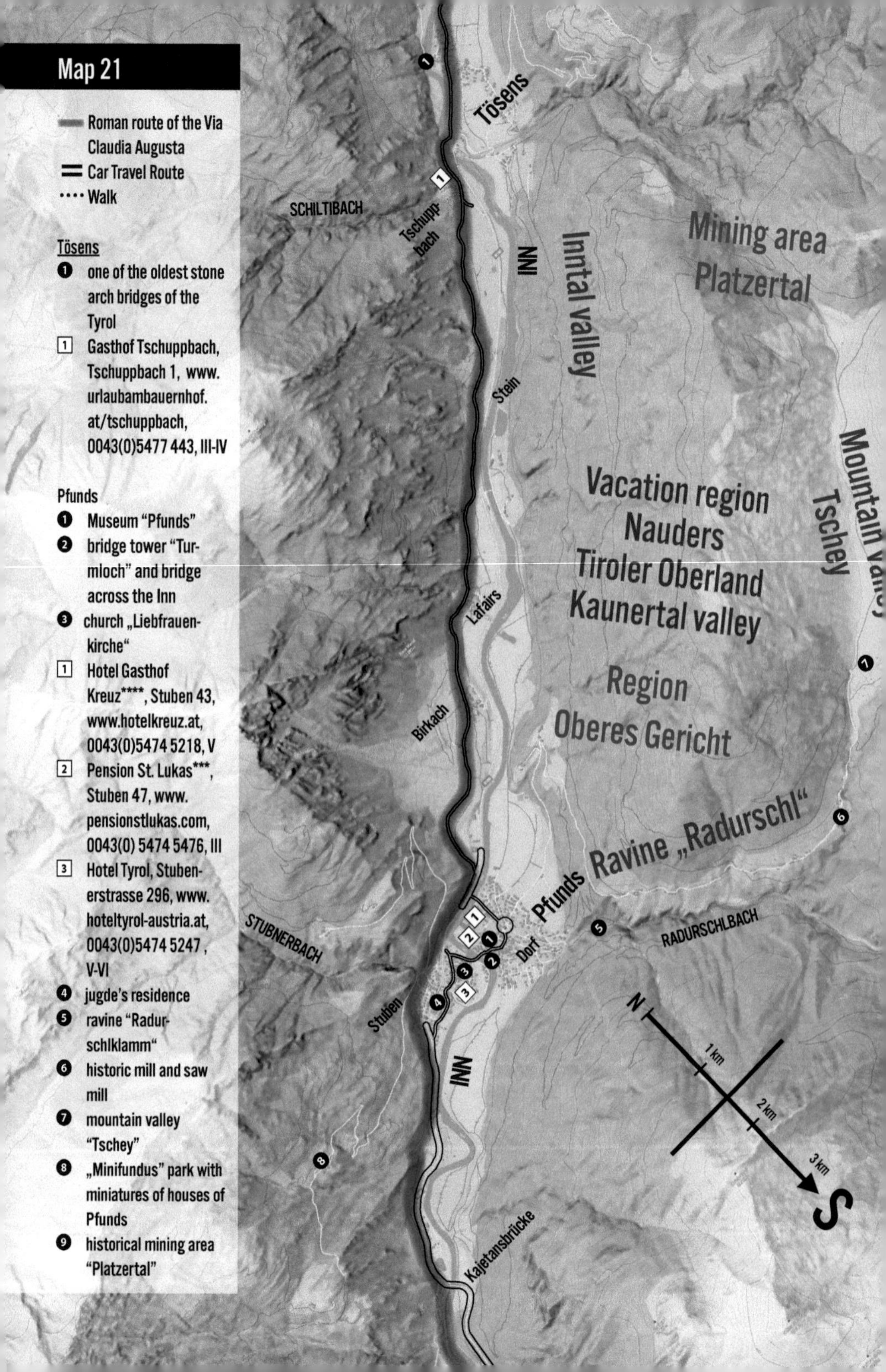

Superior Court.

One of the oldest stone bridges in Tyrol in Tösens

The „Turmloch“ and the bridge over the Inn between Pfunds and Stuben

Siegmundsried Castle in Ried

Altfinstermünz

20 The Reschenpass: the roof of the route (maps 22, 23)

In the olden days, the Alpine passes were extremely challenging. That is why the Romans liked to build rest stations before and after each pass. At an altitude of 1507, meters, the Reschenpass is the highest point of the Via Claudia Augusta. Its peak is in Italy. The Austrian municipality of Nauders, a little to the north, used to be the site of the only Roman road station documented in writing: Inutrium. Today, holidaymakers flock to the high valley. They enjoy the beautiful mountainscapes around Nauders, Reschen/Resia, Graun/Curon, and St. Valentin/San Valentino in summer and winter alike. These four towns are in two countries and tourism regions, but they are all part of the geographical region of the Vinschgau valley. Visitors also appreciate the reservoirs that were created on the pass. The steeple of the submerged Altgrauner church protruding from the water is one of the most popular photo motifs on the route.

The route to Nauders on the Reschenpass

After the Kajetansbrücke over the Inn river, the Reschen national road ascends the rocky slope. The road was built in 1856. Before its construction, the government spent decades discussing whether to improve the existing direttissima, which followed the Roman road from Altfinstermünz to Nauders, or build a more modern road with a steady incline, landslide guards and tunnels. As you travel along the result of all those years of planning, you are constantly treated to spectacular views of the Altfinstermünz ensemble in the Inn gorge. On the side of the road, you will see what is left of the Hotel Hochfinstermünz. Once a high-class hotel, it has been all but abandoned. From the hotel parking lot, follow the hiking trail into the Innschlucht gorge and continue for about 20 minutes to reach Altfinstermünz. Above the gorge, the Reschen national road takes you through a narrow which marks the geographical boundary between the Inntal valley and the Vinschgau valley. The next high valley is already part of the latter. The Nauders fortress thrones above the narrow. Built close to the rockface, it used to be the northernmost fortress complex of the Austria-Hungarian empire and a defense against Italy. Today, it houses an exhibition about traffic over the Reschenpass. ■ +43 (0)50225400, opens upon arrangement.

Inutrium & Schloss Naudersberg castle

To see the center of the touristic town of Nauders on the Reschenpass, which used to be a road station on the Roman road, start at the entrance of the town. It is even mentioned in Ptolemy's World Map, which was created in Alexandria in 150 A. D. The St. Valentin parish church dates to the 4th century and is dedicated to the apostle of the Roman province of Rhaetia. It was redesigned in the Baroque/Romanesque Revival style later but still retains its original Gothic tower from 1509. The small Heiliger Geist hospital church in the lower area of the village belonged to a hostel for poor travelers built in 1140. The road through the town is lined with buildings whose past as inns is quite obvious. Schloss Naudersberg castle, which thrones on a hill in the north of the village, is a fortress from the 13th/14th century that was expanded in the 15th/16th century. The Roman road passes the eastern foot of the hill. Not long ago, it was the Reschen national road. Today, it is the domain of cyclists and the locals who live around it. From Naudersberg, you can see the entire border valley. The jurisdiction of the former seat of the court also covered the upper Vinschgau valley. Today, the castle houses a museum and a restaurant. The St. Leonhardskapelle, a chapel in the southern part of the castle, boasts one of the most significant Romanesque frescoes. ■+43(0)50225400, guided tours available as per the current schedule and upon prior arrangement.

Reschenpass, Reschensee and Haidersee lakes

The former border stations clearly mark the national boundary, which is located just before the pass plateau and the nearby watershed. In the 19th century, the last bear of South Tyrol was shot dead in the town of Reschen/Resia, which is the first Italian stop of our travel route. Its inhabitants are lovingly called 'Bärenschießer' ('bear shooters'). Thanks to its excellent wind conditions, the Reschensee lake is the most popular kite surfing and kite skiing destination in the Alps. Every year, national and international kite events are held here. Spend some time by the shore of the lake and watch the kite surfers glide across the water. Dammed in 1950, the lake combined the Reschensee and

Mittersee into a single body of water with a length of 6 kilometers. It even replaced the old village of Graun/Curon. To this day, its steeple protrudes from the water near the eastern shore of the lake, creating one of the best-known postcard motifs. Apart from the listed, Romanesque steeple, the Late Gothic chapel from 1521 on a small hill near the modern town center also evokes the early days of Graun/Curon. Before you reach St. Valentin auf der Haide/San Valentino alla Muta, the travel route takes you along the striking dam. Behind it lies the Haidersee, the only one of the three original lakes that remained in its natural state. The town museum of Graun/Curon documents how the Reschensee lake was dammed and how the town of Graun was submerged and rebuilt afterwards. ■ 39027 Graun, +39 0473 633 127.

History(s):

In prehistory and early history, people had a close relationship with nature. Springs with special water were among the special places where they drew strength. In order to find such places, people paid attention to the springs where animals liked to drink and stay, especially when they were sick. People tasted, listened to their bodies and observed the effect on others. Mysticism and religion also played an important role. In ancient times, for the first time, people had the means to scientifically investigate ingredients and effects. Perhaps it was already known then that the water of the „Prutzer Sauerbrunnen" contains important minerals such as iron, calcium, magnesium as well as sulfur, and even a little natural carbonic acid, which makes it sparkling and fresh. With the fall of the Roman Empire, much knowledge was lost, replaced in the Middle Ages by feeling and faith. The Prutz people noticed the extraordinary taste of the water. They also observed that it was good for them - especially for problems with digestive organs. Since then, many come to get from the water - an impulse for early tourism. Today we know a lot and some people even think they know everything. What sometimes falls a little short is the ability to observe constantly and patiently, to listen, to feel and also simply to believe. If we do not know or understand something, it does not mean that it does not exist. With that in mind, „Bless you!"

Regional cuisine like 2000 years ago

■ Hotel Restaurant Post
6543 Nauders,Tschiggfrey-Str. 37, 0043(0)5473 87 20 20
■ Gasthof „Zum Goldenen Löwen"
6543 Nauders 36, 0043(0)5473 87 208
■ Hotel Restaurant Central
6543 Nauders, Unterdorfweg 196, 0043(0)5473 87 22 10
■ Hotel Restaurant „Schwarzer Adler"
6543 Nauders,Tschiggfrey-Str. 33,0043(0)5473 87 25 40
■ Hotel Restaurant „Mein Almhof"
6543 Nauders, Tschiggfrey-Str. 314, 0043(0)5473 87 313
■ Gasthof Martha
6543 Nauders 296, 0043(0)5473 87 33 80

Overnight and camping possibilities in the appendix and in the maps

Questions and information about the subsection

■ Touristinfo Nauders am Reschenpass, 6543 Nauders, Doktor-Tschiggfrey-Str. 66,0043(0)50225400
■ Touristinfo Reschen
39037 Reschen, Hauptstraße 22, 0039 0473 633 101
■ Touristinfo St. Valentin
39037 St. Valentin, Hauptstraße 61, 0039 0473 634 603
■ Hotline Via Claudia Augusta 0043(0)664 27 63 555

Map 22

- Roman route of the Via Claudia Augusta
- Car Travel Route
- Walk

Finstermünz

❶ Altfinstermünz historic customs station

Nauders am Reschenpass

❶ fortress Nauders

1 Haus Sonneck, Hinterdorf 267, www.haus-sonneck.at, 0043(0)5473 87541, I

2 Pension Amontara, Spitzwiesenweg 243, www.amontanara.at, 0043(0) 5473 87323, II

3 Ferienhaus Auer, Dr. Tschiggfreystr. 446, www.ferienhaus-auer.at, 0043(0)5473 86158, I

4 Apart-Bauernhof Rosenhof, Kleinhansgasse 93, www.rosenhof-nauders.at, 0043(0)5473 86165, II

5 Apart-Pension Haus Arina, Dr. Tschiggfreystr. 392, www.arina.at, 0043(0)5473 87765, I-II

6 Gästehaus Vergissmeinnicht, Nauders 357, www.zimmer-ferienwohnungen.at, 0043(0)5473 87426, I

7 Haus Jung, Kleinhansgasse78, www.haus-jung.at, 0043(0)5473 87360, I

8 Gasthof Zum Goldenen Lö¦wen***, Postplatz 36, www.loewen-nauders.com, 0043(0)5473 87208, III-IV

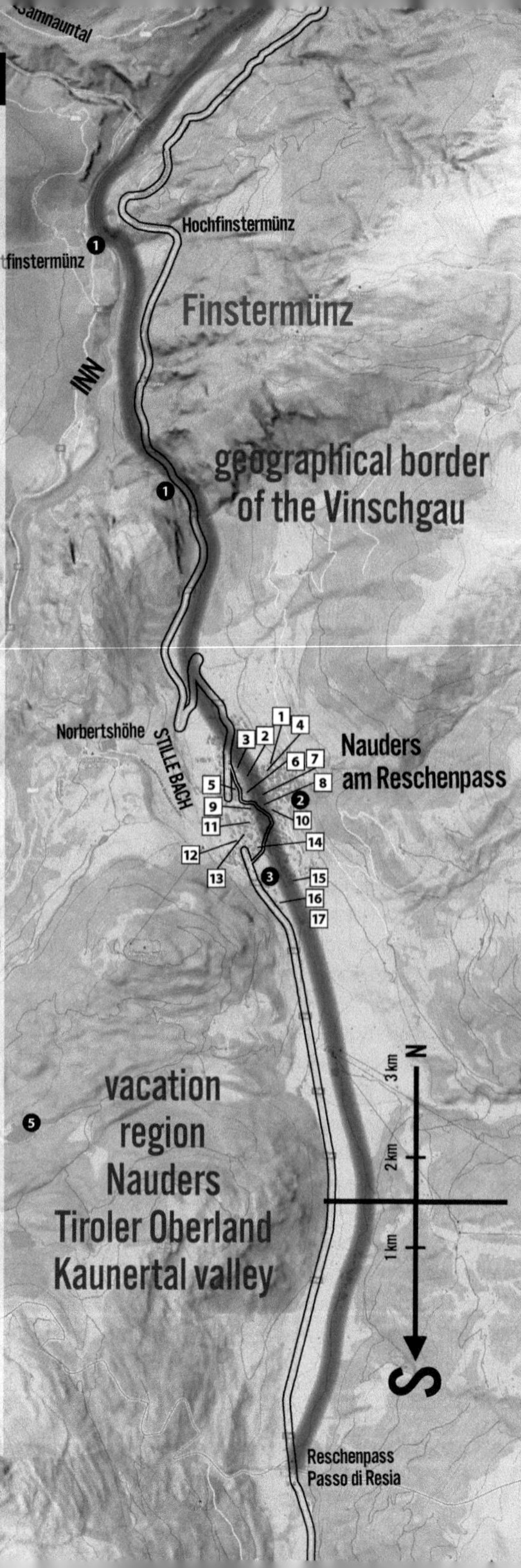

Nauders am Reschenpass

❷ parish church „Sankt Valentin“

9 Hotel Post ****, Dr.-Tschiggfrey-Str. 37, www.post-nauders.com, 0043(0)5473 872020, III-IV

10 Aktivhotel Schwarzer Adler ****, Dr.-Tschiggfrey-Str. 33, www.adlerhotel.at, 0043(0)5473 872540, III-IV

11 Hotel Central ****, Unterdorfstraße 196, www.hotel-central.at, 0043(0)5473 872210, IV-V

12 Haus Ferienglück, Sandbichl 455, www.haus-ferienglueck.at, 0043(0)650 6543455, II-III

13 Pension Garni Alpenhof, Nauders 229, www.alpenhof-nauders.at, 0043(0)5473 87263, IV-V

14 Hotel Restaurant Mein Almhof****, Dr.-Tschiggfrey-Str. 314, www.meinalmhof.at, 0043(0)5473 387313, IV-V

❸ castle „Naudersberg“

15 Hotel Neue Burg****, Alte Strasse 370, www.neue-burg.at, 0043(0)5473 87700, V

16 Gasthof Martha***, Nauders 296, http://www.gasthofmartha.at, 0043(0)5473 87338, III

17 Apart Bergkastelblick, Bundesstraße 287, www.bergkastelblick.at, 0043(0)676 9369873, III

❹ adventure world „Goldwasser“

❺ lake „Schwarzer See“

Nauders am Reschenpass, the first village in the high valley. Photo: Nauders am Reschenpass / Manuel Baldauf

Fortress Nauders.

Naudersberg Castle. Photo: Daniela Zangerl

The tower of Altgraun in the Reschensee.

Top kite spot Reschensee

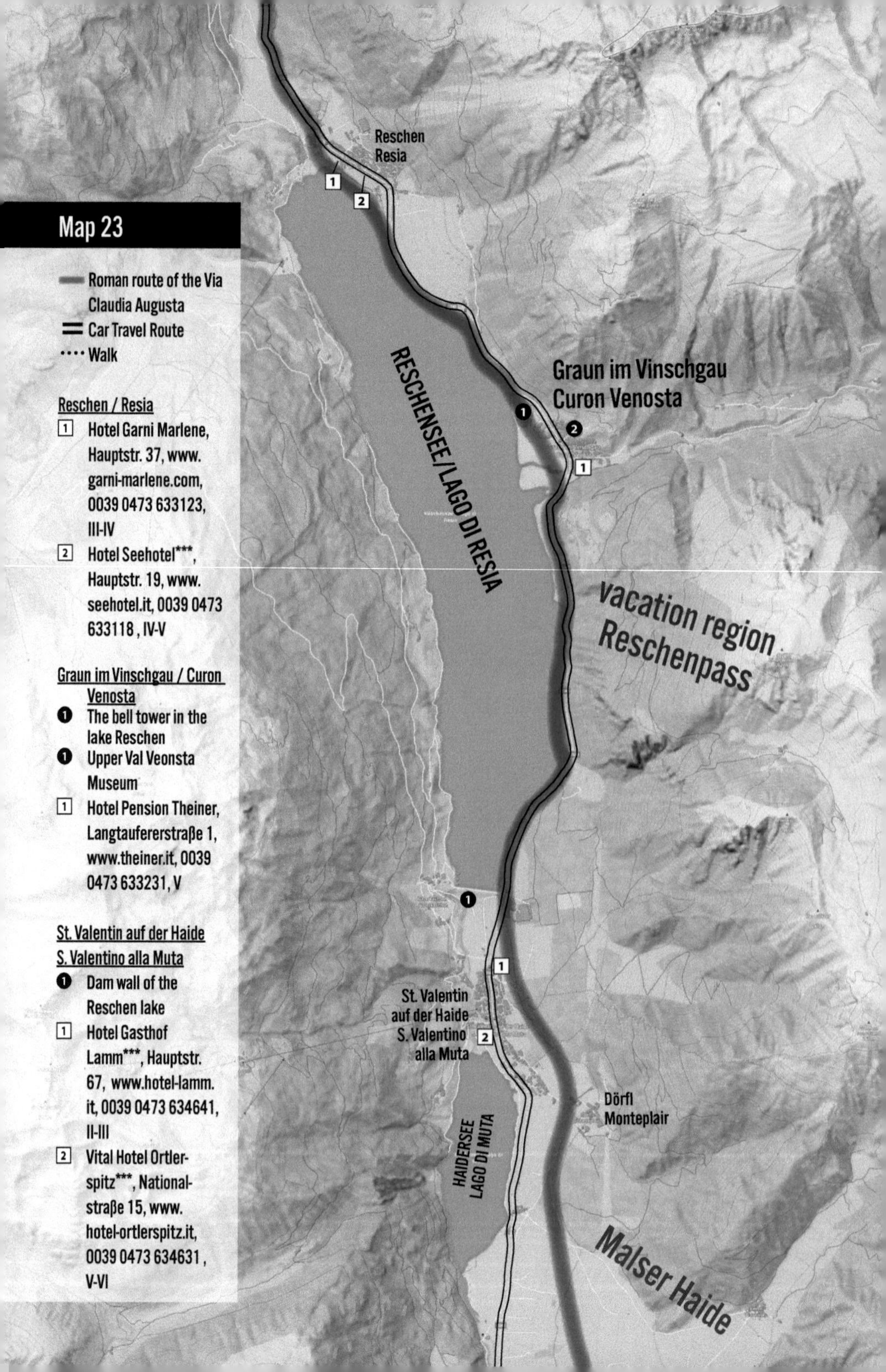
Map 23
Roman route of the Via Claudia Augusta
Car Travel Route
Walk
Reschen / Resia
1 Hotel Garni Marlene, Hauptstr. 37, www.garni-marlene.com, 0039 0473 633123, III-IV
2 Hotel Seehotel***, Hauptstr. 19, www.seehotel.it, 0039 0473 633118 , IV-V
Graun im Vinschgau / Curon Venosta
1 The bell tower in the lake Reschen
1 Upper Val Veonsta Museum
1 Hotel Pension Theiner, Langtaufererstraβe 1, www.theiner.it, 0039 0473 633231, V
St. Valentin auf der Haide
S. Valentino alla Muta
1 Dam wall of the Reschen lake
1 Hotel Gasthof Lamm***, Hauptstr. 67, www.hotel-lamm.it, 0039 0473 634641, II-III
2 Vital Hotel Ortler-spitz***, National-straβe 15, www.hotel-ortlerspitz.it, 0039 0473 634631 , V-VI
Reschen
Resia
RESCHENSEE/LAGO DI RESIA
Graun im Vinschgau
Curon Venosta
vacation region
Reschenpass
St. Valentin
auf der Haide
S. Valentino
alla Muta
HAIDERSEE
LAGO DI MUTA
Dörfl
Monteplair
Malser Haide

21 The upper Vinschgau valley, where each town is prettier than the next (map 23, 24, 25)

This region is filled with historical town centers and buildings like few others along the Via Claudia Augusta. Due to its favorable climate, the Vinschgau valley has been a popular place of human settlement since long before the Romans arrived. Its name is derived from the Venostes, a Rhaetian tribe settled on the Tartscher Bichl and the Ganglegg above Schluderns/Sluderno among other sites. The historical route of the Via Claudia Augusta led across the Mals heath, where archaeologists have identified a former Roman road station, and followed the sunny side of the valley after Mals/Malles. In the 10th century, Romanic farmers populated the region more densely and made the ground arable. Marienberg monastery supported them from the 12th century onwards. Multiple castles, the medieval town of Glurns/Glorenza with its fully preserved walls, and the centers of the surrounding villages bear witness to those times. Building on its rich heritage, the Vinschgau valley presents itself as a historically significant cultural region of South Tyrol.

Malser Haide, Burgeis, Mals

Cross the imposing Mals heath (the largest scree of the Alps) and its striking canals to get to Mals/Malles. About halfway, you pass the town of Burgeis/Burgusio, which was first mentioned in records from the 12th century. It has the Fürstenburg castle, picturesquely narrow alleyways, and a plethora of houses decorated with frescoes, portals, free-standing staircases and bay windows. Marienberg monastery, Europe's highest-altitude Benedictine monastery, thrones on the hill above. The local museum screens an interesting film that brings 900 years of monastic history to life. ■ 39024 Burgeis, Schlinig 1, +39 0473 843 980, open 15 March to 31 October: Mon–Sat, 10 am–5 pm; 27 December to 5 January: Mon–Sat 10 am–5 pm. The little church of St. Stefan dates to the 5th century. Excavations near the 9th-century St. Benedikt church in the north of the extensive old town have proven that Mals/Malles has Roman origins. In the 12th century, it became the seat of the court; in 1642, it was granted market privileges. To this day, the town has an unusually large number of steeples. In fact, there used to be two more. Not far from the village is the prominent Tartscher Bichl, which is considered the landmark of the Vinschgau and on which, according to legend, there was a rich settlement that sank because of the dissolute life of its inhabitants.

The town of Glurns/Glorenza

The small town of Glurns, situated a little further south, with its still completely preserved town walls, is one of the smallest towns in the Alps with just under 900 inhabitants. Strategically located and supported by the Tyrolean sovereigns, it achieved considerable wealth, but then fell more and more into obscurity. The Laubengassen are particularly worth seeing.

Schluderns/Sluderno and Prad/Prato

Schluderns/Sluderno is located on the sunny slope below the partially reconstructed Rhaetian settlement on the Gangledd mountain and the Churburg, a 13th-century castle that is considered the best-preserved fortress in all of South Tyrol. Since 1504, the castle has been owned by the Counts Trapp, who showcase an impressive collection of armors there. ■ 39020 Schluderns, Churburg 1, +39 0473 615 241, Guided tours between 10 March and 31 October: 10 am–12 noon and 2–4:30 pm. Closed on Mondays except public holidays, www.churburg.com. In the historical town center, the Vinschger Museum is worth a visit if you want to learn about the history of the valley. ■ 39020 Schluderns, Meranerstr. 1, 0039 0473 615 590, open 20 March to 31 October: 10 am–12 noon and 3–6 pm. Closed on Mondays except public holidays. www.vintschgermuseum.com. In the town center of Prad am Stilfserjoch/Prato Allo Stelvio, the permanent exhibition 'Unter Fischen – eine Reise in fremde Welten' at the Aquaprad visitor center of the national park gives you insights into the fish of the Stilfserjoch national park. Its 12 aquariums are designed to represent different habitats, from mountain lakes to Alpine streams and rivers. ■ 39026 Prad am Stifserjoch, Kreuzweg 4/c, +39 0473 618 212, open Tue–Fri: 9 am–12 noon and 2:30–6 pm. Sat, Sun, public holidays: 2:30–6 pm, closed on Mondays, www.aquaprad.com

Overnight and camping possibilities in the appendix and in the maps

Questions and information about the subsection

■ Hotline Tourist-Info Vinschgau, 0039 0473 620480

■ Hotline Via Claudia Augusta, 0043 664 27 63 555

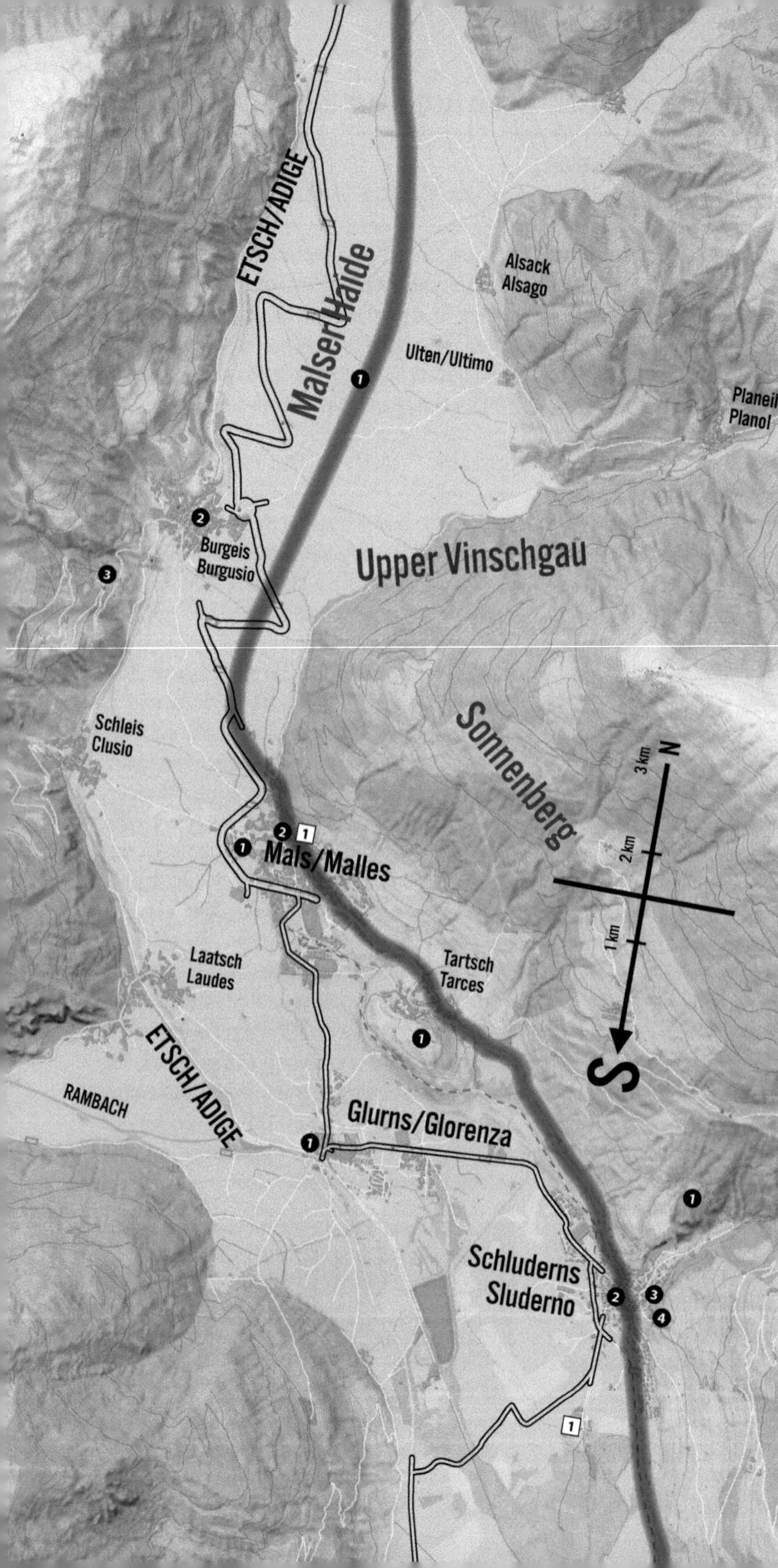

Map 24

- Roman route of the Via Claudia Augusta
- Car Travel Route
- Walk

Burgeis/Burgusio

1. The Mals heath, largest debris cone of the Alps
2. Town centre of Burgeis
3. Monastery „Marienberg“

Mals/Malles Venosta

1. Church „St.-Benedikt“
2. Historical centre of Mals

[1] Hotel Greif***, Gen. Verdroβstraβe 40/A, www.hotel-greif.com, 0039 0473 831189, V-VI

Tartsch / Tarces

1. historic settlement site

Glurns / Glorenza

1. The medieval town Glurns with completely preserved city walls

Schluderns/Sluderno

1. Partially reconstructed prehistoric hilltop settlement at Ganglegg
2. Historical centre of Schluderns
3. Museum of the Venosta Valley
4. Churburg with a large collection of armours

[1] Garni am Bauernhof Hausergut, Auenweg 3, www.miavalvenosta.it/de/obervinschgau/hausergut/, 0039 0473 615326, III

Malser Haide. Photo: Frieder Blickle

Marienberg and the Prince's Castle.

Churburg. Photo (2): Frieder Blickle

In the small town of Glurns. Photo: Vinschgau Marketing / Frieder Blickle

The Vintschgermuseum documents the history of the valley.

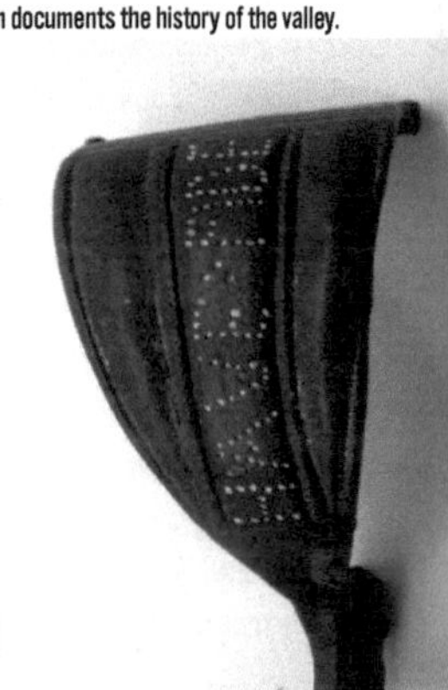

Ganglegg.

Acquaprad gives insight into the water world of the nature park.

22 Schlanders and Laas, the heart of the fruitful Vinschgau valley (map 25, 26)

The heart of the fruitful Vinschgau valley lies on the foothills of the Sonnenberg mountain. The Roman road is likely to have passed this area, where the marble village of Laas/Lasa and the regional capital, the market town of Schlanders/Silandro, are located today. Nomadic herders and hunters were present here as early as the Neolithic, attracted by sunny weather and low rainfall due to the high mountain ranges in the north and south. Since Roman times or earlier, the locals have mined the famous marble of Laas/Lasa and Göflan/Covelano. The milestone of the Via Claudia Augusta found at Rabland/Rablà provides evidence of this. Schlanders/Silandro and Laas/Lasa are first mentioned in writing in records from the late 11th and early 12th century. In the 14th century, Schlanders/Silandro became the seat of the court.

Laas/Lasa, a town of marble and apricots

On a little hill at the entrance to Laas/Lasa stands the picturesque and ancient St. Sisinus church. The Romanesque Hl. Johannes der Täufer parish church houses an altar mensa from the Early Middle Ages, decorated with a relief depicting the martyrs Sisinus, Alexander and Martyrius. Another noteworthy architectural monument of the area is the Kandlwaal irrigation canal, which crossed the Etsch river on tall stone pillars. A fire in 1907 left it in ruins. The Nörderberg in the south of Laas/Lasa has been a white-marble quarry since time immemorial, and the local marble is known to be particularly hard, resilient and weather-resistant. An inclined elevator transports it down into the valley; the marble blocks are stored on the factory grounds of Lasa Marmo. There are several processing companies in the town, too. Even the town square consists entirely of white marble. But Laas/Lasa is also the center of the growing region that produces Vinschgau apricots. Every year, a festival celebrates the local treasures, marble and apricots.

Schlanders/Silandro, the district capital

The hamlet of Kortsch/Corzes has an attractive, rural center overlooked by the Ägidus church, well visible from afar. It is a lovely place for a leisurely walk: its pedestrian area has plenty of little shops and cafés to explore. The former garrison town also offers lovely alleyways and many old buildings that were established between the 13th and 20th century: Schloss Schlandersburg castle, the Gothic parish church Mariä Himmelfahrt, the even older Michaelskapelle chapel at the cemetery, the Kapuzinerkirche church and the associated monastery of the Order of Friars Minor Capuchin, and various manors. Schloss Schlandersberg castle, built in the 13th century, thrones on the Sonnberg hill above the market town.

Regional cuisine like 2000 years ago

■ Historischer Gasthof Adler, Vinschgaustraβe 53, 0039 0473 626140

Overnight and camping possibilities in the appendix and in the maps

Questions and information about the subsection

■ Touristinfo Laas, 39023 Laas, Bahnhofstraβe 3
0039 0473 730 155
■ Touristinfo Schlanders, 39028 Schlanders, Kapuzinerstraβe 10, 0039 0473 730 155
■ Hotline Via Claudia Augusta, 0043664 27 63 555

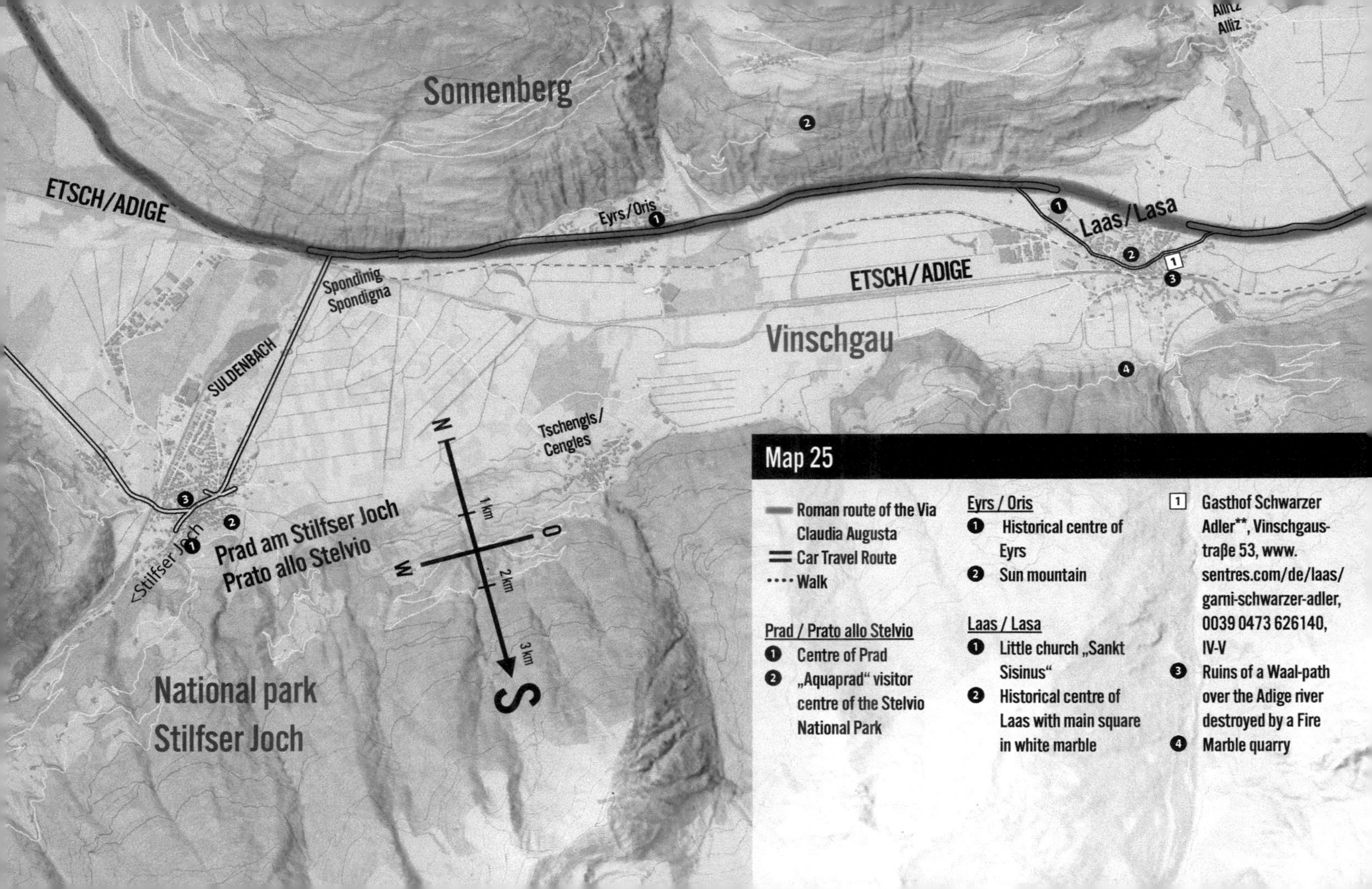
Sonnenberg
ETSCH/ADIGE
Eyrs/Oris
Laas/Lasa
Alliz
ETSCH/ADIGE
Spondinig
Spondigna
Vinschgau
SULDENBACH
Tschengls/
Cengles
N
O
W
S
1 km
2 km
3 km
Prad am Stilfser Joch
Prato allo Stelvio
<Stilfser Joch
National park
Stilfser Joch
Map 25
Roman route of the Via Claudia Augusta
Car Travel Route
Walk
Prad / Prato allo Stelvio
1 Centre of Prad
2 „Aquaprad" visitor centre of the Stelvio National Park
Eyrs / Oris
1 Historical centre of Eyrs
2 Sun mountain
Laas / Lasa
1 Little church „Sankt Sisinus"
2 Historical centre of Laas with main square in white marble
1 Gasthof Schwarzer Adler**, Vinschgaus-traße 53, www. sentres.com/de/laas/ garni-schwarzer-adler, 0039 0473 626140, IV-V
3 Ruins of a Waal-path over the Adige river destroyed by a Fire
4 Marble quarry

Goldrain Castle.

Sculptor from Lasa. Photo: SMG / Alex Filz

Silandro and Lasa are also centers of apple growing. Photo: Frieder Blickle

Castelbello.

Castelbello. Photos: Frieder Blickle, Christoph Tschaikner

Schlanders

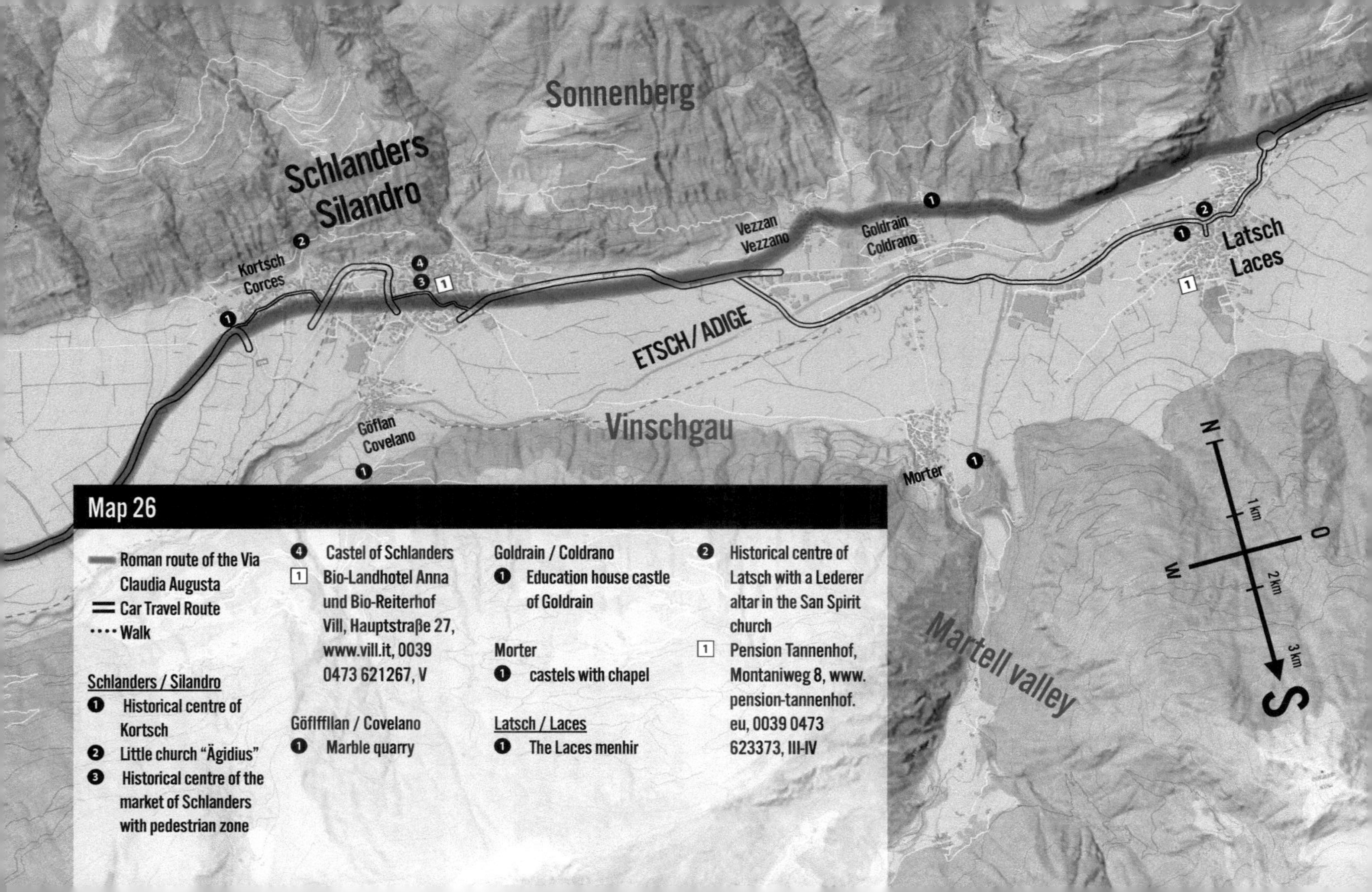

Map 26

Roman route of the Via Claudia Augusta
Car Travel Route
Walk

Schlanders / Silandro

1 Historical centre of Kortsch
2 Little church "Ägidius"
3 Historical centre of the market of Schlanders with pedestrian zone
4 Castel of Schlanders
[1] Bio-Landhotel Anna und Bio-Reiterhof Vill, Hauptstraße 27, www.vill.it, 0039 0473 621267, V

Göflfflan / Covelano

1 Marble quarry

Goldrain / Coldrano

1 Education house castle of Goldrain

Morter

1 castels with chapel

Latsch / Laces

1 The Laces menhir
2 Historical centre of Latsch with a Lederer altar in the San Spirit church
[1] Pension Tannenhof, Montaniweg 8, www.pension-tannenhof.eu, 0039 0473 623373, III-IV

23 The gorge at Goldrain, Latsch and Kastelbell (map 26, 27)

There are about ten fortress complexes and stately homes dotted around the narrow pass in the middle of the geographical Vinschgau valley region, which stretches up all the way to the Töll/Tel valley step. They were built very close to each other and helped secure this strategically important location. The most important structures are Schloss Goldrain castle, the educational and cultural center of the Vinschgau valley, Kastelbell/Castelbello with its permanent exhibition on the Via Claudia Augusta, and Reinhold Messner's summer residence of Juval, high up on the mountain. Blessed with a diverse microclimate offering plenty of sunshine, low precipitation and cool breezes at night, the region is home to a relatively recent tradition of growing a wide variety of quality wines. Kastelbell-Tschars/Castelbello-Ciardes is the largest wine-growing area in the valley, spanning an area of 25.5 hectares. Chardonnay, Pinot Blanc, Pinot Grigio, Gewürztraminer, Riesling, Vernatsch, Zweigelt and Pinot Noir ripen here.

Schloss Goldrain castle and Latsch/Laces

The market town of Latsch/Laces consists of a main district, the two subdivisions of Goldrain/Coldrano and Morter in the valley, and Tartsch/Tarres on a debris flow cone. Make sure you visit the hospital church of Latsch/Laces to see its winged altar, designed by Jörg Lederer. The mountain chapel of St. Stefan near Obermontan and Untermontan in Morter is considered the 'Sistine Chapel of South Tyrol' thanks to its splendid murals. Schloss Goldrain castle, built gradually from 1475 onwards, is worth visiting for its enclosing wall, portals, free-standing staircases and recessed balconies. All important construction parts are made from white marble. Also have a look at the 5000-year-old menhir (standing stone) of Latsch/Laces. It can be viewed every Monday at the Bichlkirche near the entrance to the village, where it was originally found.

Kastelbell/Castelbello and Tschars/Ciardes

Its location at the narrowest part of the valley and the castle on the promontory by the road give the village a particularly striking appearance. ■ 39020 Kastelbell, Staatsstraße 5, +39 0473 624 193, Guided tours available from 17 June to 14 September: Tue–Sun, 11 am, 2 pm, 3 pm and 4 pm. Minimum group size: 4 people, www.schloss-kastelbell.com. The canal path is worth a detour. Tschars/Ciardes, which was merged with Kastelbell/Castelbello in 1928, is located on a debris flow cone on the sunny side of the valley, which is a little wider again here. Reinhold Messner's summer residence Juval, just above the entrance to the Schnalstal valley, houses the Tibetika collection at the Messner Mountain Museum. ■ Kastelbell, Juval 3, +39 348 443 38 71, open between the fourth Sunday of March to 30 June and from 1 September to the first Sunday in November, 10 am–4 pm, closed on Wednesdays, www.messner-mountain-museum.it (to be found in the map after next!)

Regional cuisine like 2000 years ago

Here could be an inn that has at least one dish on the menu continuously as it was 2000 years ago.

Overnight and camping possibilities in the appendix and in the maps

Questions and information about the subsection

■ Hotline Vinschgau, 0039 0473 620480
■ Hotline Via Claudia Augusta, 0043664 27 63 555

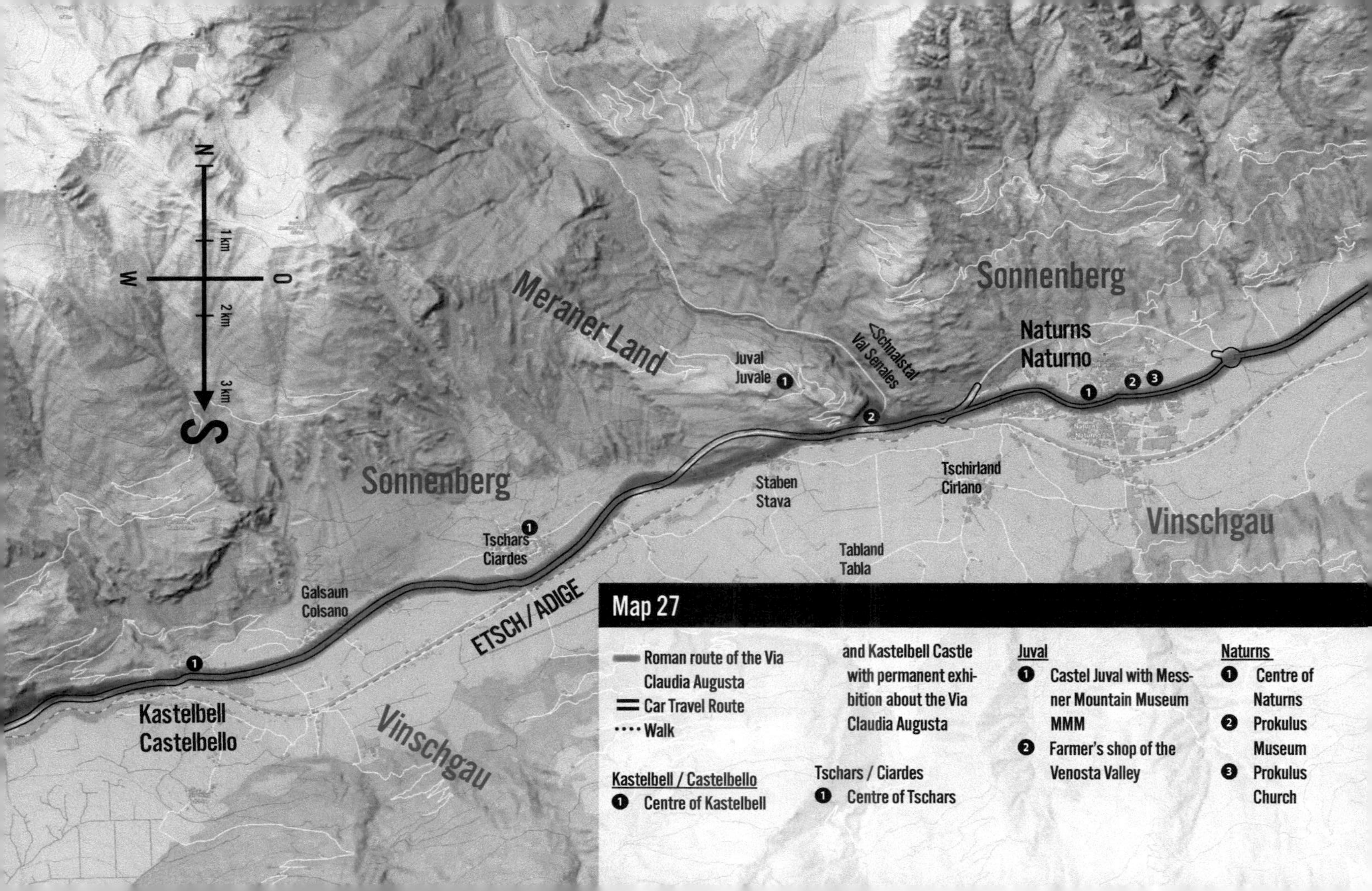
N
W
O
S
1 km
2 km
3 km
Meraner Land
Sonnenberg
Sonnenberg
Juval
Juvale
<Schnalstal
Val Senales
Naturns
Naturno
Staben
Stava
Tschirland
Cirlano
Tabland
Tabla
Vinschgau
Vinschgau
Tschars
Ciardes
Galsaun
Colsano
ETSCH / ADIGE
Kastelbell
Castelbello
Map 27
Roman route of the Via Claudia Augusta
Car Travel Route
Walk
Kastelbell / Castelbello
1 Centre of Kastelbell and Kastelbell Castle with permanent exhibition about the Via Claudia Augusta
Tschars / Ciardes
1 Centre of Tschars
Juval
1 Castel Juval with Messner Mountain Museum MMM
2 Farmer's shop of the Venosta Valley
Naturns
1 Centre of Naturns
2 Prokulus Museum
3 Prokulus Church

While the municipalities of Naturns/Naturno, Plaus and Partschins/Parcines are geographically part of the Vinschgau valley, they belong to the administrative district of Burggrafenamt and the tourism association of the Meran/Merano and environs. The earliest evidence of human settlement found on the southern mountain pass date back to the Mesolithic. The name 'Naturns' comes from the Celts and translates to 'settlements on the meadow'. Human settlement of this region has continued uninterrupted. One of the two milestones of the Via Claudia Augusta was found in Rabland/Rablà. The Prokuluskirchlein, a little church in the eastern part of Naturns/Naturno, dates back to the 7th century. Its inner frescoes were probably painted in the 8th century, making them the oldest in the German-speaking cultural sphere. Visit the St. Prokulus museum to learn about the history of the region from its multimedial exhibition.

Naturns/Naturno, Plaus

Naturns/Naturno is a vibrant hotspot of tourism and trade and an excellent place for a walk, a shopping trip or a meal. Its central street is lined with buildings that used to be inns. For a historical and cultural highlight, visit St. Proculus' Church and the Proculus Museum. ■ Naturns, St.-Prokulus-Straße, +39 0473 673 139, open from 1 April to 2 November, Tue–Sun and public holidays: 10 am–12:30 pm and 2:30–4:30 pm, closed on Mondays, www.naturns.it/prokulus. Head a little further into the valley and cross the Etsch river to get to Plaus, a little municipality first mentioned in records from the 13th century.

Rabland/Rablà, Partschins/Parcines, Töll/Tel

Near the Hotel Hanswirt in Rabland/Rablà, one of the two milestones marking the Via Claudia Augusta was found. Today, you can still see a replica of the milestone here. The original is kept at the Civic Museum of Bolzano/Bozen. Just around the corner, you can view the largest model railway in South Tyrol. Partschins/Parcines has the largest elevation span of all the towns in the Vinschgau valley: from the valley at 525 meters to the Roteck peak at 3337 meters. In is picturesque center, visit the Late Gothic parish church of St. Peter and Paul, the 13th-century castle winery and the typewriter museum, dedicated to Peter Mitterhofer from Partschins/Parcines, the inventor of the typewriter. ■ Partschins, Kirchplatz 10, +39 0473 967 581, open from April to October: Mon 2–6 pm, Tue–Fri 10 am–12 noon and 2–6 pm, Sat 10 am–12 noon, www.schreibmaschinenmuseum.com.

Regional cuisine like 2000 years ago

Here could be an inn that has at least one dish on the menu continuously as it was 2000 years ago.

Overnight and camping possibilities in the appendix and in the maps

Questions and information about the subsection

■ Touristinfo Naturns
39025 Naturns, Rathausstraße 1, 0039 0473 666 077
■ Touristinfos Rabland & Partschins
39020 Partschins, 0039 0473 967 157
■ Hotline Via Claudia Augusta, 0043664 27 63 555

Mountain farms above Naturno. Photo: Tschaikner

Proculus church. photos (2): Lois Lammerhuber

Proculus Museum.

Replica of the milestone of the Via Claudia Augusta at the site in Rabland.

Typewriter Museum

25 The old bridge over the Etsch river in Algund, Marling and Meran (map 28)

The 200-meter terrace near Töll/Tel takes you from the Vinschgau valley into the Mediterranean garden village of Algund/Lagundo. Its lower altitude and sheltered location make this region one of Italy's warmest: palm trees, cypresses and olive trees grow alongside birch trees and sycamores. There are many gardens with southern plants here. They give the village a feeling of existing simultaneously in the Alps and the Mediterranean. The Roman road had a bridge here. It crossed the Etsch river near Schloss Forst castle, then headed back up the hill and onwards to the panoramic village of Marling/Marlengo on the western slopes above Meran/Merano. To this day, there are bridges over the Etsch river between Algund/Lagundo and Marling/Marlengo. The Brückenkopf museum in Algund/Lagundo tells the story of the historical ones. Two of the most beautiful canal paths lead through the beautiful landscapes dotted with vineyards and apple orchards, the Algunder Waal and the Marlinger Waal. In and around Meran/Merano, you will also find the only wellness spa along the Via Claudia Augusta, the gardens of Schloss Trauttmansdorf castle, and Schloss Tirol castle. The area is a holistic region of well-being awash with mother nature's ripest bounty.

Garden village Algund at the old Etsch bridge

At the Etsch lock at Töll/Tel, our route forks to the left and follows the old country road to Algund/Lagundo, which corresponds to the Roman road. Right after the fork, there is a parking lot that marks the beginning of the Algunder Waalweg hiking trail. From here, you have wonderful views of the garden village and the city of Meran/Merano. The same vistas present themselves when you stand at the picturesque rest stop just by the road, where the locals have erected the huge 'Trauttmansdorff Thrones'. Algund/Lagundo has an attractive, modern church. Although many of its houses have been rebuilt and renovated, you can still feel that the continuation of the Alte Landstraße used to lead to the spa town. The new Brückenkopf Museum on the Etsch river is dedicated to the historical roads that all crossed the river in this spot. Today, there is still a bridge here. Visitors can cross it on foot to get to the district of Forst with its eponymous castle and private brewery.

The spa town of Meran/Merano

Meran/Merano used to be the site of the Castrum Maiense fortress in Late Antiquity, and it still has a lot to offer beyond its lovely old town and beautiful arcades. A two-hour walk from the parking lot at the Frauenmuseum will take you past nearly all of its sights, including the new wellness temple Therme Meran and the Sisi Gardens. The ancestral seat of the Counts of Tyrol and the famous Trauttmansdorff Castle Gardens throne above the town.

Panoramic village of Marlengo on the western slope above Merano

Nestled picturesquely in the slope, Marling/Marlengo has a well-preserved old town. The village and the canal path, which is the longest of its kind in South Tyrol at a length of 12 kilometers, give you spectacular views of the spa town below. Schloss Lebenberg is one of South Tyrol's most beautiful castles. While privately owned, parts of it are open to the public.

Regional cuisine like 2000 years ago

Here could be an inn that has at least one dish on the menu continuously as it was 2000 years ago.

Overnight and camping possibilities in the appendix and in the maps

Questions and information about the subsection

■ Touristinfo 39022 Algund, Hans-Gamper-Platz 3, 0039 0473 448 600

■ Touristinfo 39020 Marling, Kirchplatz 5, 0039 0473 447 147

Via Claudia Augusta Hotline, 0043664 27 63 555

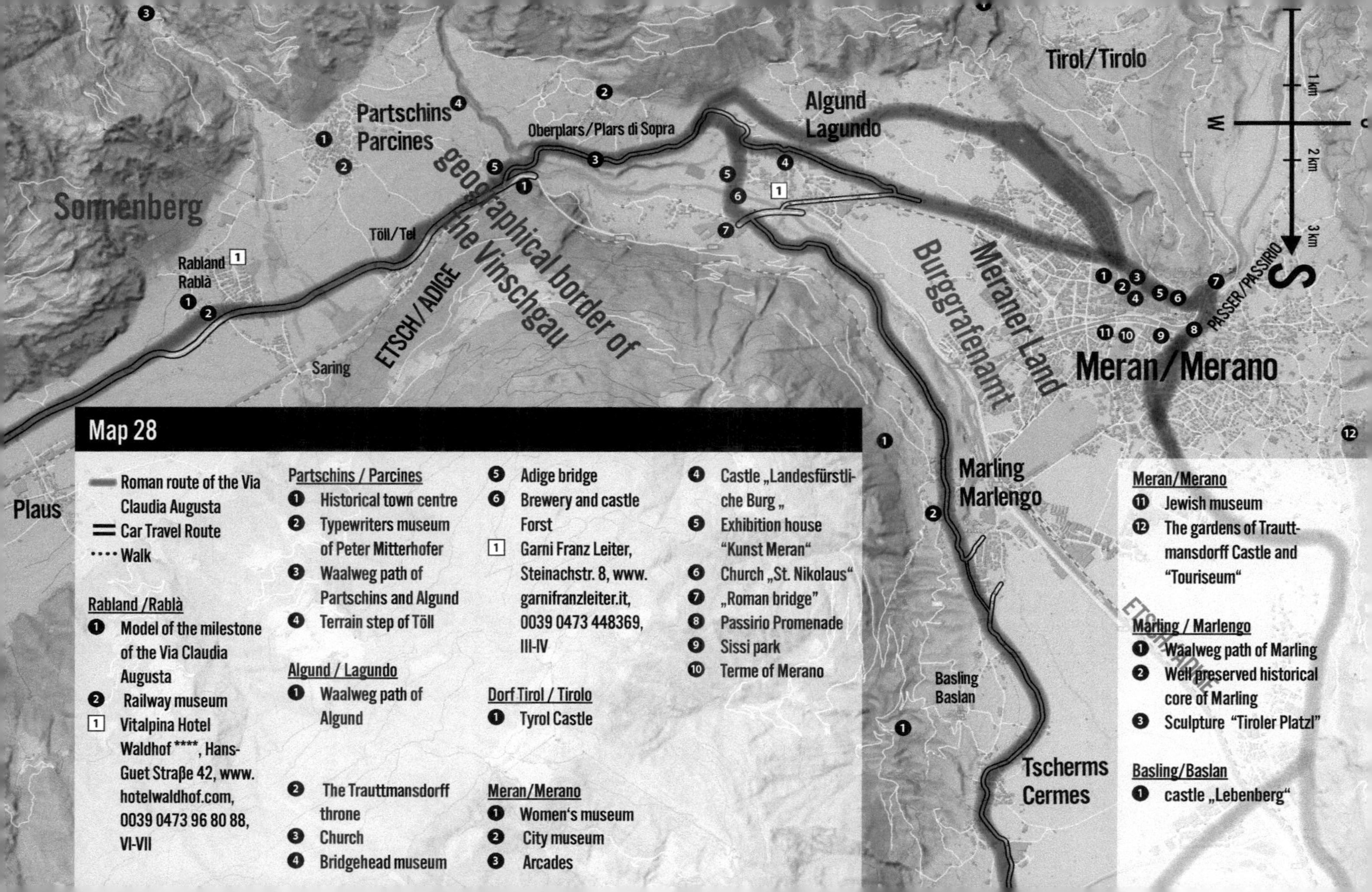
Map 28
Roman route of the Via Claudia Augusta
Car Travel Route
Walk
Rabland / Rablà
1 Model of the milestone of the Via Claudia Augusta
2 Railway museum
1 Vitalpina Hotel Waldhof ****, Hans-Guet Straße 42, www.hotelwaldhof.com, 0039 0473 96 80 88, VI-VII
Partschins / Parcines
1 Historical town centre
2 Typewriters museum of Peter Mitterhofer
3 Waalweg path of Partschins and Algund
4 Terrain step of Töll
Algund / Lagundo
1 Waalweg path of Algund
2 The Trauttmansdorff throne
3 Church
4 Bridgehead museum
5 Adige bridge
6 Brewery and castle Forst
1 Garni Franz Leiter, Steinachstr. 8, www.garnifranzleiter.it, 0039 0473 448369, III-IV
Dorf Tirol / Tirolo
1 Tyrol Castle
Meran/Merano
1 Women's museum
2 City museum
3 Arcades
4 Castle „Landesfürstliche Burg „
5 Exhibition house "Kunst Meran"
6 Church „St. Nikolaus"
7 „Roman bridge"
8 Passirio Promenade
9 Sissi park
10 Terme of Merano
Meran/Merano
11 Jewish museum
12 The gardens of Trauttmansdorff Castle and "Touriseum"
Marling / Marlengo
1 Waalweg path of Marling
2 Well preserved historical core of Marling
3 Sculpture "Tiroler Platzl"
Basling/Baslan
1 castle „Lebenberg"
Tirol/Tirolo
Partschins
Parcines
Algund
Lagundo
Oberplars/Plars di Sopra
Sonnenberg
Töll/Tel
Rabland
Rablà
geographical border of the Vinschgau
ETSCH / ADIGE
Saring
Meraner Land
Burggrafenamt
Meran/Merano
PASSER/PASSIRIO
Marling
Marlengo
Basling
Baslan
Tscherms
Cermes
Plaus
W
S
1 km
2 km
3 km

The panoramic village of Algund and the garden village of Algund on the Roman road ,south and north of the Roman bridge over the Adige river. Photo: Tschaikner

The historical bridgehead in Algund.

Oversized Trauttmansdorff throne chairs in the garden village Algund

Today's bridge over the Adige between Algund and Forst with the brewery.

Merano spa town

The Merano Thermal Baths.

Panoramic village Marlengo

Trauttmansdorff Castle with its famous gardens

26 Between Meran/Merano and Bolzano/Bozen: a land of castles (map 28, 29, 30)

Between Meran/Merano and Bolzano/Bozen, the Roman road crossed the Etschtal valley along its western slope. Prehistoric settlements existed on its many hills. In Nals/Nalles, archaeologists discovered a house with a underfloor heating system, bathing complex and apsis from late antiquity. The Aschbach river in Gargazon/Gargazzone marked the boundary between the Roman provinces of Rhaetia I and Rhaetia II. To this day, this region is a border region. From the 13th century onwards, countless fortresses sprang up, giving the area the highest density of castles in Europe. Some of the towns in the region are very old: St. George's Church and St. Margaret's Church in Lana both date back to the 9th century, for instance. The locals lived off the produce of their land and business which the road brought; some worked in mining. Important silver mines existed in Nals/Nalles and Terlan/Terlano. In the 15th century, as many as 1000 miners were digging for ores in more than 30 pits in Terlan/Terlano alone. From Andrian/Andriano onwards, the Etsch river was navigable, facilitating the transport of silver to the south.

Tscherms/Cermes, Lana, Burgstall/Postal, Gargazon/Gargazzone

The border area was inhabited at a very early stage. But the municipality of Lana was only created when Vill, Oberlana/Lana di Sopra and Niederlana/Lana di Sotto were merged in 1850. Besides the castles, palaces and stately homes of the town, attractions include the parish church Mariä Himmelfahrt in Niederlana with its Schnatterpeck altar and the South Tyrolean Museum of Fruit-Growing. The Roman provincial boundary of Aschbach river with several waterfalls makes for a lovely day out in nature.

The wine and rose village of Nals/Nalles and Andrian/Andriano

Today, Nals/Nalles is a relatively small municipality, but it has an extensive town center that reminds visitors of its historical significance. Its countless roses have earned it the nickname 'rose village'. Andrian/Andriano, one of South Tyrol's smallest communities, was incorporated into Nals/Nalles by the King in 1928. It regained independence in 1953. Between them, the two little towns have five castles: Stachelburg, Schloss Payrsberg, Schwanburg with its winery, Burg Wolfsthurn, and the ruins of Burg Festenstein.

The old mining town and modern asparagus-growing area of Terlan/Terlano

Terlan/Terlano, which includes Vilpian/Vilpiano to the north and Siebeneich/Settequerce in the south, used to be an important mining town. The Gothic parish church Maria Himmelfahrt from the 14th century with its multi-coloured steeple shingles dates back to that era. The ruins of Burg Maultasch thrones over the town as its symbol. Today, it is best known for its asparagus.

Regional cuisine like 2000 years ago

■ Gasthof Schwarzer Adler
39010 Andrian, St. Urban-Platz 4, 0039 0471 510 288

Overnight and camping possibilities in the appendix and in the maps

Questions and information about the subsection

■ Hotline Meraner Land, 0039 0473 200 443
■ Via Claudia Augusta Hotline, 0043664 27 63 555

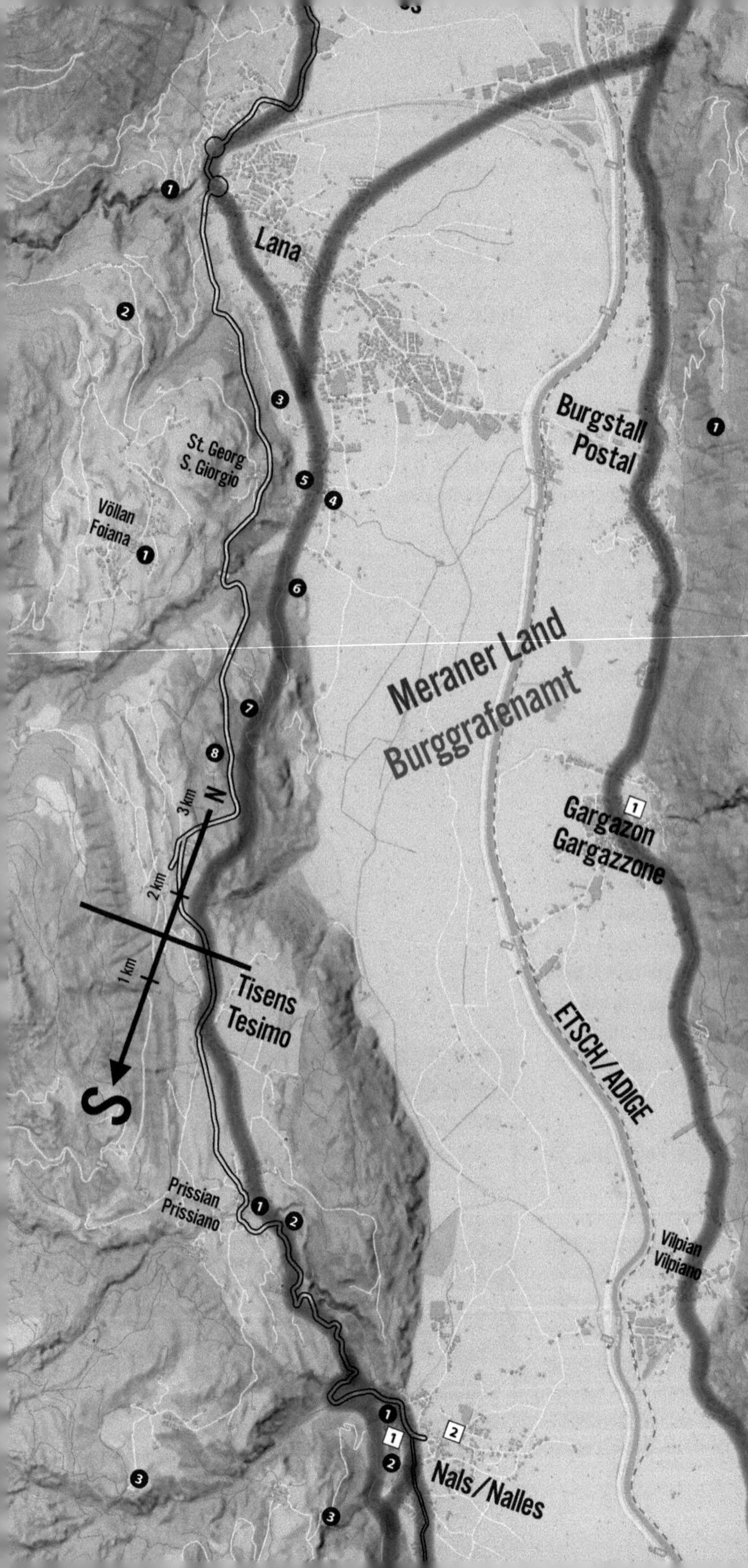

Map 29

- Roman route of the Via Claudia Augusta
- Car Travel Route
- Walk

Lana

1. castle „Braunserberg“
2. castle „Werrenberg“
3. Church with Schnatterbeck altar
4. Southtyrolean museum of fruit trees
5. castle „Brandis“
6. castle of Lana

Völlan

1. castle „Mayenburg“

Burgstall / Postal

1. Castle ruins of the Counts of Volkmar

Gargazon

[1] Pension Sonnheim, Vöranerweg 11, www.sonnheim.com, 0039 0473 292347, III-IV

Tisens, Prissian / Tesimo, Prissiano

1. castle „Fahlburg“
2. castle „Werrenberg“

Nals.+Tisens / Nalles+Tesimo

1. castle „Stachelburg“

[1] Boutique Hotel Zum Rosenbaum, Goldgasse 3, www.rosenbaum.it, 0039 0473 678636, V

2. castle „Schwanburg“ with winery
3. castle „Payrsberg“

[2] Garni Rebhof, Vilpianer Straße 19, www.garni-rebhof.eu, 0039 0473 678924, III

The area between Merano and Bolzano is the richest in castles in Europe. The picture shows the Festenstein Castle in Andrian.

St. Leonburg in the border area near Lana. Photo: Tschaikner

The South Tyrolean Fruit Tree Museum in Lana

The Schnatterbeck altar in the parish church in Niederlana.

In the rose village of Nals.

Testimony to the mining past. Photo: Terlan Tourist Association

Eppan Castle and "Kreideturm" Tower

27 Bolzano/Bozen, the capital on the assumed Pons Drusi (map 30)

Researchers believe that the Pons Drusi, a bridge on the Roman road that is mentioned in early records, was located at the spot where today's Drusus Bridge crosses the Eisack river, a little way to the west of its confluence of the Talfer and the Eisack. Before, it crossed the Etsch and the valley basin at the foot of Siegmundskron castle. The valley basin is occupied entirely by the capital of the autonomous province today. Between 1170 and 1180, the town was built as a planned market settlement with a central street and a marketplace (the Kornplatz). It was expanded several times later.

Taking the Drususallee/Viale Druso to the city center

In Frangart/Frangarto at the foot of Schloss Siegmundskron, where the Messner Mountain Museum Firmian explores the relationship between humans and the mountains, the historical route and our travel route turn towards the town center. They cross the Etsch river and the wide valley basin. The alley and the bridge that lead towards the old town are named after Drusus, who once led the Romans across the Alps and ordered the expansion of the existing paths to create a road. ■ MMM Firmian, Bozen, Sigmundskronerstraße 53, +43 0471 631 264, open from the first Sunday in March until the third Sunday in November, 10 am–6 pm, closed on Thursdays, last entry at 5 pm, www.messner-mountain-museum.it.

A walk through the city

During a walk through the city, the traveler leaves his car in the parking garage P8 behind the train station, in the small parking garage near the Rittner cable car or in the underground parking garage at Waltherplatz, where the described walk starts. Waltherplatz and the monument in the center of the square are dedicated to the minnesinger Walther von der Vogelweide. From there there is also a shuttle to the „Bilderburg" Runkelstein Castle in the north of the city, with some of the most important secular frescoes in the Alpine region. Kornplatz used to be the site of the corn and grain market. In the middle of the picturesque Laubengasse is the Mercantile Museum, which tells the economic history of the country in the former Chamber of Commerce. At the east end of the boulevard is the town hall. A little further on, the Museum of Nature South Tyrol awaits. If you want to enjoy a beautiful view of the city, it's best to take the Ritten cable car up to the Ritten plateau, which is just a few minutes' walk away. Franziskanerstraße leads to the Franciscan church, the Franciscan monastery and finally to the east side of Laubengasse. A little to the west are the South Tyrol Museum of Archaeology with „Ötzi" and the City Museum with one of the two original milestones that provide written evidence of the Via Claudia Augusta and the South Tyrol Museum of Archaeology with „Ötzi". Crossing the Talvera Bridge, you reach the Victory Monument, one of the last remaining monuments erected during the fascist period. Over the new bicycle and pedestrian bridge the route crosses the Talfer again and leads directly to the „Museion", which presents modern and contemporary art. Municipal theater and concert hall form a unit near the Eisack river. The worthy conclusion of the city tour is the Gothic Cathedral of the Assumption of Mary from the 12th century, with the Cathedral Treasury. It once stood outside the city walls.
■ Bolzano City Museum, +39 0471 997 960, Tue-Sun 10 a.m.-6 p.m. ■ South Tyrol Museum of Archaeology, +39 0471 320 100, daily 10 a.m.-6 p.m. in July, Aug. and Dec. Other months Mon off, last admission 5:30 p.m., www.iceman.it. ■ Museum of Nature South Tyrol, +39 0471 412 964, open Tue - Sun. 10 a.m.-6 p.m., www.naturmuseum.it. ■ Rittner cable car, operating year-round, www.ritten.com. ■ Mercantile Museum, +39 0471 945 702, Mon - Sat, 10 am - 12:30 pm. ■ Cathedral Treasury, +39 0471 978 676, Tue - Sat 10 am - 12 noon. ■ Museion, +39 0471 223 413, open Tue - Sun 10am - 6pm, last admission 5:30pm, Thu 10am - 2pm,free admission 6pm - 10pm, free guided tour 7pm, last admission 9:30pm, www.museion.it. ■ Runkelstein Castle, +39 0471 329 808, Tue - Sun, through March 15 10 a.m. - 5 p.m. (last admission 4:30 p.m.), from March 16 10 a.m. - 6 p.m. (last admission 5:30 p.m.), www.runkelstein.info.

Traveling south

The travel route takes you across the Loretobrücke bridge, following the Roman road to Laives/Leifers, the southernmost town of South Tyrol.

Questions and information about the subsection

■ Touristinfo Verkehrsamt der Stadt Bozen, 39100 Bozen, Waltherplatz 8, 0039 0471 307000
■ Via Claudia Augusta Hotline, 0043664 27 63 555

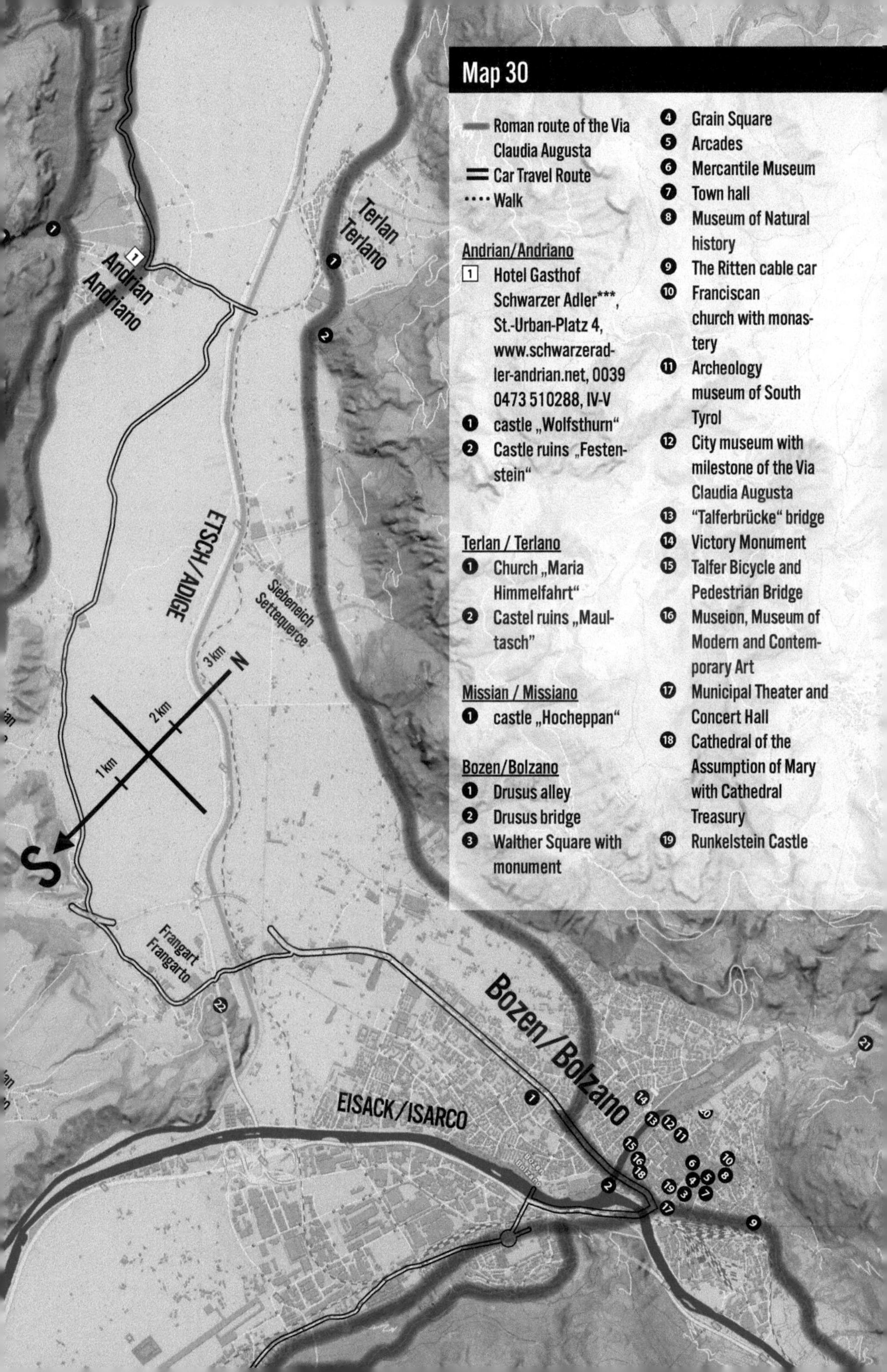
Map 30
Roman route of the Via Claudia Augusta
Car Travel Route
Walk
Andrian/Andriano
1 Hotel Gasthof Schwarzer Adler***, St.-Urban-Platz 4, www.schwarzerad-ler-andrian.net, 0039 0473 510288, IV-V
❶ castle „Wolfsthurn"
❷ Castle ruins „Festen-stein"
Terlan / Terlano
❶ Church „Maria Himmelfahrt"
❷ Castel ruins „Maul-tasch"
Missian / Missiano
❶ castle „Hocheppan"
Bozen/Bolzano
❶ Drusus alley
❷ Drusus bridge
❸ Walther Square with monument
❹ Grain Square
❺ Arcades
❻ Mercantile Museum
❼ Town hall
❽ Museum of Natural history
❾ The Ritten cable car
❿ Franciscan church with monas-tery
⓫ Archeology museum of South Tyrol
⓬ City museum with milestone of the Via Claudia Augusta
⓭ "Talferbrücke" bridge
⓮ Victory Monument
⓯ Talfer Bicycle and Pedestrian Bridge
⓰ Museion, Museum of Modern and Contem-porary Art
⓱ Municipal Theater and Concert Hall
⓲ Cathedral of the Assumption of Mary with Cathedral Treasury
⓳ Runkelstein Castle
Andrian
Andriano
Terlan
Terlano
ETSCH/ADIGE
Siebeneich
Settequerce
N
S
1 km
2 km
3 km
Frangart
Frangarto
Bozen/Bolzano
EISACK/ISARCO

BOZEN
Rittner Seilbahn
Altstadt
TALFER / TALVERA
EISACK / ISARCO
Bolzano Bozen
N
S
100 m
200 m
300 m
400 m
500 m
Via dei Vanga - Wangergasse
Via Andreas Hofer - Andreas-Hofer-Straße
Via Piave - Piavestraße
Via Renon - Rittner Straße
Via Laurino - Laurinstraße
Via Rosmini - Rosministraße
Via Dante Alighieri - Dantestraße
Via Carducci - Carduccistraße
Via Venezia - Venediger Straße
Via Zara - Zarastraße
Via Trento - Trienter Straße
Via Josef Mayr Nusser - Josef-Mayr-Nusser-Straße
Pie di Virgolo - Untervirgl
Roman route of the Via Claudia Augusta
Car Travel Route
Walk
Bozen/Bolzano
1 Drusus alley
2 Drusus bridge
3 Walther Square with monument
4 Grain Square
5 Arcades
6 Mercantile Museum
7 Town hall
8 Museum of Natural history
9 The Ritten cable car
10 Franciscan church with monastery
11 Archeology museum of South Tyrol
12 City museum with milestone of the Via Claudia Augusta
13 Talferbrücke
14 Siegesdenkmal
15 Talfer-Rad- und Fußgängerbrücke
16 Museion, Museum für moderne und zeitgenössische Kunst
17 Stadttheater und Konzerthaus
18 Gotischer Dom Maria Himmelfahrt mit Domschatzkammer
19 Schloss Runkelstein

Walther Square, Walther Monument and Gothic Cathedral in Bolzano. Photo: Thomas Stankievicz

Milestone of the Via Claudia Augusta in the City Museum. Photo: SMG

Bozen. Photo: Luca Ognibeni

„Ötzi" in the archaeological museum. Photo: Tourist Office Bolzano / Ochsenreiter

Talfer Bridge and Museion. Photo: Seehauser

The arcade

Bridges used to be expensive and difficult to build and maintain. That is why they were few and far between, and a road had to be built into the slopes on both sides of the river. A Roman road probably ran along today's South Tyrolean Wine Road, crossing the well-known wine-growing villages of St. Pauls/San Paolo, St. Michael/San Michele, Kaltern am See/Caldaro, Tramin/Termeno, Kurtatsch/Cortaccia, Margreid/Magrè, and Kurtinig/Cortina. The Via Claudia Augusta itself is likely to have clung to the eastern slope on its way to the south. It would have led from the foot of the striking Castelfeder hill in Auer/Ora, which has been a site of human settlement for millennia, to the proven Roman road station of Endidae in the modern village of Neumarkt/Egna and onwards to Salorno/Salurn, where the famous Salurner Klause used to be. From Bronzolo/Branzoll near South Tyrol's southernmost and most recently built city, Laives/Leifers, the Etsch river was navigable by raft. Until the construction of the railway, it was the most important transportation route for the economy of South Tyrol and Trentino.

Laives/Leifers, Bronzolo/Branzoll and Vadena/Pfatten

Leifers, Branzoll and Pfatten are - apart from Bolzano - one of the few places inhabited by a majority of Italian-speaking South Tyroleans. The center of Laives, which was only elevated to the status of a town in 1985, already exudes a bit of Italian flair. In the long village of Pfatten on the right and left side of the Adige River, archaeologists discovered important Late Bronze Age and Early Iron Age burial grounds. It was first mentioned as Vatina as early as 860.

Auer/Ora and Castelfeder

Auer lies at the foot of the historically and biologically interesting hill Castelfeder. The prominent hill also offers a good overview of the valley, offered protection and was therefore settled long before the birth of Christ and also in Roman times. The market center of Auers, which is mostly situated uphill, has numerous cobblestone alleys with stone walls higher than man.

Neumarkt/Egna and Laag/Laghetti

For a long time, the Roman road station Endidae in the north of Neumarkt was the only recorded station in South Tyrol. Part of the excavations in today's residential area are still open and can be visited. The extensive historic center of the market town with its arcades dates back mainly to the 16th century. Founded in 1189 by the bishops of Trento, the town owed its visible prosperity mainly to the flourishing year-round trade, along the important road and the Adige river. The village of Laag, located to the south, may have taken its name from a lake to which the debris of the Noce River had dammed the Adige. The historical center of Laag is smaller than that of Neumarkt, but also worth seeing.

Salurn/Salorno at the much sung hermitage

At Salurn, the Etschtal narrows to the Salurner Klause, which separates the South Tyrolean Unterland from the adjoining Piana Rotaliana. The villages of Salurn and Buchholz date back to Roman settlements. Salurn was first mentioned in documents as early as 575 BC. The municipality owed its importance to its strategic position. Not only was there a dam at the mouth of the valley. There also began the path over the Sauchsattel into the Cembratal. Salurn captivates with a picturesque old village center, over which the Haderburg towers.

Eppan on the wine route

Several villages together form the large municipality of Eppan in the north of the so-called „Überetsch", a hilly landscape raised above the valley floor. Graves, ramparts and a late Bronze Age settlement show that it was settled early on. Historians suspect that the name Appiano comes from the Roman landowner Appius. In 2005, archaeologists discovered the remains of a Roman villa with floor mosaics from the 4th century and a thermal bath complex in St. Pauls, which they assume may have been the residence of Appius. The village was mentioned for the first time as early as 590. In the High Middle Ages the Counts of Appiano fought with those of Tyrol for supremacy in South Tyrol. Today the area is the richest in castles and residences in Europe. Today's main town of St.

Michael and also the original main town of St. Pauls, with one of the highest church towers in the country, have a picturesque historic center. Eppan is the largest wine-growing community in South Tyrol.

Kaltern/Caldaro on the lake

The wine village of Kaltern am See with its picturesque traffic-calmed center lies at the foot of the slopes of the Mendel ridge in the southern part of the „Überetsch" and is separated from the river by the Mitterberg. South of the main town, the landscape, characterized by viticulture, descends to the natural jewel of Lake Kaltern, considered the warmest bathing lake south of the Alps. As the largest natural lake in South Tyrol and the most important wetland in the region, it provides the ideal habitat for a variety of species. The biotopes of Lake Kaltern and the ice holes are integrated in the protected area network „Natura 2000", an initiative of the European Union.

Tramin/Termeno, Kurtatsch/Cortaccia, Margreid/Magrè and Kurtinig/Cortina

Tramin is famous for the Gewürztraminer grape variety. It has an extensive old village center with magnificent churches nestled on the hillside. Kurtatsch was already inhabited in the Mesolithic period, as archaeological finds testify. Already in the 4th century the village was brought to the Christian faith by St. Vigilius, to whom a Romanesque pilgrimage church from the 1300 century is dedicated. Margreid shows that it has always been characterized by fruit and wine growers. The picturesque village center with its winding alleys shows southern influences. The small municipality of Kurtinig, which is limited to the valley and has an altitude difference of only 4 meters, was already considered a productive hunting and fishing area in the Stone Age and Roman times.

Special: Roman road station Endidae-Neumarkt

During some excavation works in the „Kahn" field, starting in 1983, the remains of a large structure from the Roman period were brought to light. It is very probable that it belongs to the „Endidae Mansio", which appears in the „Itinerarium Antonini". The large building, with a floor area of737 m2, had a rectangular shape and was characterized by a large columned entrance and a central courtyard, partly covered, around which were distributed a series of smaller rooms, probably resting rooms (cubicula) and a kitchen.

Overnight and camping possibilities in the appendix and in the maps

Questions and information about the subsection

■ Touristinfo 39055 Leifers (including Branzoll and Pfatten)
Kennedystraße 75/D, 0039 0471 950 420
■ Touristinfo 39040 Auer (including Neumarkt and Salurn)
Hauptplatz 4, 0039 0471 81 02 31
■ Touristinfo 39052 Kaltern an der Weinstraße
Marktplatz 8, 0039 0471 96 31 69
■ Touristinfo 39040 Tramin an der Weinstraße
Mindelheimerstraße 10A, 0039 0471 860 131
■ Touristinfo 39040 Kurtatsch (including Margreid and Kurtinig), Hauptmann-Schweiggl-Pl. 8, 0039 0471 880 100
■ Hotline Via Claudia Augusta 0043 664 27 63 555

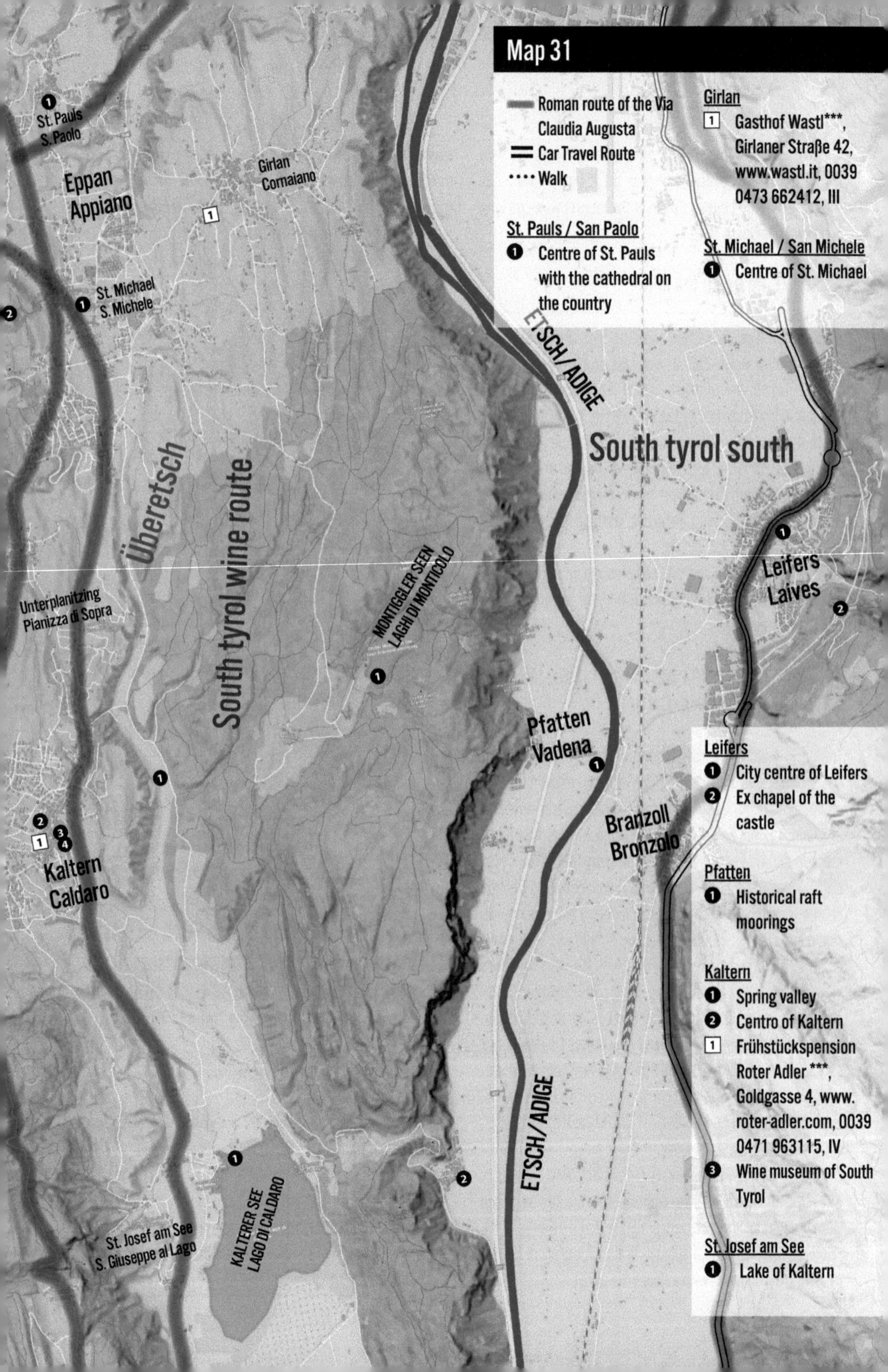
Map 31
Roman route of the Via Claudia Augusta
Car Travel Route
Walk
St. Pauls / San Paolo
1 Centre of St. Pauls with the cathedral on the country
Girlan
1 Gasthof Wastl***, Girlaner Straße 42, www.wastl.it, 0039 0473 662412, III
St. Michael / San Michele
1 Centre of St. Michael
Leifers
1 City centre of Leifers
2 Ex chapel of the castle
Pfatten
1 Historical raft moorings
Kaltern
1 Spring valley
2 Centro of Kaltern
1 Frühstückspension Roter Adler ***, Goldgasse 4, www.roter-adler.com, 0039 0471 963115, IV
3 Wine museum of South Tyrol
St. Josef am See
1 Lake of Kaltern
St. Pauls
S. Paolo
Eppan
Appiano
Girlan
Cornaiano
St. Michael
S. Michele
Überetsch
South tyrol wine route
ETSCH/ADIGE
South tyrol south
Unterplanitzing
Pianizza di Sopra
MONTIGGLER SEEN
LAGHI DI MONTICOLO
Leifers
Laives
Pfatten
Vadena
Branzoll
Bronzolo
Kaltern
Caldaro
KALTERER SEE
LAGO DI CALDARO
St. Josef am See
S. Giuseppe al Lago

View from Castelfeder in south direction. Photo: Castelfeder Tourist Office

Endidae. Roman road station in Neumarkt. Photo: SMG

Lake Kaltern. Photo: TV Kaltern

Arbors of Neumarkt.

The Haderburg above Salurn

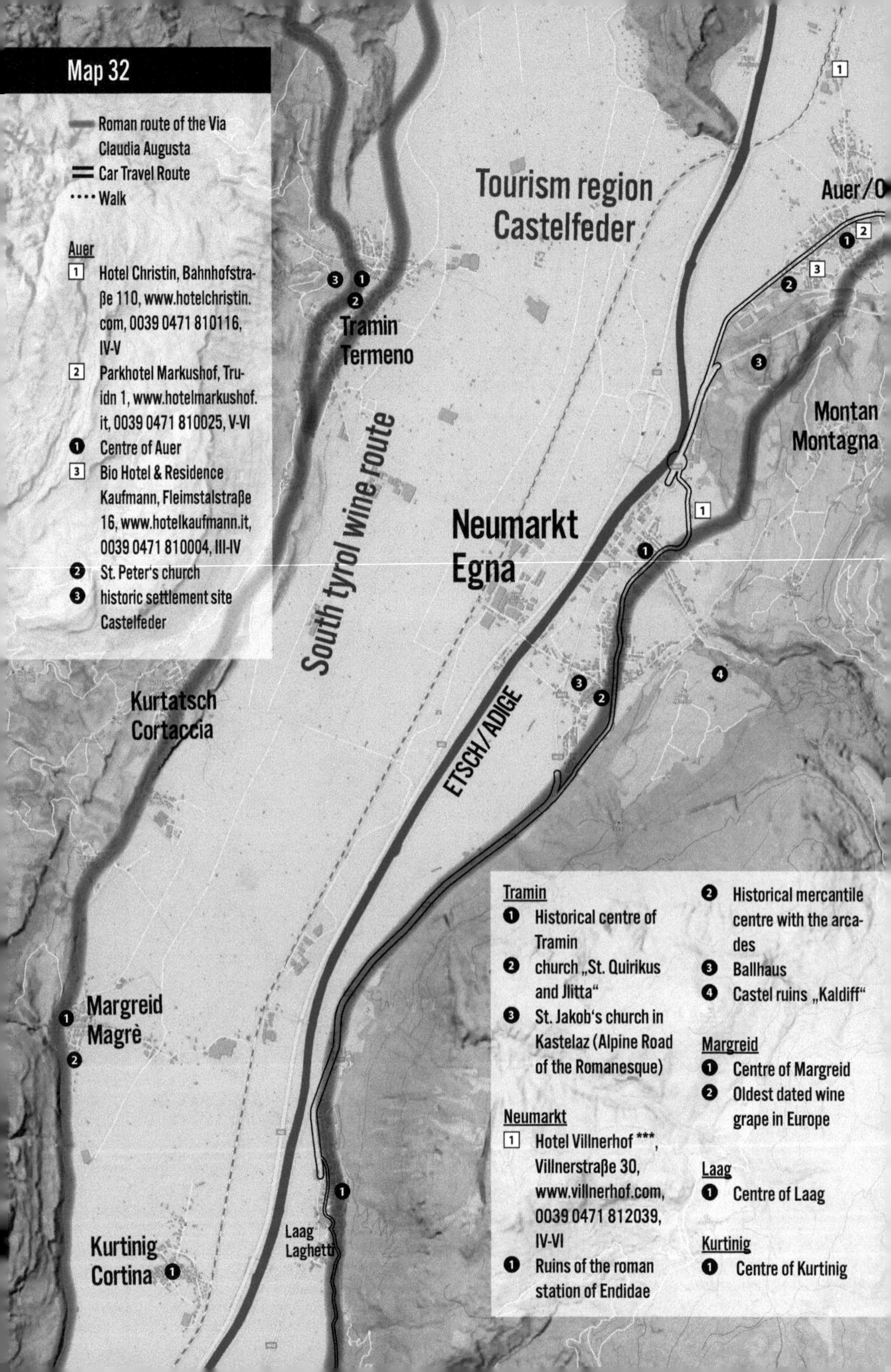

Map 32
Roman route of the Via Claudia Augusta
Car Travel Route
Walk
Auer
1 Hotel Christin, Bahnhofstraβe 110, www.hotelchristin.com, 0039 0471 810116, IV-V
2 Parkhotel Markushof, Truidn 1, www.hotelmarkushof.it, 0039 0471 810025, V-VI
❶ Centre of Auer
3 Bio Hotel & Residence Kaufmann, Fleimstalstraβe 16, www.hotelkaufmann.it, 0039 0471 810004, III-IV
❷ St. Peter's church
❸ historic settlement site Castelfeder
Tourism region Castelfeder
Auer / O
Tramin Termeno
South tyrol wine route
Montan Montagna
Neumarkt Egna
ETSCH / ADIGE
Kurtatsch Cortaccia
Margreid Magrè
Kurtinig Cortina
Laag Laghetti
Tramin
❶ Historical centre of Tramin
❷ church „St. Quirikus and Jlitta“
❸ St. Jakob's church in Kastelaz (Alpine Road of the Romanesque)
Neumarkt
1 Hotel Villnerhof ***, Villnerstraβe 30, www.villnerhof.com, 0039 0471 812039, IV-VI
❶ Ruins of the roman station of Endidae
❷ Historical mercantile centre with the arcades
❸ Ballhaus
❹ Castel ruins „Kaldiff“
Margreid
❶ Centre of Margreid
❷ Oldest dated wine grape in Europe
Laag
❶ Centre of Laag
Kurtinig
❶ Centre of Kurtinig

29 Piana Rotaliana, the fertile wine plain at the language border (map 33, 34)

The drift washed up by the Noce river from the Nonstal valley dammed the Etsch river, creating a large lake that filled the entire valley. It formed a natural border between the municipalities in the south of South Tyrol, those of the Nonstal valley, and those to the north of Trento. This made it more difficult for the people of the various localities to interact with each other and contributed to the emergence of the language border between the German-speaking and Italian-speaking areas. Today, the inhabitants of the Piana Rotaliana all speak Italian. But the water also created a border across the region: Mezzocorona (Kronmetz), today's agricultural center, is culturally more German, while the traditional mercantile centers of Mezzolombardo at the entrance to the Nonstal valley and Lavis at the entrance of the Avisio valley are culturally Italian with impressive palazzi. The lake no longer exists. The soil on the drift from the Noce river is particularly fertile. All of the Piana Rotaliana and its slopes are covered in vineyards, where the famous Teroldego grapes ripen – a regional specialty. The former Foundation of San Michele all'Adige contributed considerably to the flourishing of this region. To this day, its Istituto Agrario is the agricultural competence center of the entire Trentino, and its local-history museum documents the customs and traditions of the state. Of all the palaces and fortresses in the region, the San Gottardo grotto castle behind Mezzocorona is the best known.

Across the language border to Roveré della Luna

Bridges were expensive and difficult to maintain. Therefore there were not many of them and consequently there had to be - also in Roman times - a main road west and east of the Adige river and also of the Adige lake dammed by the Noce. After Salurn, the itinerary changes to the western side of the valley, where the first Italian-speaking village, Roverè della Luna, awaits. In the picturesque old village center, the former cemetery chapel of St. Anna from the late 15th century is particularly worth seeing.

Agricultural Center Mezzocorona

From Roverè della Luna, along the presumed Roman road route, the itinerary leads along the rocky slope to Mezzocorona, which is the agricultural center of the region with the largest wineries, including the modern „Cittadella del Vino“. Prehistoric findings show that the place was inhabited before the Romans. As excavations show, it was also an important waypoint on the Roman road. On the site of a Roman villa there are residential blocks today. In the front area, however, an information center „Domus Romana“ has been established, from which the initiative for the regular traveling exhibition „Incontri D'Arte“ along the Via Claudia Augusta originates. Mezzocorona also has a wide church square worth seeing. A few meters away, a gondola lift leads to a plateau at the top of the rugged Monte mountain range, from where you can enjoy a splendid view. In the rock face is the cave castle of San Gottardo, which unfortunately can only be viewed from below due to the danger of falling rocks.

Mezzolombardo, commercial center for the Non-Valley

The itinerary does not only go a little bit into the Val di Non to show Mezzolombardo to the traveler. The western route of the Romans could not cross the Noce river directly in the estuary. The town of Mezzolombardo, leaning on the hillside, with its picturesque closed rows of houses and numerous palazzi, is the commercial center along the ancient road to the Val di Non. In the town, at the foot of the church of San Pietro and the castle Castello della Torre, the visitor can stroll beautifully, drink coffee, enjoy an ice cream and shop in small stores where also the population stores.

Agricultural Competence Center San Michele all'Adige

In 1144/45 the Counts of Eppan and the Bishop of Trentino founded the Augustinian Canons' Monastery of St. Michael, around which the village developed. From the beginning, the monastery was an impulse center for the development of agriculture. When it was dissolved in the course of secularization in 1807, the construction of the precursor of today's

Istituto agrario di San Michele all'Adige began in the former monastery building while it was still under the Austro-Hungarian Empire. Today it is a teaching and research center for the entire Trentino region and also houses the Trentino Folklore Museum „Museo degli Usi e Costumi della Gente Trentina". ■ Via Mach 2, +39 046 650 314, open daily 9:00 a.m. - 12:30 p.m. and 2:30 p.m. – 6 p.m., closed only Nov 1, Dec 25 and Jan 1. www.museosanmichele.it.

Faedo, Nave San Rocco und Zambana

Like most of the Roman road, the eastern route ran through the region slightly above the valley floor where the lush vineyards now lie. The itinerary shows a bit of this, leading almost up to the wine village of Faedo, which towers over the valley like an eagle's nest. Before reaching the ferry and rafting village of Nave San Rocco, the itinerary crosses the Adige River once again, where the Roman road also once crossed the valley. The scattered farmsteads of Nave San Rocco indicate the Germanic domain. The next village, Zambana, was also once a station on the Adige waterway, which was the center of the Trentino economy until the construction of the railroad. In 1955 a catastrophic landslide completely buried the old village. From the original site, now called „Zambana Vecchia" (Old Zambana), only the church was rebuilt. The new village of Zambana was built further from the hillside, in the center of the valley. Incidentally, the municipality is best known for the white asparagus of Zambana.

Lavis, at the entrance to the valley of Avisio

Finally, Lavis awaits before crossing the Avisio torrent into the urban area of Trento. The town has a picturesque old core with many buildings worth seeing. Particularly noteworthy is the mysterious hanging garden of the „Ciucioi", which dominates the valley below with its romantic ruins.

Regional cuisine like 2000 years ago

■ Hotel Garnì B&B „La Vigna", Via Postal 49a,
38010 San Michele all'Adige, 0039 0461 650276

Overnight and camping possibilities in the appendix and in the maps

Questions and information about the subsection

■ Touristinfo Consorzio Turistico Piana Rotaliana-Königsberg, 38017 Mezzolombardo, Corso del Popolo 35, 0039 0461 175 25 25 (italian and english)
■ Hotline Via Claudia Augusta, 0043664 27 63 555

Map 33

Roman route of the Via Claudia Augusta
Car Travel Route
Walk

Salurn

1. (□) Jugendhaus Dr. Josef Noldin, Dr. Josef-Noldin-Straße 20, www.noldinhaus.org, 0039 0471 884356, III-IV

❶ Centre of Salurn

❷ castle „Haderburg“

Roverè della Luna

❶ chapel „St. Anna“

Cadino

1. (□) B&B La Ferrata, Dr. Loc. Cadino 1, www.laferrata.com, 0039 0461 650409, IV

Mezzocorona

❶ zona archeologica „Domus Romana“

1. (□) Hotel Drago***, Piazza San Gottardo 46, www.hoteldrago.it, 0039 0461 603824, V

2. (□) B&B La Masera, Corso del Popolo 35, www.pianarotaliana.it/Dormire/B-B/B-B-La-Masera, 0039 0461 1752525

❷ Main square of Mezzocorona

❸ Gondola to Monte, with great views of the valley

❹ Firmian castle

❺ cave castle San Gottardo

Masetto

❶ old winery of castle Königsberg

❷ castle „Königsberg“

Faedo

❶ wine village Faedo on the mountainside

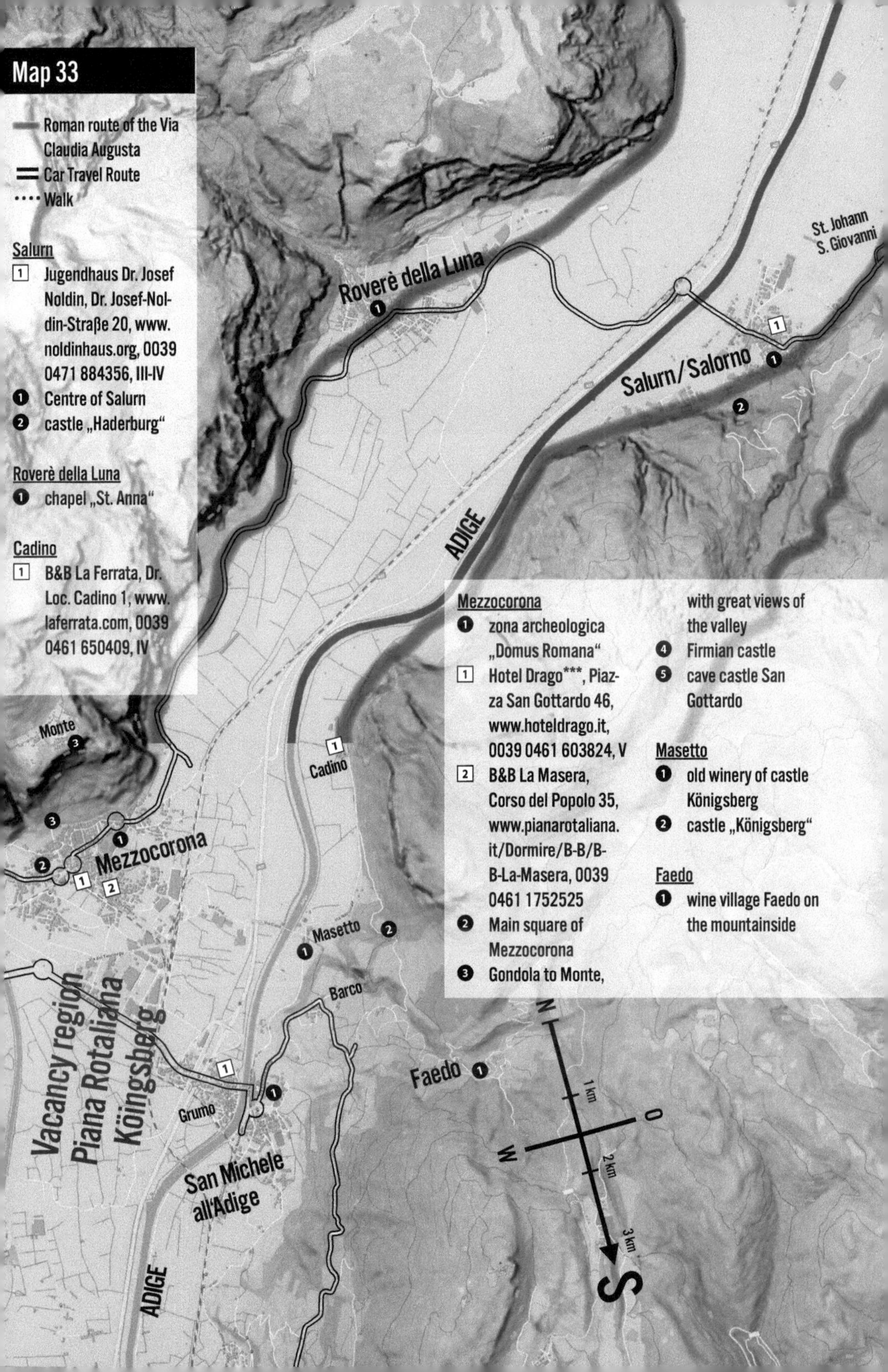

Piana Rotaliana

Cave castle (Corona). Photo: Tschaikner

The former monastery of San Michele all'Adige.

Hanging garden of the „Ciucioi" above Lavìs. Photo: A. Ceolan

Mezzolombardo

The Roman Tridentum below the old town.

The Trento Cathedral

The cityscape of Trento shaped during the Renaissance. Photo (3): APT Trento

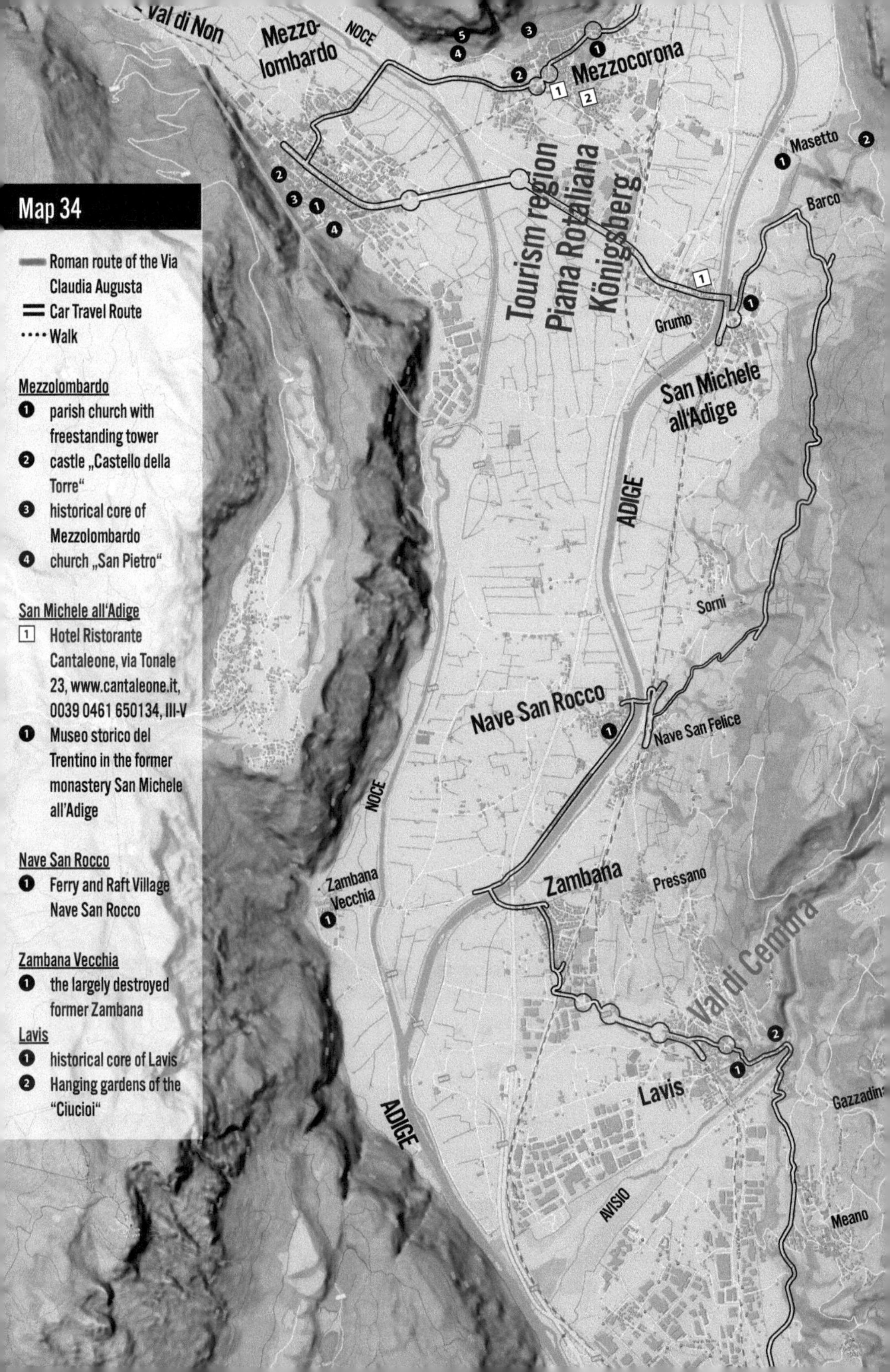
Map 34
Roman route of the Via Claudia Augusta
Car Travel Route
Walk
Mezzolombardo
1 parish church with freestanding tower
2 castle „Castello della Torre“
3 historical core of Mezzolombardo
4 church „San Pietro“
San Michele all‘Adige
[1] Hotel Ristorante Cantaleone, via Tonale 23, www.cantaleone.it, 0039 0461 650134, III-V
1 Museo storico del Trentino in the former monastery San Michele all’Adige
Nave San Rocco
1 Ferry and Raft Village Nave San Rocco
Zambana Vecchia
1 the largely destroyed former Zambana
Lavis
1 historical core of Lavis
2 Hanging gardens of the “Ciucioi“
Val di Non
Mezzo-lombardo
NOCE
Mezzocorona
Tourism region Piana Rotaliana Königsberg
Masetto
Barco
Grumo
San Michele all'Adige
ADIGE
Sorni
Nave San Rocco
Nave San Felice
NOCE
Zambana Vecchia
Zambana
Pressano
Val di Cembra
Lavis
Gazzadina
ADIGE
AVISIO
Meano

31 Traffic hub Tridentum / Trento, towards Feltre, Treviso, Altino, Venice (map 35)

As the name suggests, Trento has Rhaetian origins. It was already an important traffic hub during their time. In Tridentum, the Via Claudia Augusta forked. One section, the Via Claudia Augusta Altinate, led to the Adriatic port town of Altinum near today's Venice. The other section, the Via Claudia Augusta Padana, continued to the riverport of Ostiglia on the Po. From there, another road led to Rome. The later historical significance of the city is primarily due to the Council of Trent (1545–1563). It initiated the Counter-Reformation and delineated its intellectual foundations. The map of today's Old Town was shaped significantly during that period. Later, Baroque buildings were added to the Renaissance-style district. Until the invasion of the Napoleonic Troops, the prince-bishops of Trento rules over the city and the surrounding region from the their base in the majestic Buonconsiglio Castle.

The route to the old town

The city begins at the bridge across the Avisio river in Lavis. In Roman times, the old road towards Altino near Venice led up the hill to the Valsugana. Our route largely follows the historical route into the town of Meano, where you can catch your first glimpse of the birthplace of the Council of Trent. After that we go back to the valley and straight to the Renaissance old town.

Trento, the Roman Tridentum

During a walk through the city, the visitor is best to leave his car in the parking garage at Via Torre Verde 40, right on the edge of the old town. Upon entering the historic part of the city, the tourist information office and the contemporary city gallery await the visitor. Not far away, below Battisti Square, the underground excavations of the Roman Tridentum await. Via Belenzani, lined with Renaissance palazzi, with the Town Hall in Palazzo Thun, the visitor reaches Piazza Duomo. The parallel alleys Via Cavour to the west and Via Oss Mazzurana to the east compete with it. Directly on Piazza Duomo are also the Diocesan Museum and the Cathedral of Vigilio. Finally, the walk leads to the Buonconsiglio Castle, which also houses the Historical Museum of Trento.

Across the Altinate in Valsugana

Passing by the Buonconsiglio castle and then at the large crossroads on the left, the route leaves the city in the direction of Valsugana. From the top there is another beautiful view of the places you leave behind.

Via the „Padana" in Vallagarina

If one wants to continue the journey along the „Via Claudia Augusta Padana" in the direction of Ostiglia, the traveler must follow the bank of the Adige River to the south.

Regional cuisine like 2000 years ago

Here could be an inn that has at least one dish on the menu continuously as it was 2000 years ago.

Overnight and camping possibilities in the appendix and in the maps

Questions and information about the subsection

■ Touristinfo APT Trent, Monte Bodone, Valle dei Laghi
38122 Trento, Via Manci 2, 0039 0461 216 000
■ Hotline Via Claudia Augusta, 0043664 27 63 555

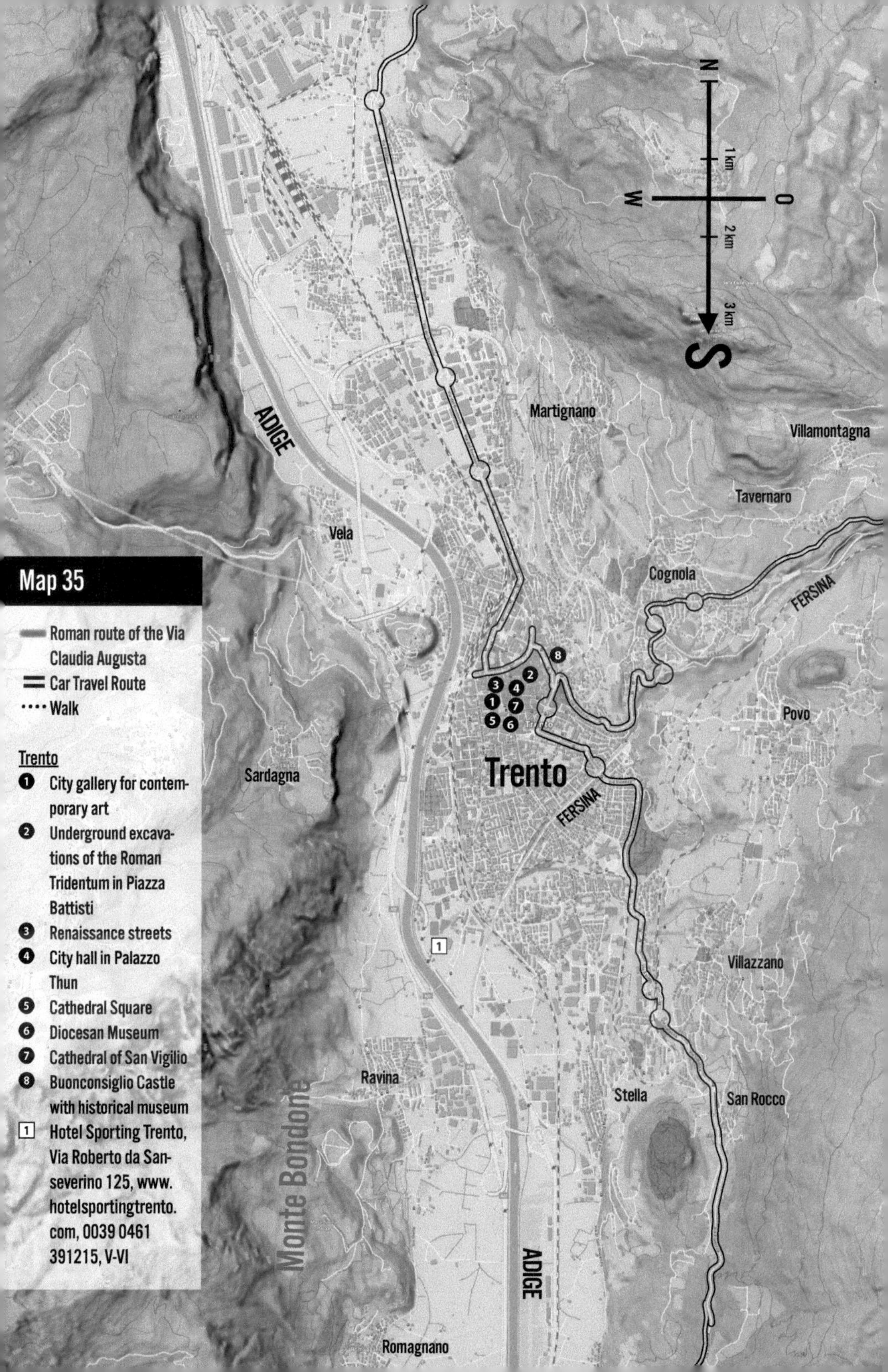
Map 35
Roman route of the Via Claudia Augusta
Car Travel Route
Walk
Trento
1 City gallery for contemporary art
2 Underground excavations of the Roman Tridentum in Piazza Battisti
3 Renaissance streets
4 City hall in Palazzo Thun
5 Cathedral Square
6 Diocesan Museum
7 Cathedral of San Vigilio
8 Buonconsiglio Castle with historical museum
1 Hotel Sporting Trento, Via Roberto da Sanseverino 125, www.hotelsportingtrento.com, 0039 0461 391215, V-VI
N
W
O
S
1 km
2 km
3 km
ADIGE
Martignano
Villamontagna
Tavernaro
Vela
Cognola
FERSINA
Povo
Sardagna
Trento
FERSINA
Villazzano
Ravina
Stella
San Rocco
Monte Bondone
ADIGE
Romagnano

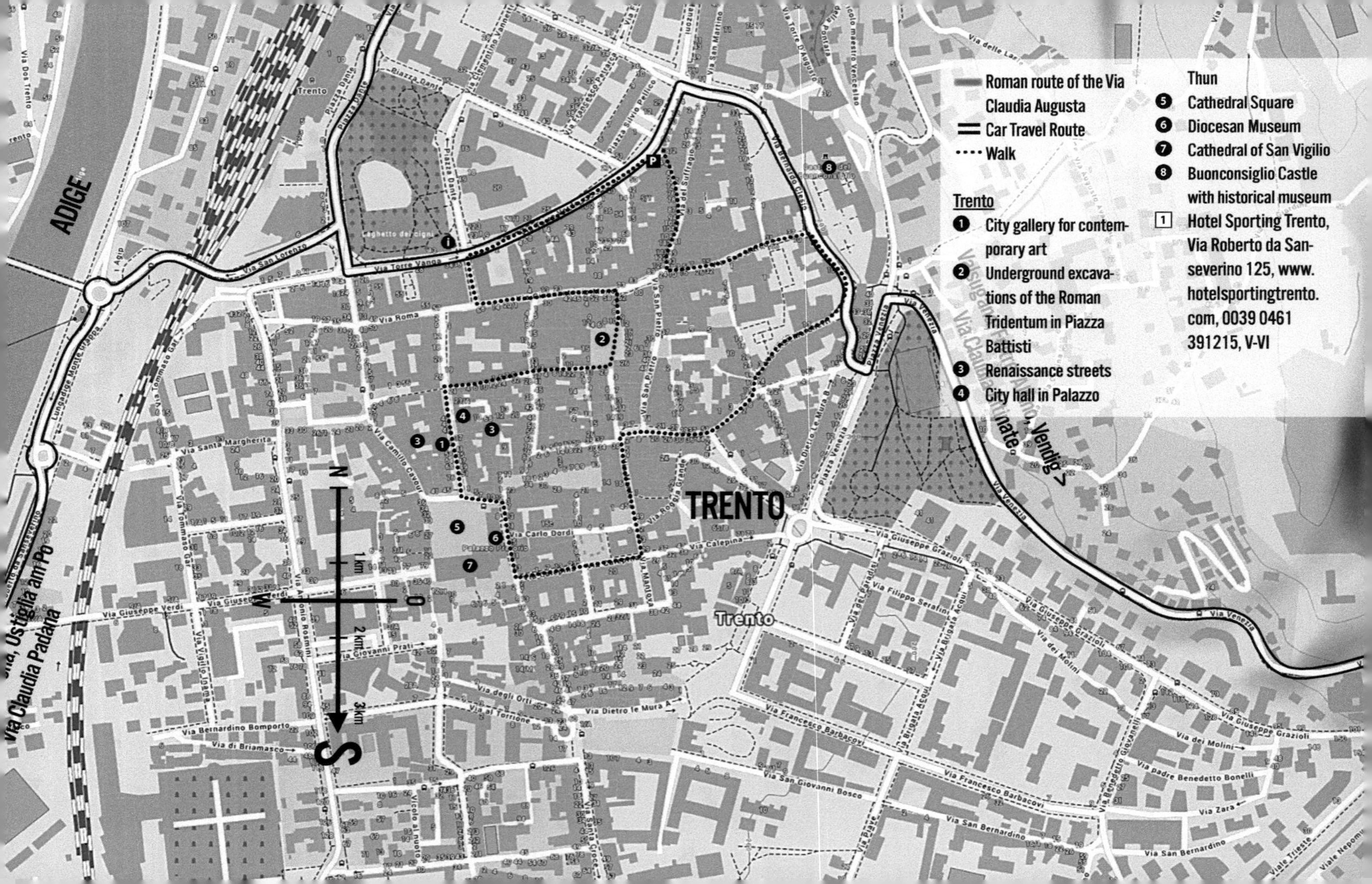

Roman route of the Via Claudia Augusta
Car Travel Route
Walk
Trento
1 City gallery for contemporary art
2 Underground excavations of the Roman Tridentum in Piazza Battisti
3 Renaissance streets
4 City hall in Palazzo Thun
5 Cathedral Square
6 Diocesan Museum
7 Cathedral of San Vigilio
8 Buonconsiglio Castle with historical museum
1 Hotel Sporting Trento, Via Roberto da Sanseverino 125, www.hotelsportingtrento.com, 0039 0461 391215, V-VI
TRENTO
ADIGE
Valsugana, Feltre, Altino, Via Claudia Altinate
Vendig >
Via Claudia Padana
..., Ostiglia am Po
N
S
O
W
1 km
2 km
3 km

32a Upper Valsugana: land of lakes and the Habsburgs' spa destination (map 35, 36, 37)

Archaeological excavations have produced evidence of early human settlement in the valley between Trento and Veneto. Castles, such as that towering above Pergine, helped their inhabitants monitor the crucial road. The Alta Valsugana has been in Trento's sphere of influence ever since. During the First World War, the region was a fiercely contested battleground: the border between Austro-Hungary and Italy was right around the corner, to the south of the high plateau of Lavarone. Countless fortress complexes bear witness to that period. Two large swimming lakes, the Caldonazzosee and Levicosee, characterize the area. The Valsugana has been a popular spa destination since the time of the House of Habsburg, offering the spa towns of Levico Terme and Roncegno Terme.

To Civezzano, Pergine and Levico Terme

Our travel route leads up a slop to the Valsugana. As you enter the valley, you are immediately greeted by the first of many Austro-Hungarian fortresses from the First World War. Inside the church in the picturesque old town center of Civezzano, you can see Trentino's oldest church organ. This town also offers the Ecomuseo Argentario, which tells the story of the medieval silver mining business. The region of Pergine Valsugana has been inhabited since prehistoric times. At its heyday, it was a mining center. Today's municipality was created when 13 communities were merged in 1928. The old town with its splendid town hall and the Renaissance street Via Maier give you a glimpse of its former glory. Pergine is overlooked by the eponymous castle, which is believed to have Roman origins. The historical route of the Via Claudia Augusta is believed to have run along the mountain ridge in Tenna between the Caldonazzo and Levicosee lakes. That is where the milestone was found. Our travel route takes us along the slope to the north of the Levicosee lake to the eponymous spa town. Alternatively, you can head south to drive around the Caldonazzo lake.

The Habsburg spa town of Levico Terme

The House of Habsburg granted Levico town privileges, making it the only town in the Alta Valsugana. It used to be a garrison town and a popular holiday destination that attracted the Habsburgs and the upper classes of Austro-Hungary. At the center of its extensive old town with its many picturesque alleyways, you will find the spa gardens and the Grandhotel Terme. You can also view a Roman sarcophagus in Levico.

Overnight and camping possibilities in the appendix and in the maps

Questions and information about the subsection

- Hotline tourist board APT Valsugana
  0039 0461 727760
- Tourist-Info Pergine Valsugana
  38057 Pergine Valsugana, Piazza Serra 10
- Tourist-Info Levico Terme
  38056 Levico Terme, Viale Vittorio Emanuele III 3
- Hotline Via Claudia Augusta, 0043 664 27 63 555

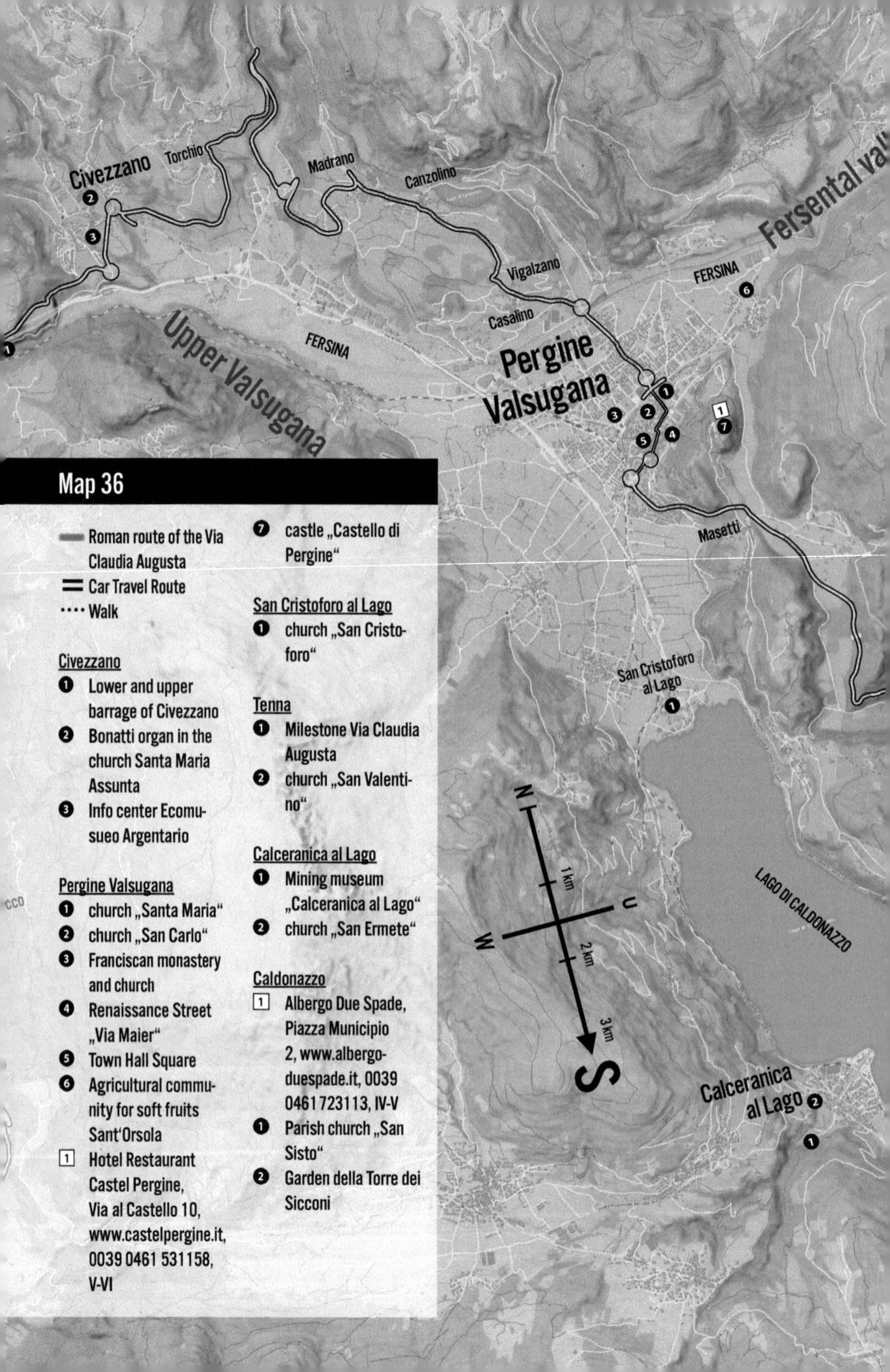

Map 36

- Roman route of the Via Claudia Augusta
- = Car Travel Route
- ···· Walk

Civezzano

1. Lower and upper barrage of Civezzano
2. Bonatti organ in the church Santa Maria Assunta
3. Info center Ecomuseo Argentario

Pergine Valsugana

1. church „Santa Maria“
2. church „San Carlo“
3. Franciscan monastery and church
4. Renaissance Street „Via Maier“
5. Town Hall Square
6. Agricultural community for soft fruits Sant'Orsola

[1] Hotel Restaurant Castel Pergine, Via al Castello 10, www.castelpergine.it, 0039 0461 531158, V-VI

7. castle „Castello di Pergine“

San Cristoforo al Lago

1. church „San Cristoforo“

Tenna

1. Milestone Via Claudia Augusta
2. church „San Valentino“

Calceranica al Lago

1. Mining museum „Calceranica al Lago“
2. church „San Ermete“

Caldonazzo

[1] Albergo Due Spade, Piazza Municipio 2, www.albergo-duespade.it, 0039 0461 723113, IV-V

1. Parish church „San Sisto“
2. Garden della Torre dei Sicconi

The Caldonazzo and the Levico lake. Photo: APT Valsugana

The Grandhotel Imperial in the spa park of Levico. Photo: APT Valsugana

The fortress of Pergine dominates the Alta Valsugana

Arte Sella Art Park. Photo: Arte Sella / Giacomo Bianchi

Castle Telvana

Borgo Valsugana already exudes a little Venetian flair

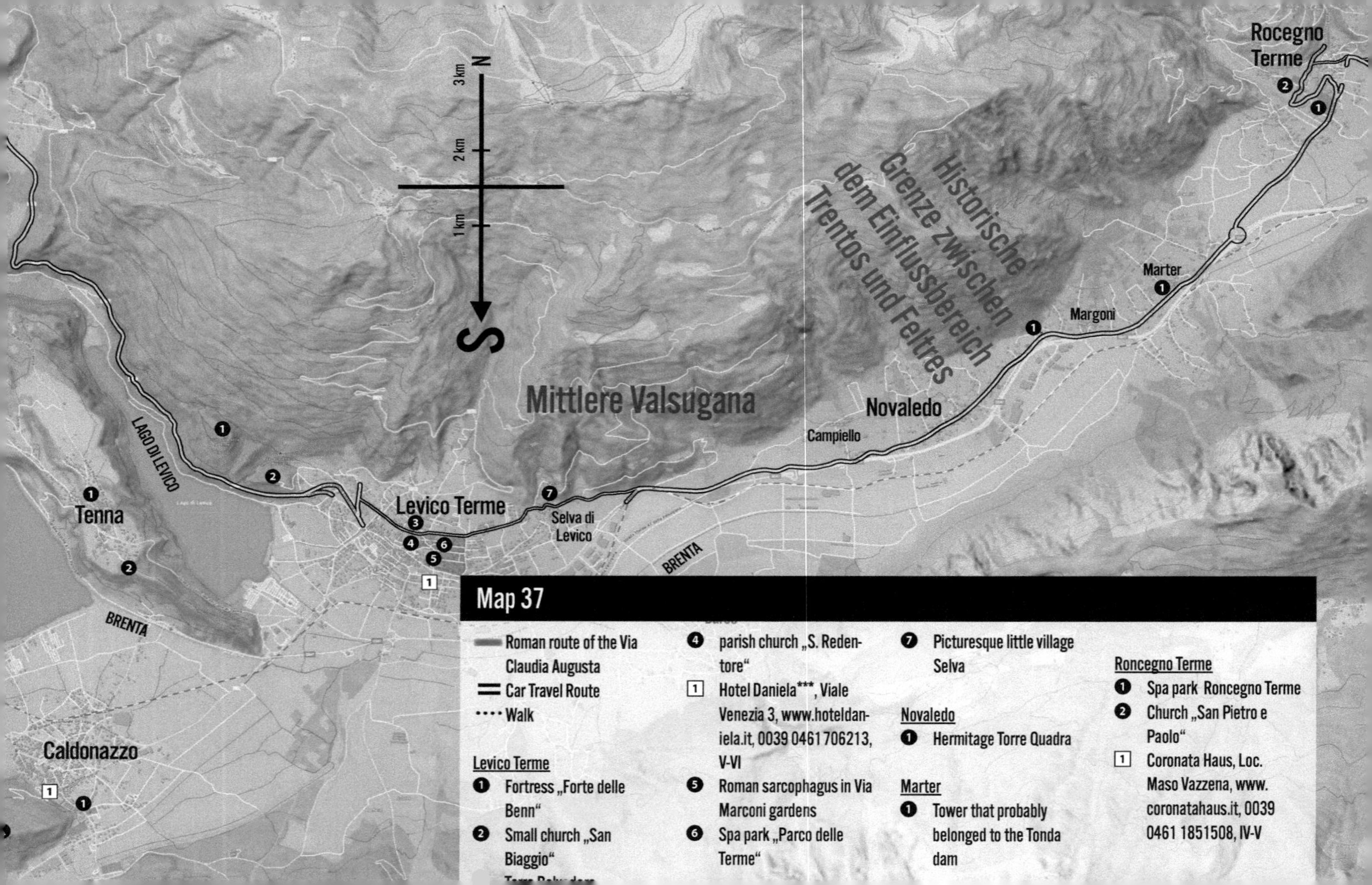

Map 37

- Roman route of the Via Claudia Augusta
- = Car Travel Route
- ···· Walk

Levico Terme

1. Fortress „Forte delle Benn“
2. Small church „San Biaggio“
4. parish church „S. Redentore“

[1] Hotel Daniela***, Viale Venezia 3, www.hoteldaniela.it, 0039 0461 706213, V-VI

5. Roman sarcophagus in Via Marconi gardens
6. Spa park „Parco delle Terme“
7. Picturesque little village Selva

Novaledo

1. Hermitage Torre Quadra

Marter

1. Tower that probably belonged to the Tonda dam

Roncegno Terme

1. Spa park Roncegno Terme
2. Church „San Pietro e Paolo“

[1] Coronata Haus, Loc. Maso Vazzena, www.coronatahaus.it, 0039 0461 1851508, IV-V

The Torre Quadra, a tower on the meadow next to the road leading up to Novaledo, is a remnant of the dam that used to cross the valley here. This is where Trento's sphere of influence bordered that of Feltre. You will notice the Venetian influence in the medieval commune of Borgo Valsugana immediately. It is likely that the Roman road also ran along the sunny slopes of the central Valsugana. Several fortresses line its path. In the valley basin to the east of Borgo, the Via Claudia Augusta ascended towards the mountain again: the Brenta river used to flood the valley here, making it impassable on a regular basis.

Heading to Borgo via Novaledo and Roncegno Terme

On the way to Borgo, our travel route clings to the sunny slope as it crosses Selva, a district of Levico. The Roman road is believed to have followed the same route. Novaledo, Marter and Roncegno Terme, the smaller of two spa towns in the valley. Apart from the Torre Quadra, the town of Marter just past Novaledo still has ruins of medieval fortresses. They continue on the slopes; some of them are still visible. Afterwards, the travel route leads you through the pretty center of the spa town of Roncegno Terme before continuing to Borgo Valsugana, overlooked by Telvana castle. While you can easily spot the castle from afar, its interior is unfortunately closed to the public.

Borgo Valsugana

Borgo was shaped by the Brenta river and a long arcade on its shore. Its Venetian influences are unmistakable. The sights of Borgo include the large Piazza Degasperi with the town hall and the Chiesa di Sant'Anna. From the latter, cross the Venetian bridge to the Corso Ausugum, the old road through the town. Much like Levico, Borgo Valsugana used to be a garrison town during the time of the Austro-Hungarian Monarchy. Besides the picturesque old town on the River Brenta, the art park Arte Sella in the Sella valley, eight kilometers away from here, is an excellent place for discovery, photography and relaxation.

From Borgo to Strigno

Borgo is located in a narrow section of the Sugana valley. Past the town, the valley widens once more before narrowing further and further. In the past, the Brenta used to flood this narrow section regularly. That is why the Roman road crossed two passes to get to the Veneto region. Before the historical route and our travel route climb towards the Tesino high valley, we cross the towns of Castelnuovo, Scurelle and Strigno. Spera and Samone are located on the sunny slope a little further above. Ivano Castle thrones above the basin.

Regional cuisine like 2000 years ago

Here could be an inn that has at least one dish on the menu continuously as it was 2000 years ago.

Overnight and camping possibilities in the appendix and in the maps

Questions and information about the subsection

- Hotline Tourismusverband APT Valsugana
  +39 0461 727760
- Touristinfo Pergine Valsugana
  38057 Pergine Valsugana, Piazza Serra 10
- Touristinfo Levico Terme
  38056 Levico Terme, Viale Vittorio Emanuele III 3
- Hotline Via Claudia Augusta, +43(0)664 27 63 555

Map 38

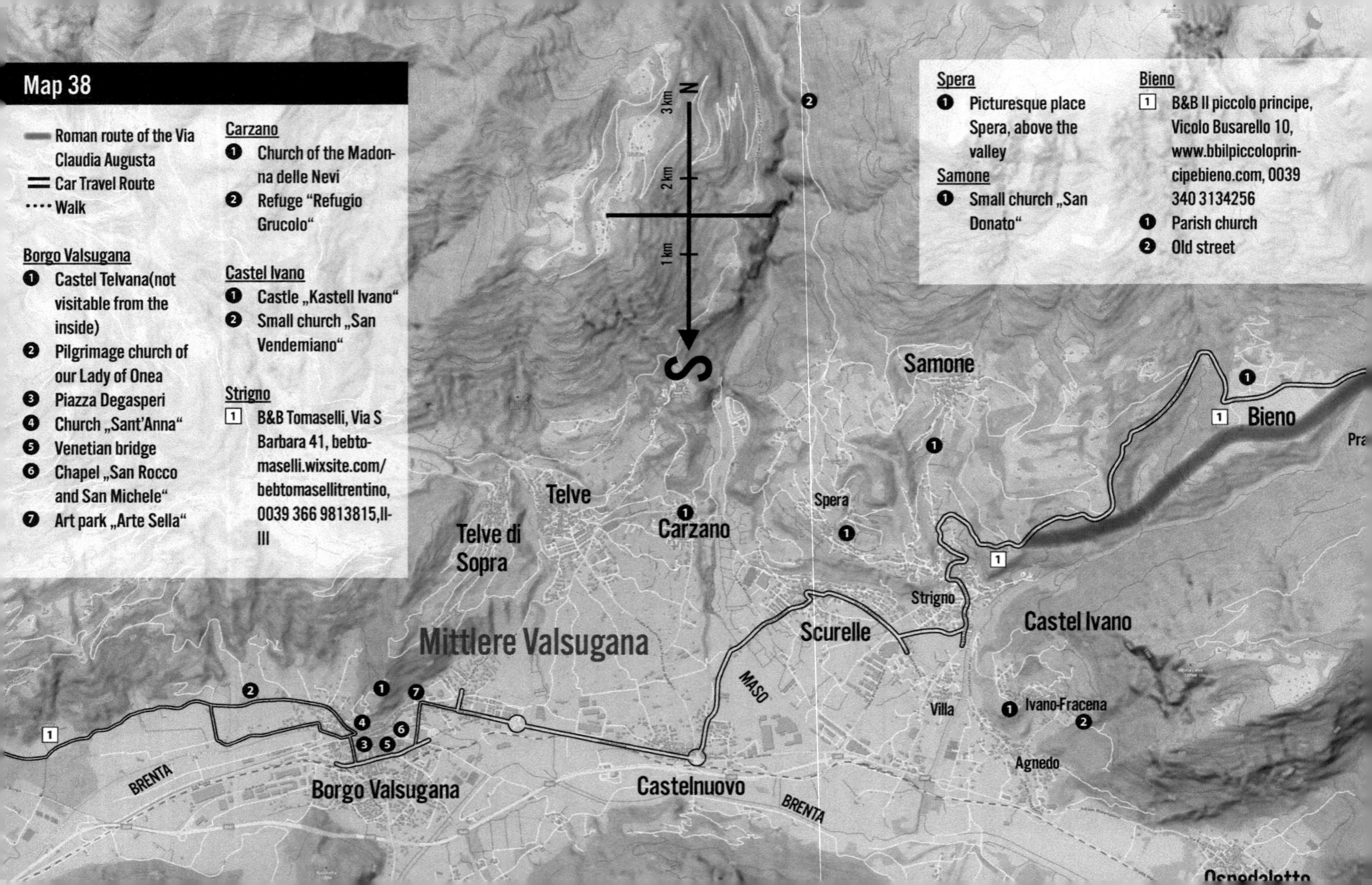

- Roman route of the Via Claudia Augusta
- Car Travel Route
- Walk

Borgo Valsugana
1. Castel Telvana(not visitable from the inside)
2. Pilgrimage church of our Lady of Onea
3. Piazza Degasperi
4. Church „Sant'Anna"
5. Venetian bridge
6. Chapel „San Rocco and San Michele"
7. Art park „Arte Sella"

Carzano
1. Church of the Madonna delle Nevi
2. Refuge "Refugio Grucolo"

Castel Ivano
1. Castle „Kastell Ivano"
2. Small church „San Vendemiano"

Strigno
[1] B&B Tomaselli, Via S Barbara 41, bebtomaselli.wixsite.com/bebtomasellitrentino, 0039 366 9813815,II-III

Spera
1. Picturesque place Spera, above the valley

Samone
1. Small church „San Donato"

Bieno
[1] B&B Il piccolo principe, Vicolo Busarello 10, www.bbilpiccoloprincipebieno.com, 0039 340 3134256
1. Parish church
2. Old street

34a Towards the Dolomites: Tesino high valley, Lamon, Sovramonte (map 38, 39, 40)

The Roman road ascended from the Valsugana to the Tesino high valley, crossing the deep river valley of the Senaiga at the regional border between Trentino and Veneto before heading across the Croce D'Aune Pass to Feltre. Following in its footsteps, the hiking route takes you through diverse landscapes and picturesque villages as it reaches the gateway to the Dolomites. The important old road has left its marks along its route. Lamon is where the internationally renowned Lamon beans are grown, by the way.

Crossing the Tesino high valley

From Strigno, the road crosses a valley and climbs steeply to the Tesino high valley. Its towns have always depended on the business brought in by the road. Today, this business comes in the form of tourists seeking to explore and enjoy the beautiful mountains. The reddish and greenish walls of the Lagorai range are of volcanic origin. From the rest spot near the bridge between Beino and Pieve Tesino, you can clearly see the old road as it crosses the wild stream below. The elongated, narrow alleyways that cross Pieve Tesino from east to west are also remnants of the road. Alcide De Gasperi's birthplace of Pieve Tesino has dedicated a museum to the Austro-Hungarian politician and founding father der European Union: ■ 38050 Pieve Tesino, +39 345 848 99 75 or +39 339 698 4804, open 1 June to 30 September: Tue–Fri 3–6 pm, Sat 1 am–12 noon and 3–6 pm, Sun 3–6 pm; 1 October to 31 May: Fri 3–6 pm, Sat 10 am–12 noon and 3–6 pm, Sun 3–6 pm. Just before Castello Tesino, there is a bridge. It stands on the old Roman road, which is still visible here, but was probably rebuilt in the Middle Ages based on its Roman predecessor. There used to be a Roman fortress above the town, where the little church of Sant'Ippolito stands today.

To Lamon and Sovramonte in Veneto

As you continue to Lamon, you are treated to breathtaking views of the deep gorges cut into the virtually uninhabited borderlands by its wild streams. On the opposite site, the Via Claudia Augusta used to cross the Senaiga stream. Below San Donato, which sprang up and developed on the Roman road, archaeologists discovered an ancient cemetery. The opulent grave goods are exhibited at the little archaeological museum in Lamon, where you can learn about the history of human settlement in the region. ■ Central Lamon, +39 328 311 83 36, fixed opening hours during summer, open upon arrangement during the remaining year. ■ At the end of the deep gorge in the border area, you will find a stalactite cave. It is only accessible upon prior arrangement – call +39 0461 593 322. Our route now takes you along the southern edge of the Dolomiti Bellunesi national park and through the little villages of the Sovramonte municipality.

Regional cuisine like 2000 years ago

Here could be an inn that has at least one dish on the menu continuously as it was 2000 years ago.

Overnight and camping possibilities in the appendix and in the maps

Questions and information about the subsection

- ■ Touristinfo Castello Tesino - Visit Valsugana, Via Dante 10, +39 0461 593 322
- ■ Hotline Ufficio Turistico di Feltre - Consorzio Dolomit Prealpi, +39 0439 2540
- ■ Hotline Via Claudia Augusta, +43(0)664 27 63 555

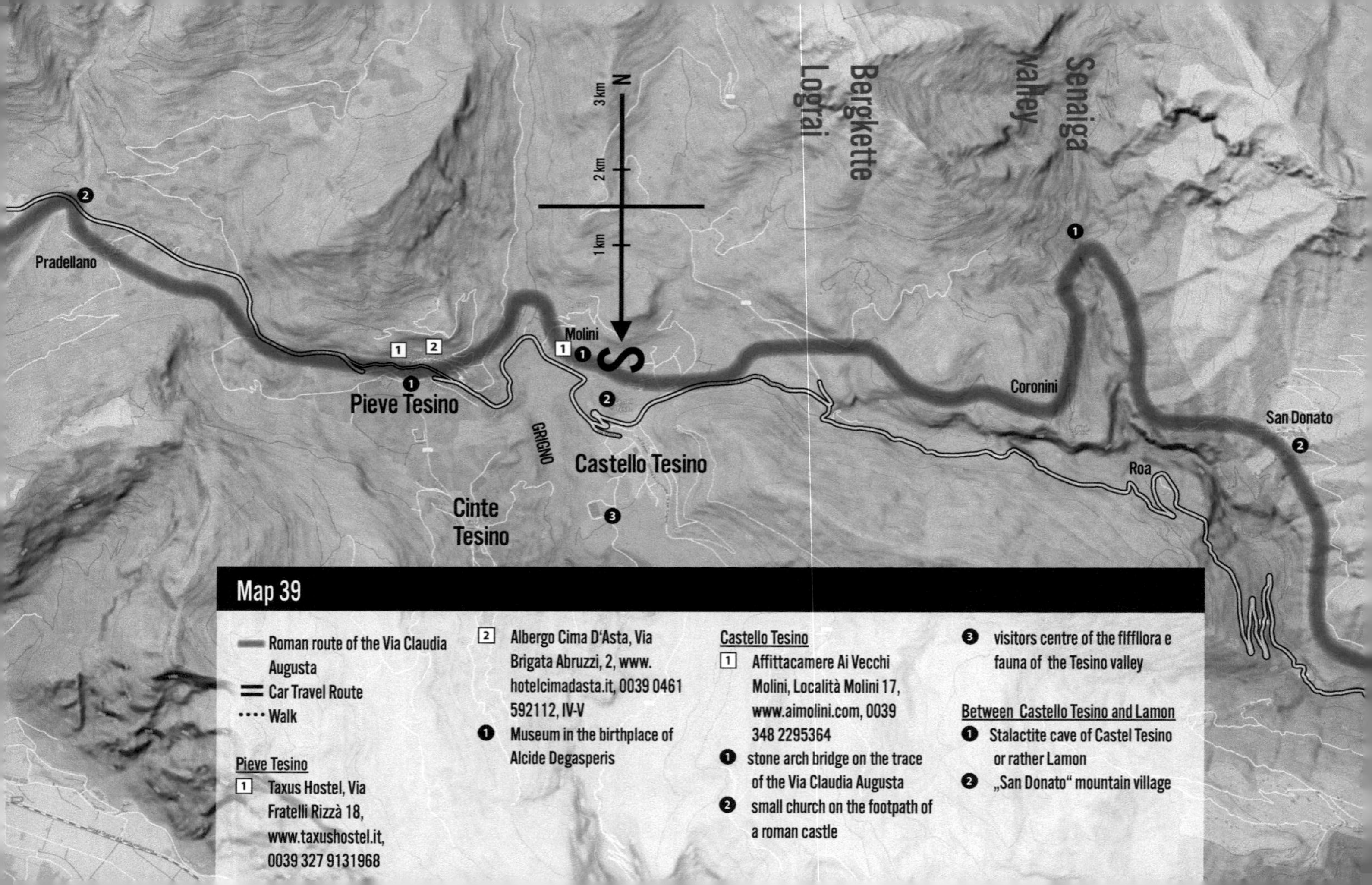

Map 39

Roman route of the Via Claudia Augusta
Car Travel Route
Walk

Pieve Tesino
1 Taxus Hostel, Via Fratelli Rizzà 18, www.taxushostel.it, 0039 327 9131968
2 Albergo Cima D'Asta, Via Brigata Abruzzi, 2, www.hotelcimadasta.it, 0039 0461 592112, IV-V
❶ Museum in the birthplace of Alcide Degasperis

Castello Tesino
1 Affittacamere Ai Vecchi Molini, Località Molini 17, www.aimolini.com, 0039 348 2295364
❶ stone arch bridge on the trace of the Via Claudia Augusta
❷ small church on the footpath of a roman castle
❸ visitors centre of the fifflora e fauna of the Tesino valley

Between Castello Tesino and Lamon
❶ Stalactite cave of Castel Tesino or rather Lamon
❷ „San Donato" mountain village

The Bellunese Dolomites. Photo: Dolomiti Pre Alpi.

Castello Tesino. Photo (2): Tschaikner

The bridge of the Via Claudia Augusta before Lamon even adorns a stamp

Brew kettle at the Fabbrica Pedavena brewery. Photo: Tschaikner

The original milestone of the Via Claudia Augusta in Cesiomaggiore

Feltre. Photo: Tschaikner

Map 40

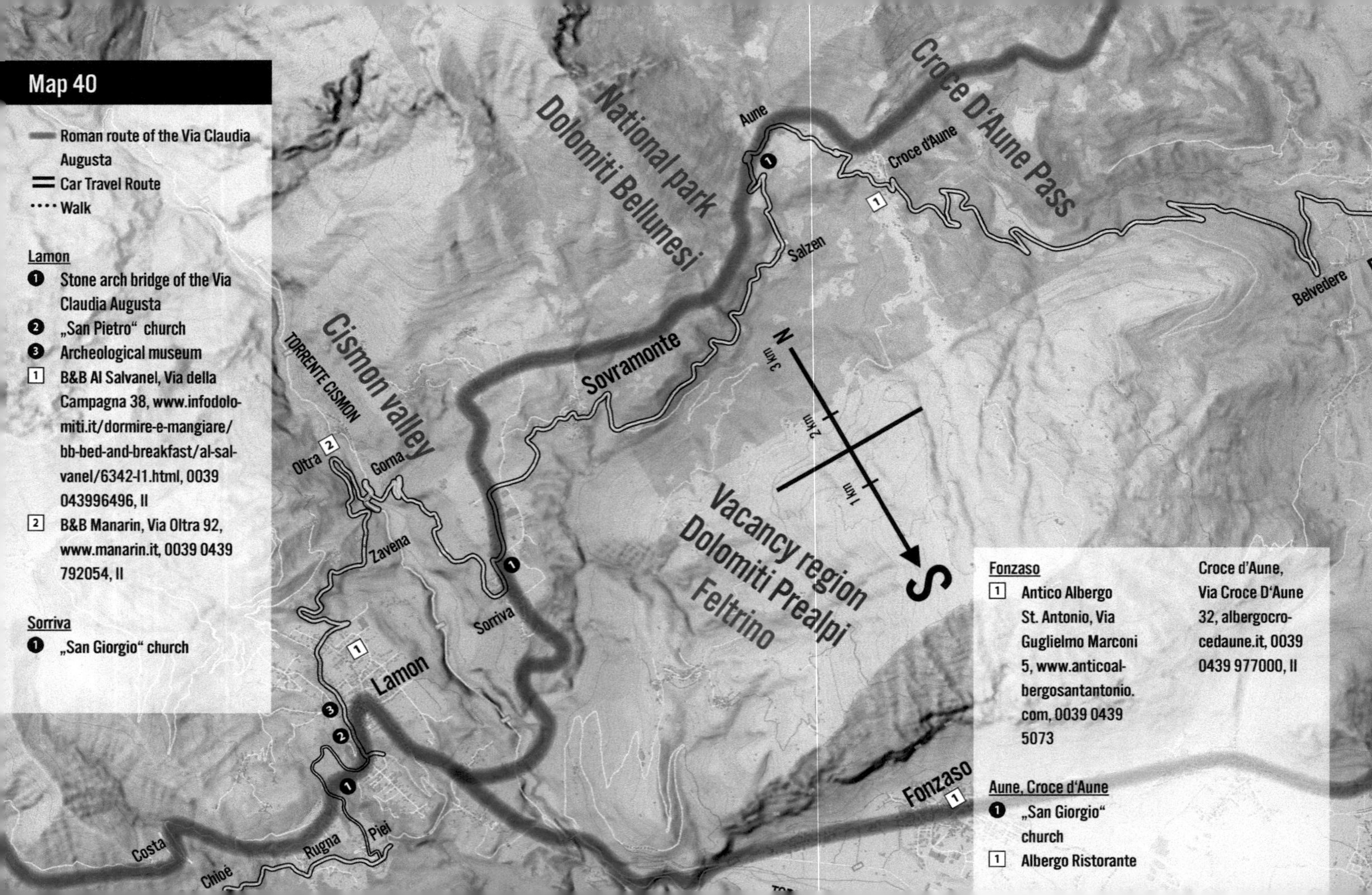

Roman route of the Via Claudia Augusta

Car Travel Route

Walk

Lamon

1. Stone arch bridge of the Via Claudia Augusta
2. „San Pietro" church
3. Archeological museum

[1] B&B Al Salvanel, Via della Campagna 38, www.infodolomiti.it/dormire-e-mangiare/bb-bed-and-breakfast/al-salvanel/6342-l1.html, 0039 043996496, II

[2] B&B Manarin, Via Oltra 92, www.manarin.it, 0039 0439 792054, II

Sorriva

1. „San Giorgio" church

Fonzaso

[1] Antico Albergo St. Antonio, Via Guglielmo Marconi 5, www.anticoalbergosantantonio.com, 0039 0439 5073

Aune, Croce d'Aune

1. „San Giorgio" church

[1] Albergo Ristorante Croce d'Aune, Via Croce D'Aune 32, albergocrocedaune.it, 0039 0439 977000, II

Feltrino, Feltre, Pedavena, Santa Giustina, Cesiomaggiore (map 40, 41)

Feltre has been a traffic hub since prehistoric times. The narrow mountain ridge on which its attractive old town stands and the surrounding sunny slopes have also been inhabited ever since. We know this because of the Etruscan name of Feltre and many archaeological findings. The Roman road Via Claudia Augusta did not lead directly into the town. Instead, it ran in a straight line from the Croce D'Aune Pass to Cesiomaggiore, clinging to the slope. Feltria was a significant Roman town. Its architecture and layout clearly exhibit the influence of the Doges of Venice. Feltre's sphere of influence reached all the way to the Valsugana at times.

From the Croce D'Aune Pass to Pedavena and Feltre

Today, the Via Claudia Augusta long-distance hiking route follows the route of the old Roman road. Our travel route takes the pass road from Croce D'Aune to Pedavena, whose old town hall houses the administration of the Dolomiti Bellunesi national park. You will pass the traditional Fabbrica di Pedavena on the way, which houses an exhibition on the history of beer-making – in Pedavena and in general. It also has Italy's largest pub, the Birreria Pedavena, where you can try their many beers along with tasty dishes.

A walk through historical Feltre

Most of the extensive old town is located on a long ridge, which you can cross by car for a quick look. Head through the gate in the southwest of the old town and leave through the other gate in the east. If you want to see more of the town, leave your car at the northern or the southern parking lot; they are connected by a pedestrian underpass. Climb the picturesque staircase of the tower on the southern town wall to reach the center. Turn right to the Museo Civico and the eastern gate. On the Piazza Maggiore, you can see the town hall and the church of the Saints Rocco and Sebastiano. The town hall houses the Teatro de La Sena, which is considered the little brother of the Teatro la Fenice in Venice. From the piazza, head uphill to the Castello di Alboino fortress. Afterwards, visit the diocesan museum and the contemporary art gallery of Carlo Rizzarda. Leave the town and visit the cathedral outside its walls. Underneath its square, you can see archaeological excavations of Roman Feltria. Cross the monastery grounds and walk back to the parking lot in the south or the pedestrian crossing.

Regional cuisine like 2000 years ago

Here could be an inn that has at least one dish on the menu continuously as it was 2000 years ago.

Overnight and camping possibilities in the appendix and in the maps

Questions and information about the subsection

- Ufficio Turistico di Feltre - Consorzio Dolomit Prealpi, Piazza Vittorio Emanuele II 21, 0039 0439 2540
- Hotline Via Claudia Augusta, 0043(0)664 27 63 555

Map 41

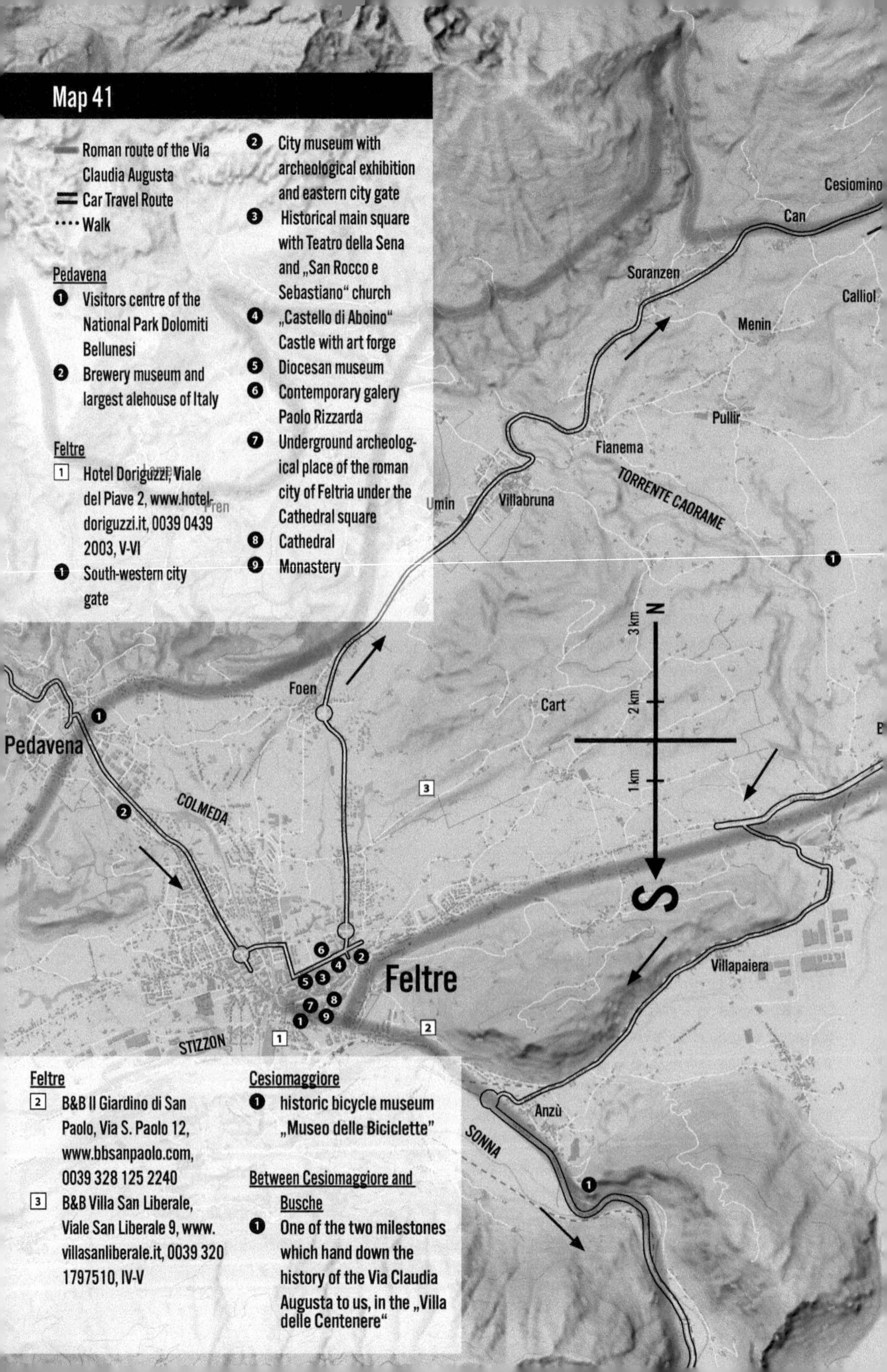
Roman route of the Via Claudia Augusta
Car Travel Route
Walk
Pedavena
1 Visitors centre of the National Park Dolomiti Bellunesi
2 Brewery museum and largest alehouse of Italy
Feltre
[1] Hotel Doriguzzi, Viale del Piave 2, www.hotel-doriguzzi.it, 0039 0439 2003, V-VI
1 South-western city gate
2 City museum with archeological exhibition and eastern city gate
3 Historical main square with Teatro della Sena and „San Rocco e Sebastiano“ church
4 „Castello di Aboino“ Castle with art forge
5 Diocesan museum
6 Contemporary galery Paolo Rizzarda
7 Underground archeological place of the roman city of Feltria under the Cathedral square
8 Cathedral
9 Monastery
Feltre
[2] B&B Il Giardino di San Paolo, Via S. Paolo 12, www.bbsanpaolo.com, 0039 328 125 2240
[3] B&B Villa San Liberale, Viale San Liberale 9, www. villasanliberale.it, 0039 320 1797510, IV-V
Cesiomaggiore
1 historic bicycle museum „Museo delle Biciclette“
Between Cesiomaggiore and Busche
1 One of the two milestones which hand down the history of the Via Claudia Augusta to us, in the „Villa delle Centenere“
Cesiomino
Can
Soranzen
Calliol
Menin
Pullir
Fianema
Villabruna
Umin
TORRENTE CAORAME
N
3 km
2 km
1 km
S
Foen
Cart
Pedavena
COLMEDA
Feltre
Villapaiera
STIZZON
Anzù
SONNA

Feltre

1 Hotel Doriguzzi, Viale del Piave 2, www.hoteldoriguzzi.it, 0039 0439 2003, V-VI

❶ South-western city gate

❷ City museum with archeological exhibition and eastern city gate

❸ Historical main square with Teatro della Sena and „San Rocco e Sebastiano“ church

❹ „Castello di Aboino“ Castle with art forge

❺ Diocesan museum

❻ Contemporary galery Paolo Rizzarda

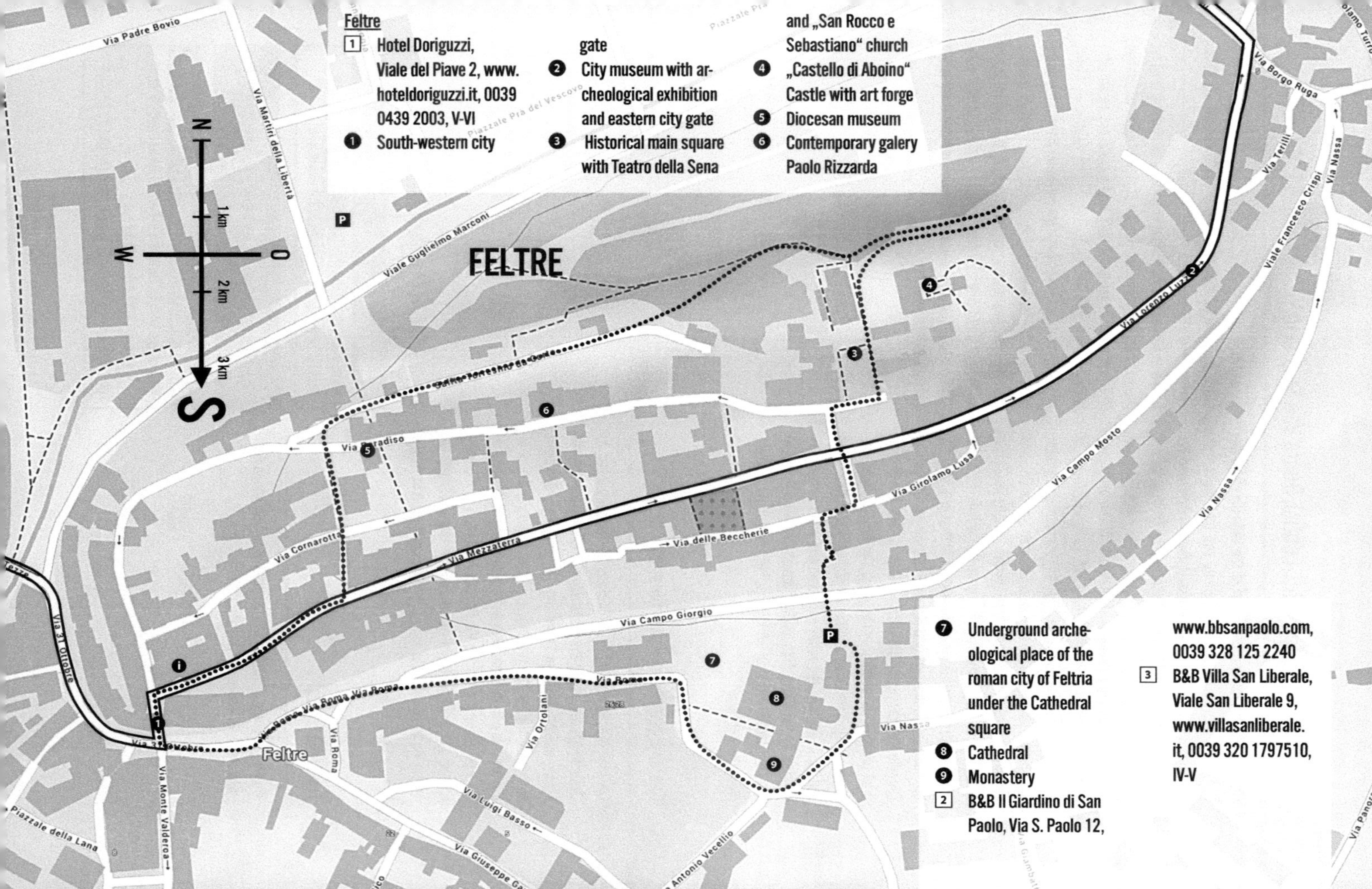

❼ Underground archeological place of the roman city of Feltria under the Cathedral square

❽ Cathedral

❾ Monastery

2 B&B Il Giardino di San Paolo, Via S. Paolo 12, www.bbsanpaolo.com, 0039 328 125 2240

3 B&B Villa San Liberale, Viale San Liberale 9, www.villasanliberale.it, 0039 320 1797510, IV-V

36a The Piave Mel, Lentiai, Quero-Vas Segusino, Alano (map 41, 42, 43)

The Valbelluna is the southern part of the Valle del Piave between the provincial capital of Belluno and the border with the province of Treviso to the south. It used to be called Val Serpentina in the past. Nestled between the foothills of the Dolomites and the last mountain ridge before the Venetian Plain, this stunning valley is dominated by the wide and largely untouched riverbed of the Piave. In Roman times as today, there have never been many bridges crossing the river. One of the few that did exist stood between Santa Giustina and the municipality of Borgo Valbelluna – strictly speaking, its capital of Mel, picturesquely located on a hill. The name 'Nave' (= ship) reminds us of the historical river crossing. On the southern slope between Mel and Lentiai, the Castello di Zumelle thrones above the valley. In this section, the Roman road climbed its southernmost pass, the Praderadego. Between Borgo Valbelluna and the municipalities of Quero Vas and Alano di Piave, the valley narrowed and was occasionally flooded by the Piave. This made it unsuitable for a road like the Via Claudia Augusta, which was built to ensure military reinforcements.

Cesiomaggiore and Santa Giustina

Over the hills in front of the Dolomites the itinerary leads to Cesiomaggiore, where the historical bicycle museum worth seeing awaits. Between Feltre and Cesiomaggiore there are numerous old country residences of the wealthy citizens of the area. In one of them, Villa delle Centenere, stands one of the two milestones of the Via Claudia Augusta. The itinerary makes a loop through the valley, passing through Santa Giustina via the back door to Mel, picturesquely perched on a hill.

The town of Mel

Mel has not only a worth seeing center with a spacious piazza. It also has a small archaeological museum.

Lentiai, Castello Zumelle and St. Vittore and Corona

Between Mel and Lentiai the Roman road climbed up the last pass. On the old pass road sits the Zumelle Castle, which has been restored in an exemplary manner. An old stone arch bridge, which can be discovered in the deciduous forest above Bardies and dates back to Byzantine times, also bears witness to the important road connection. Through Lentiai, with its spacious piazza, we finally reach the Sanctuary of St. Vittore and Corona. It was already founded in the early 11th century. The itinerary then follows the Piave River south through its narrow valley.

Regional cuisine like 2000 years ago

Here could be an inn that has at least one dish on the menu continuously as it was 2000 years ago.

Overnight and camping possibilities in the appendix and in the maps

Questions and information about the subsection

- Hotline Ufficio Turistico di Feltre - Consorzio Dolomit Prealpi, 0039 0439 2540
- Hotline Via Claudia Augusta, 0043(0)664 27 63 555

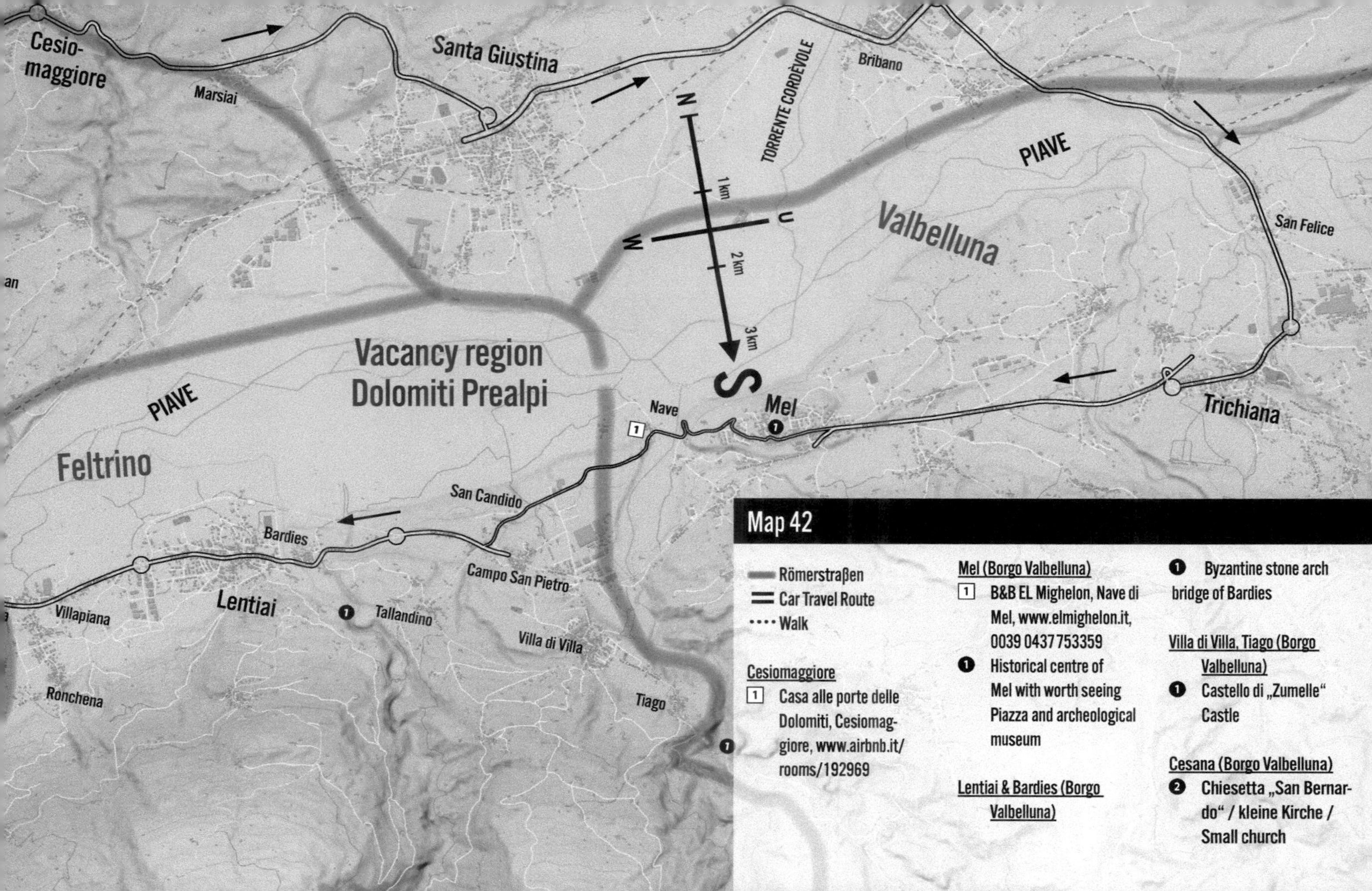

Map 42

Römerstraßen
Car Travel Route
Walk

Cesiomaggiore

1 Casa alle porte delle Dolomiti, Cesiomaggiore, www.airbnb.it/rooms/192969

Mel (Borgo Valbelluna)

1 B&B EL Mighelon, Nave di Mel, www.elmighelon.it, 0039 0437 753359

❶ Historical centre of Mel with worth seeing Piazza and archeological museum

Lentiai & Bardies (Borgo Valbelluna)

❶ Byzantine stone arch bridge of Bardies

Villa di Villa, Tiago (Borgo Valbelluna)

❶ Castello di „Zumelle“ Castle

Cesana (Borgo Valbelluna)

❷ Chiesetta „San Bernardo“ / kleine Kirche / Small church

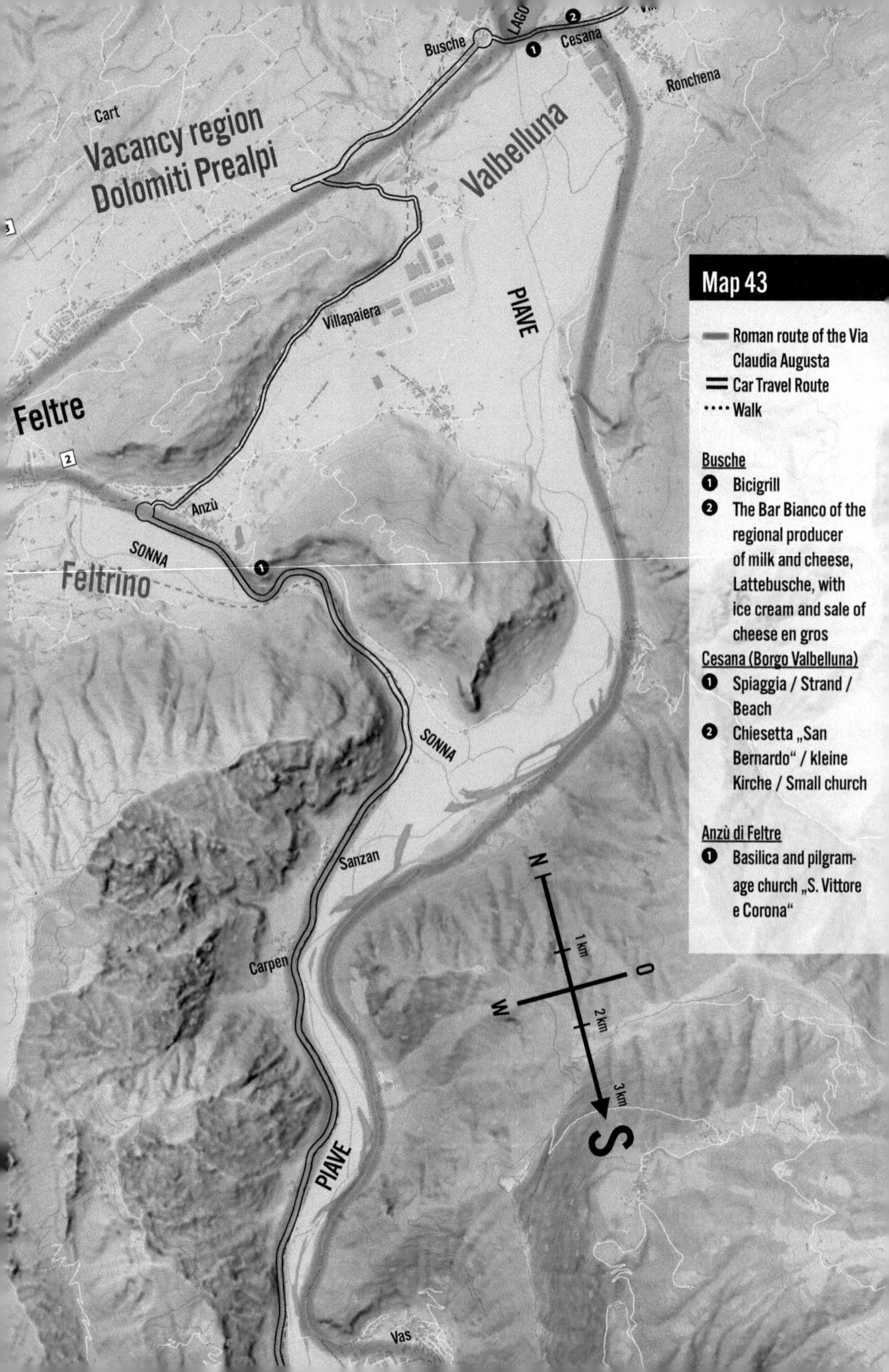
Map 43
Roman route of the Via Claudia Augusta
Car Travel Route
Walk
Busche
❶ Bicigrill
❷ The Bar Bianco of the regional producer of milk and cheese, Lattebusche, with ice cream and sale of cheese en gros
Cesana (Borgo Valbelluna)
❶ Spiaggia / Strand / Beach
❷ Chiesetta „San Bernardo" / kleine Kirche / Small church
Anzù di Feltre
❶ Basilica and pilgrimage church „S. Vittore e Corona"
Vacancy region Dolomiti Prealpi
Valbelluna
Feltre
Feltrino
Busche
LAGO
Cesana
Ronchena
Cart
Villapaiera
PIAVE
Anzù
SONNA
SONNA
Sanzan
Carpen
PIAVE
Vas
N
O
W
S
1 km
2 km
3 km

The barely regulated Piaveflfflluss still seizes large parts of the Valbelluna again and again. Photo: Via Claudia Augusta / Tschaikner

Archaeological Museum Mel. Photo (2): Via Claudia Augusta / Tschaikner

The Renaissance castle of Castelbrando. Photo: Castelbrando

The Prosecco wine hills in the Altamarca, in the north of the Veneto plain. Photo: Altamarca

37a Altamarca: the Prosecco hill at the southern edge of the Alps (map 44, 45, 46, 47)

The transition from the Alps to the Venetian Plain is gradual rather than abrupt. To the south of the last mountain ridge and the last pass of the Via Claudia Augusta lies the front garden of the Alps: the Prosecco wine hills of the Altamarca, the northernmost part of Treviso. Two wine roads snake their way through the picturesque region, taking travellers past interesting sights, pretty wine-growing villages and the best wine they will find. They are the Strada del Prosecco e Vini dei Colli Conegliano Valdobbiadene and the Strada del Vino del Montello e dei Colli Asolani.

Along the Prosecco Wine Road

The itinerary first follows the Prosecco Wine Road through the towns of the most famous Prosecco growing municipality of Valdobbiadene, with its worth seeing piazza. In the town of Follina, after the last pass, the historic route entered the hilly beginning wide plain of Veneto. Directly in the center of the village is the monastery of Follina, which is well worth seeing. A little north of Follina, above the historic road, stands the Renaissance castle of Castelbrando. It can be reached by inclined elevator from Cison di Valmarino and today houses a wellness and congress hotel as well as restaurants and several exhibitions. The next municipality, Pieve di Soligo, with an old center worth seeing, through which the wild river Soligo flows, also has an imposing piazza. The large palace in the square is to be converted into the town hall. Just before reaching the Castello Collalto, the remains of the Via Claudia Augusta can be seen on the banks of the Piave River. Between the Castello and the municipality of Susegana, the itinerary crosses picturesque pro-
secco hills. On top of one of them towers the Castello San Salvatore. On the outskirts of Susegana are the Church of Carmine and the Collalto winery. From Susegana, those interested can reach Conegliano, the capital of the region with almost 35,000 inhabitants, which is known for its traditional checkers parade with living figures in historical costumes and also has an old town worth seeing. Via the agricultural town of Santa Lucia di Piave, where annual agricultural fairs are held, the itinerary finally leads to Ponte della Priula, which belongs to Susegana, where it crosses the wide, largely natural riverbed of the Piave.

Montello and Colli Asolani Wine Route

On the opposite bank of the river, a detour is tempting along another wine route, characterized by the „Montello“ mountain and the hills of Asolo. On them, vineyards alternate with varied natural vegetation. South of Nervesa della Battaglia, the ruins of the Abbey of San Eustacchio recall the devastating battles of the 1st World War. Vineyards and wine villages line the rest of the route. Particularly worth seeing is the town of Asolo, which was already settled by the Venetians in the 6th / 7th century.

Regional cuisine like 2000 years ago

Here could be an inn that has at least one dish on the menu continuously as it was 2000 years ago.

Overnight and camping possibilities in the appendix and in the maps

Questions and information about the subsection

- Hotline Consorzio di Promozione Turistica Marca Treviso, +39 0422 54 10 52
- Hotline Via Claudia Augusta, +43(0)664 27 63 555

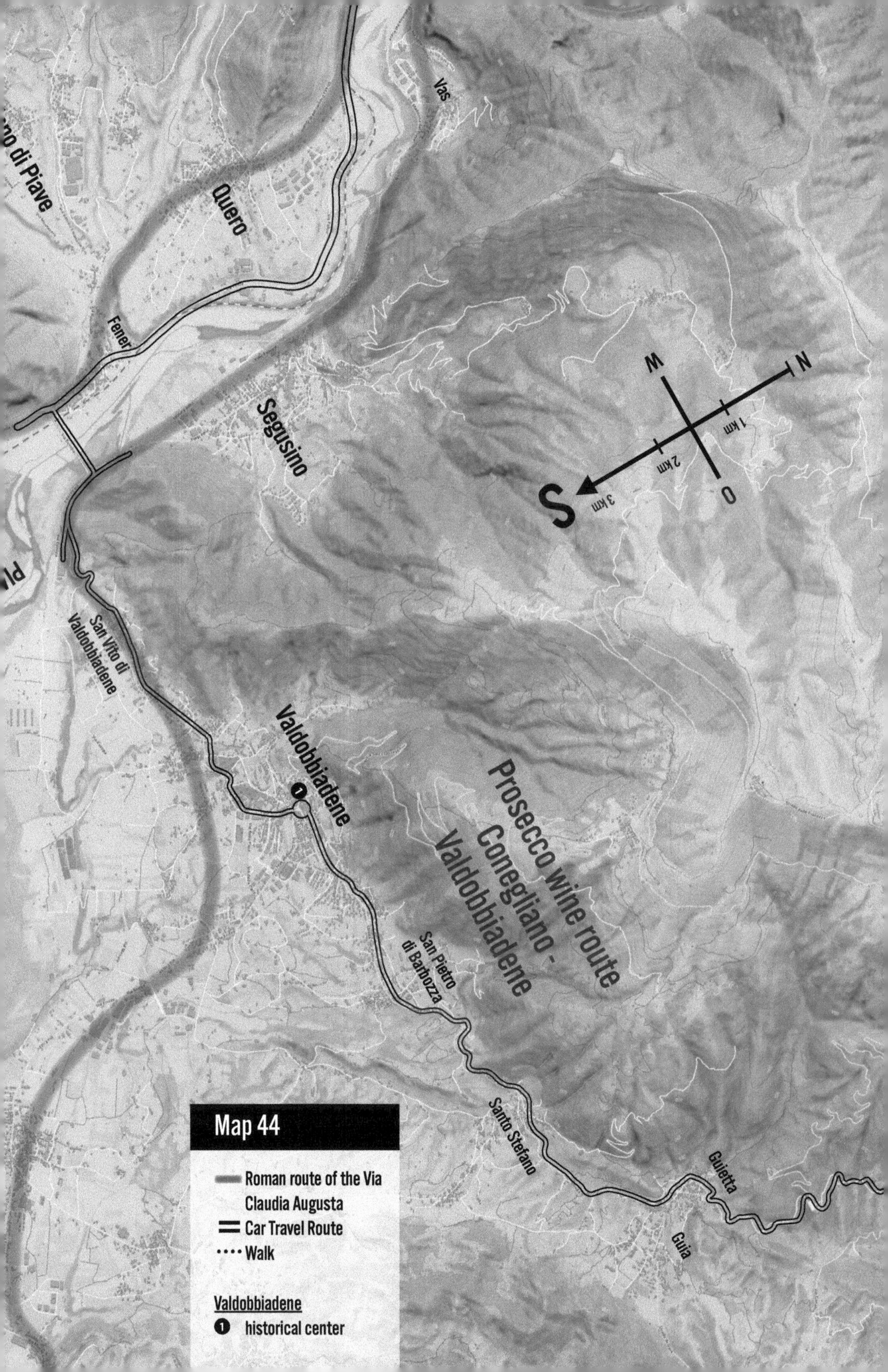
Quero
Vas
Fener
Segusino
San Vito di Valdobbiadene
Valdobbiadene
Prosecco wine route Conegliano - Valdobbiadene
San Pietro di Barbozza
Santo Stefano
Guietta
Guia
W
N
O
S
1 km
2 km
3 km
Map 44
Roman route of the Via Claudia Augusta
Car Travel Route
Walk
Valdobbiadene
1 historical center

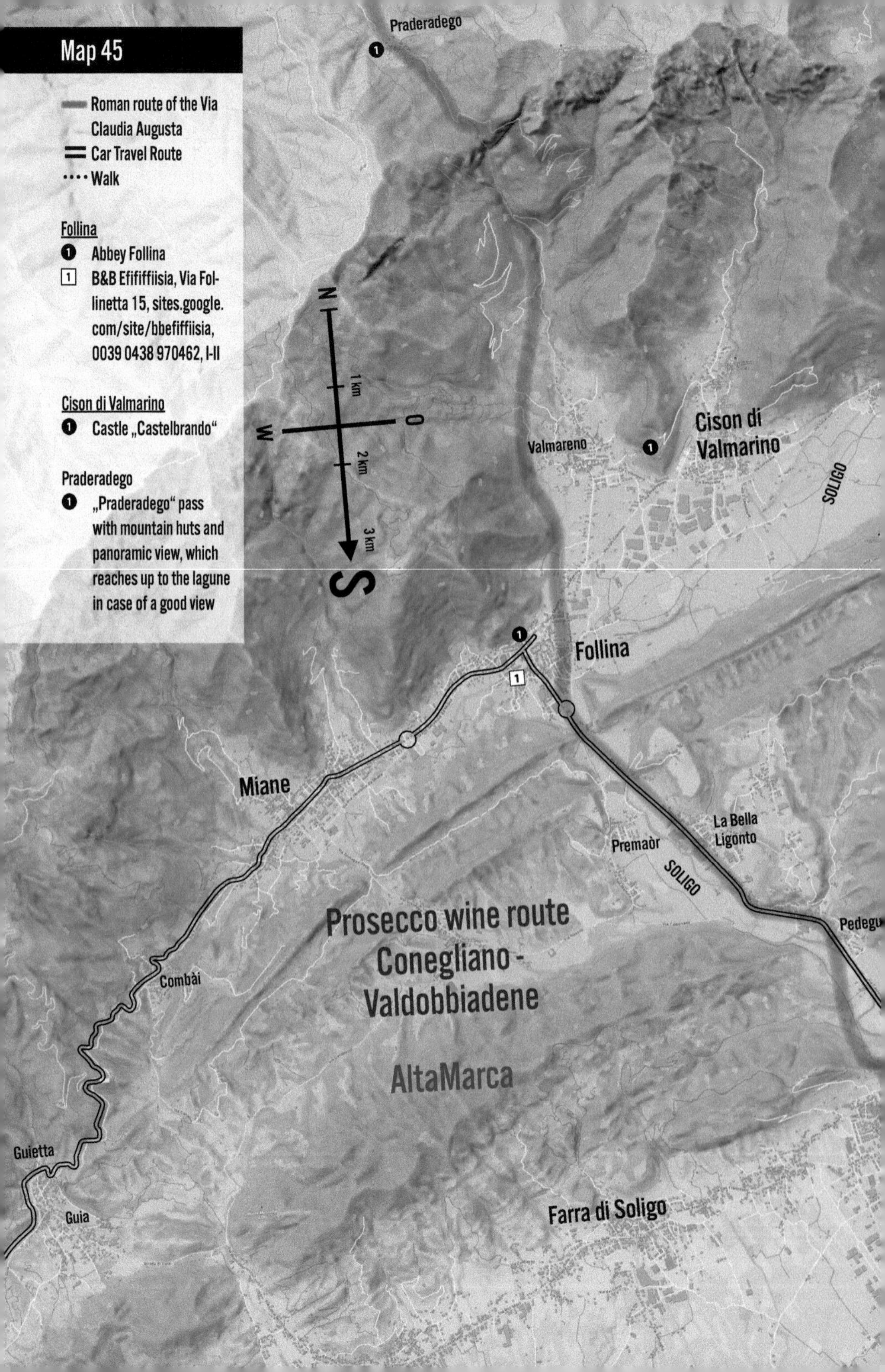
Map 45
Roman route of the Via Claudia Augusta
Car Travel Route
Walk
Follina
1 Abbey Follina
1 B&B Efififfiisia, Via Follinetta 15, sites.google.com/site/bbefiffiisia, 0039 0438 970462, I-II
Cison di Valmarino
1 Castle „Castelbrando"
Praderadego
1 „Praderadego" pass with mountain huts and panoramic view, which reaches up to the lagune in case of a good view
Praderadego
N
1 km
W
O
2 km
3 km
S
Valmareno
Cison di Valmarino
SOLIGO
Follina
Miane
Premaòr
La Bella Ligonto
SOLIGO
Pedegu
Prosecco wine route Conegliano - Valdobbiadene
Combài
AltaMarca
Guietta
Guia
Farra di Soligo

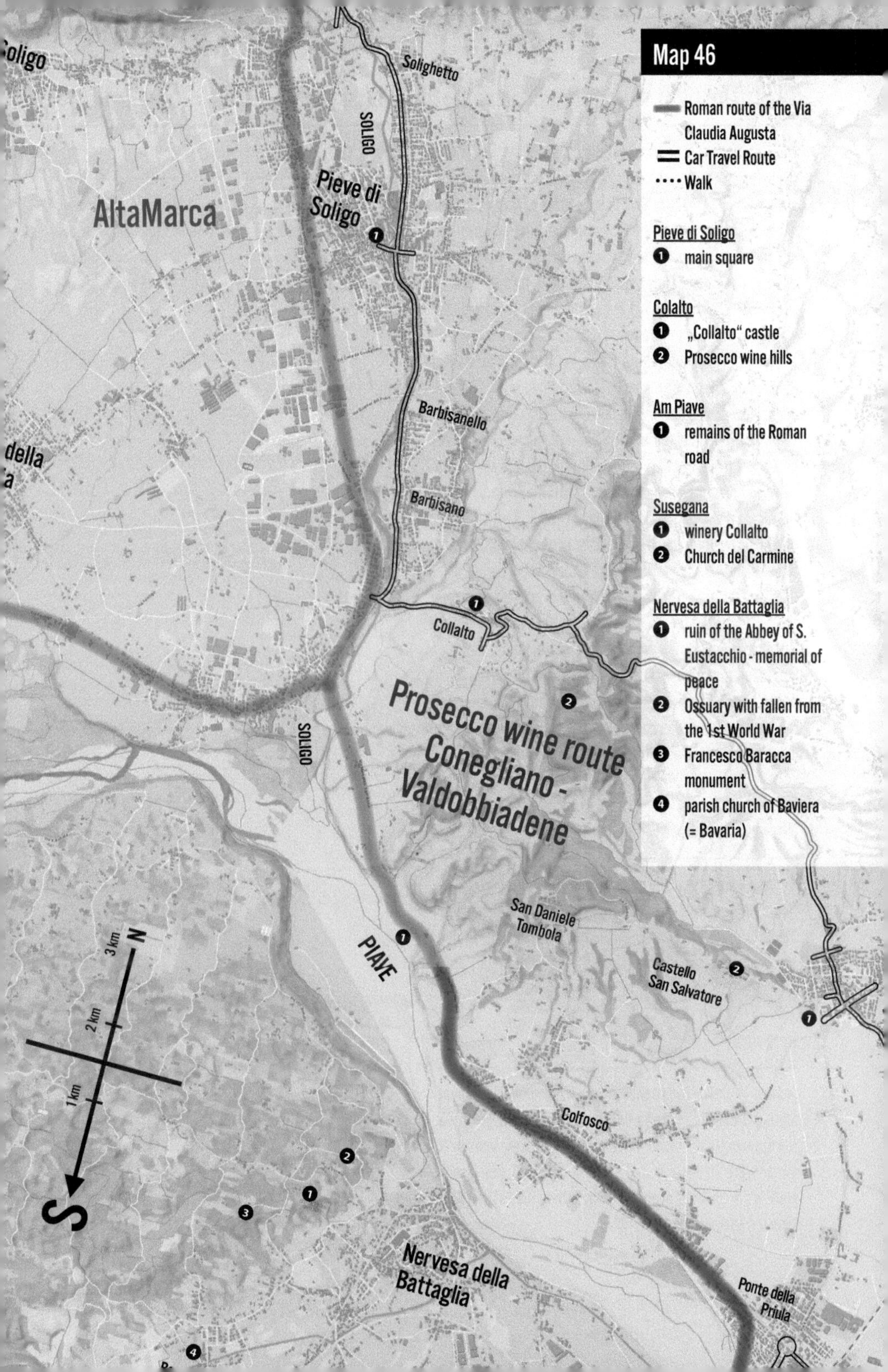
Map 46
Roman route of the Via Claudia Augusta
Car Travel Route
Walk
Pieve di Soligo
1 main square
Colalto
1 „Collalto“ castle
2 Prosecco wine hills
Am Piave
1 remains of the Roman road
Susegana
1 winery Collalto
2 Church del Carmine
Nervesa della Battaglia
1 ruin of the Abbey of S. Eustacchio - memorial of peace
2 Ossuary with fallen from the 1st World War
3 Francesco Baracca monument
4 parish church of Baviera (= Bavaria)
Soligo
Solighetto
SOLIGO
Pieve di Soligo
AltaMarca
Barbisanello
Barbisano
Collalto
Prosecco wine route Conegliano - Valdobbiadene
SOLIGO
San Daniele Tombola
PIAVE
Castello San Salvatore
Colfosco
N
3 km
2 km
1 km
S
Nervesa della Battaglia
Ponte della Priula

38a The right side of the Piave: a fertile plain on an unspoilt river (map 47, 48)

There are several theories about the course of the Via Claudia Augusta, and Italian archaeologists are yet to reach consensus on which is correct. That is why, after crossing the Prosecco Hills to the left of the Piave (teoria sinistra Piave), our cycling route follows the teoria destra Piave for a little while, running along the barely regulated, wide right-hand bank of the river. The alluvial area at the center of the Trevisan Plain was always a region of transit, influenced by a wide range of factors. It is likely that there was a settlement here during Roman times. Even the name Spresiano is said to have Roman origins. The towns of Nervesa della Battaglia, Spresiano and Villorba are documented as early as the 10th century. This region was not blessed with fertile soil. Only the ford across the Piave and the raft-making business created work for some of the local residents. The population was poor; their situation only improved after the Republic of Venice built irrigation systems. Many Ville Venete, which are typical of the region, date back to that area. The region suffered great losses during the two battles of the River Piave during the First World War. Nervesa della Battaglia, which is even named after a battle, was razed to the ground nearly completely. Today, the ruins of the 14th-century Saint Eustace Abbey remind visitors of the tragedy. The towns only began to flourish when a textile industry developed after the Second World War.

Nervesa della Battaglia

Nervesa was particularly devastated by the devastating battles of the 1st World War. As a memorial to peace, the ruins of the 14th century Abbey of San Eustacchio remind us of this. Today concerts are also held there.

Spresiano

In addition to the parish church with a monument commemorating the fallen of World War I, Villa Giustinian-Recanti is worth seeing in the main town of Spresiano. In the Visnadello fraction, the Sebbene church and Villa Gritti are to be discovered. In the fraction Lovadina among others the Palazzo Bove from the 15th century.

Villorba, place of villas

Villorba is not called so by chance. It has especially many of the famous stately Ville Venete. One of them, Villa Giovannina, is today the representative part of the municipal administration and as such is open also during office hours.

Regional cuisine like 2000 years ago

Here could be an inn that has at least one dish on the menu continuously as it was 2000 years ago.

Overnight and camping possibilities in the appendix and in the maps

Questions and information about the subsection

- Hotline Consorzio di Promozione Turistica Marca Treviso, 0039 0422 54 10 52
- Hotline Via Claudia Augusta, 0043(0)664 27 63 555

39a Tarvisium, city of water and art (map 48)

Treviso is located at the center of an agricultural region at the confluence of the Botteniga and the Sile. Humans settled here as early as the Bronze Age. In 49 B. C., the Romans granted town privileges to Tarvisium. It was mentioned as an episcopal see as early as 396 A. D. Following a long period of disputes, during which Venice demanded the liberalization of trade by the provinces of Padua and Treviso, the city was ultimately incorporated into the Republic of Venice over the course of several centuries. Its extensive old town is enclosed nearly entirely by a wall and a canal that runs along its outside. A wide network of canals inside the city gave Treviso its nickname of 'città delle acque'. It is also considered a 'città dell'arte'.

The itinerary around the old town

Our travel route runs counterclockwise around the old town, which is completely surrounded by a canal and the River Sile. Coming from the north, you directly approach the San Tommaso gate. If you want to see the old town, approach the center from the south instead: there is better parking in this part.

A walk through the old town

The old town of Treviso is a treasure trove of sights. Crossed by countless canals and lined with typically painted townhouses, it is a truly charming place. Take a leisurely walk through its alleyways to soak up the special charm of Treviso. Our suggested route is just one of many ways to see some of the town and its attractions in a short period of time. It takes you to the Sankt Nikolaus church from the 13th and 14th century and to the striking cathedral of the diocesan town. In the north, the town wall is accessible. Our walk also takes you to the Franciscan church and monastery and the Palazzo dei Trecento, a 13th-century palace with lovely frescoes situated on the picturesque Piazza dei Signori.

Regional cuisine like 2000 years ago

Here could be an inn that has at least one dish on the menu continuously as it was 2000 years ago.

Overnight and camping possibilities in the appendix and in the maps

Questions and information about the subsection

- Ufficio Turistico Treviso - Consorzio Marca Treviso, Viale degli Eroi 2, 0039 0422 54 10 52
- Hotline Via Claudia Augusta, 0043(0)664 27 63 555

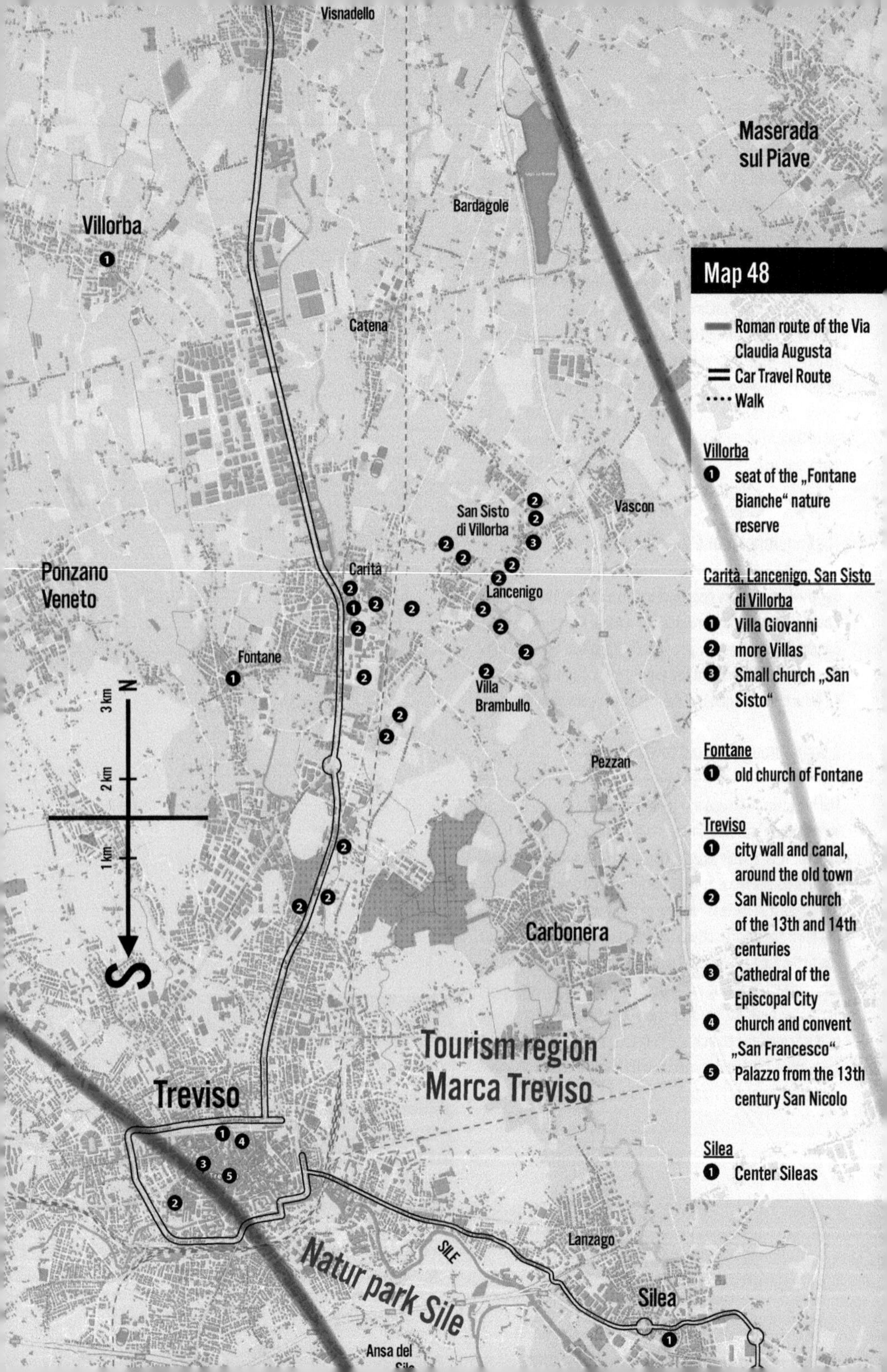
Map 48
Roman route of the Via Claudia Augusta
Car Travel Route
Walk
Villorba
❶ seat of the „Fontane Bianche“ nature reserve
Carità, Lancenigo, San Sisto di Villorba
❶ Villa Giovanni
❷ more Villas
❸ Small church „San Sisto“
Fontane
❶ old church of Fontane
Treviso
❶ city wall and canal, around the old town
❷ San Nicolo church of the 13th and 14th centuries
❸ Cathedral of the Episcopal City
❹ church and convent „San Francesco“
❺ Palazzo from the 13th century San Nicolo
Silea
❶ Center Sileas
Visnadello
Maserada sul Piave
Bardagole
Villorba
Catena
San Sisto di Villorba
Vascon
Ponzano Veneto
Carità
Lancenigo
Fontane
Villa Brambullo
Pezzan
N
S
1 km
2 km
3 km
Carbonera
Tourism region Marca Treviso
Treviso
Natur park Sile
SILE
Lanzago
Silea
Ansa del

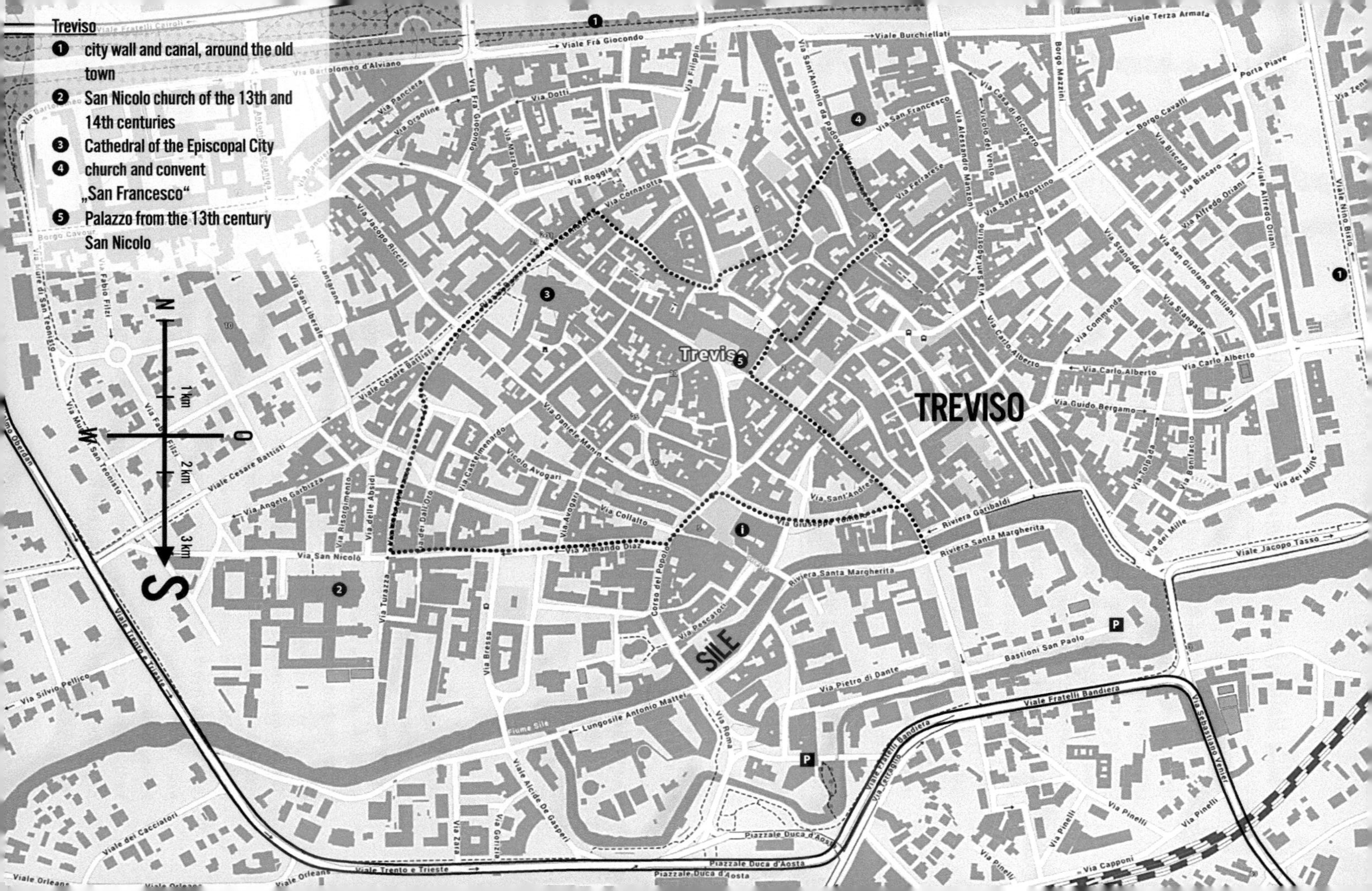
Treviso
1 city wall and canal, around the old town
2 San Nicolo church of the 13th and 14th centuries
3 Cathedral of the Episcopal City
4 church and convent „San Francesco“
5 Palazzo from the 13th century San Nicolo
N
O
W
S
1 km
2 km
3 km
TREVISO
Treviso
SILE
Viale Terza Armata
Viale Burchiellati
Viale Frà Giocondo
Via Bartolomeo d'Alviano
Borgo Mazzini
Porta Piave
Viale Nino Bixio
Viale Alfredo Oriani
Borgo Cavalli
Via San Francesco
Via Sant'Antonio da Padova
Via Casa di Ricovero
Vicolo del Vento
Via Alessandro Manzoni
Via Sant'Agostino
Via Ferrarese
Via Stangade
Via San Girolamo Emiliani
Via Commenda
Via Carlo Alberto
Via Guido Bergamo
Via Tolpada
Via Bonifacio
Via dei Mille
Viale Jacopo Tasso
Riviera Garibaldi
Riviera Santa Margherita
Bastioni San Paolo
Via Pietro di Dante
Viale Fratelli Bandiera
Via Sebastiano Venier
Via Pinelli
Via Capponi
Via Sant'Andrea
Via Giuseppe Tomea
Via Armando Diaz
Corso del Popolo
Via Pescatori
Via Collalto
Via Avogari
Vicolo Avogari
Via Daniele Manin
Via Castelmenardo
Via dall'Oro
Via delle Absidi
Via Risorgimento
Via Turazza
Via San Nicolò
Via Bressa
Lungosile Antonio Mattei
Fiume Sile
Via Roma
Piazzale Duca d'Aosta
Viale Trento e Trieste
Viale Alcide De Gasperi
Via Zara
Via Gorizia
Viale dei Cacciatori
Viale Orleans
Via Silvio Pellico
Viale Oberdan
Via Angelo Garbizza
Viale Cesare Battisti
Via Fabio Filzi
Via Mure di San Teonisto
Via San Liberale
Via Cantarane
Borgo Cavour
Via Jacopo Riccati
Via Roggia
Via Cornarotta
Via Marzolo
Via Dotti
Via Fra' Giocondo
Via Orsoline
Via Panciera
Via Filippin
Viale Fratelli Cairoli

40a Natural Park of the River Sile, Silea, Roncade,Quarto D'Altino (map 48, 49)

The villages to the south of Treviso are connected by the old road and by the natural park that stretches along the Sile. This picturesque river is truly unique: it remains calm during storms, maintains the same temperature all year round and carries very little debris. Its soil is ideal for water plants. House boats and excursion cruisers travel along this natural jewel between Venice and Treviso. Human settlements have existed in the area along the river since the Neolithic. Its oldest towns were mentioned as early as the 11th and 12th century, and they are all on the route of the old Roman road. Today, a tarmac road follows some of the old track. In Roncade, consider visiting the Castello di Roncade, which stores and sells its very own wines.

The Sile Nature Park and Silea

The Sile river has always been an important communication and trade route. Today, tourist boats navigate it, too. Until 1970, the river was used by burci, large boats used to transport heavy goods. You can still see them at the Burci Cemetery in Casier on the shore opposite Silea. Silea, which has a population of more than 10,000 today, has been inhabited since the 2nd century A. D. Its oldest settlements were in the modern districts of Sant'Elena and Cendon on the old Roman road. The same two towns were the first to be mentioned in medieval records, too. Silea used to be called Melma and was only named after the river in 1935.

Roncade and the Castello di Roncade

Roncade, today home to 14,000 people, has been a site of human settlement since the Neolithic. In Roman times, most of the population was concentrated in the district of Musestre, where the Via Claudia Augusta used to cross the Sile river. After its incorporation into the Republic of Venice, the town began to develop rapidly after 1500 A.D.. Several villas bear witness to that economic boom. The Renaissance villa Giustinian at the Castello di Roncade, which is also a renowned winery, is the most significant of them all. Other sights include the parish church and chapel at the Kastell, which house an important cycle of Baroque paintings. The winery '47 Anno Domini' (named after the year in which the Via Claudia Augusta was completed) is situated between Roncade and Silea, right on the historical route of the Roman road. It skillfully blends the tradition of wine-making with modern technology and the latest trends.

Regional cuisine like 2000 years ago

Here could be an inn that has at least one dish on the menu continuously as it was 2000 years ago.

Overnight and camping possibilities in the appendix and in the maps

Questions and information about the subsection

- Hotline Consorzio di Promozione Turistica Marca Treviso, 0039 0422 54 10 52
- Hotline Via Claudia Augusta, 0043(0)664 27 63 555

The Sile Flusspark. Photo: Club Unesco Venice

The center of the city of Roncade. Photo: City of Roncade

Die Villa Giustinian im Kastell di Roncade. Photo: Stadti Roncade

Roman road. Photo: Via Claudia Augusta

Archaeological Museum in Altino. Photo: Tschaikner

In the lagoon. Photo: Lammerhuber

41a Altino, a Roman Adriatic port on the Lagoon (maps 49, 50/1, 50/2)

Can you imagine? Venice did not exist during Roman times. Back then, the ancient port city on the lagoon, right at the mouth of the Sile river, was called Altinum. Several Roman roads started and ended here, which shows the commercial significance of the city. Only after the fall of the Roman Empire did the settlements move to the more sheltered area of the lagoon. But the Roman road remained in use, as shown by the various towns and villages founded along its route. Today, the hamlet of Altino in the municipality of Quarto D'Altino (a part of the listed port area) is home to an excavation site and an archaeological museum. As the area has dried up, it is no longer located next to the water. From the nearby port, you can take boat trips to Venice and Treviso along the Sile.

Quarto D'Altino

The municipality of Quarto d'Altino used to be home to the Roman port. Before our travel route finishes at its center, it crosses the Sile on a relatively narrow bridge. As soon as you reach the other side of the bridge, you are treated to a lovely view of the river and Musestre. The small town center has the municipal offices, a parish church, a few restaurants and some shops. Take the underpass to cross the railway line, which takes travelers to Venice in mere minutes, and follow the perfectly straight route of the Via Claudia Augusta for a little while. The last part of the route leads across the Lagoon, taking hikers and cyclists straight to the ancient port and the museum. Road trippers have to take a detour.

The former ancient port at the Lagoon

The site of the ancient port town has moved a little further inland due to progressive sedimentation. Only a few buildings are left there. One of them is a relatively compact archaeological zone, which gives you some insights into the long history of the area. There is also an old and new archaeological museum and a simple inn. ■ Museum, Via Sant'Eliodoro 37, +39 0422 82 9008, open daily from 8:30 am–7:30 pm. ■ New archaeological museum: Via Sant'Eliodoro 56, +39 0422.789443, apr.-set. mar-dom dalle 8.30 alle 19.30; lun chiuso; ott.-mar. mer, ven, sab, dom dalle 8.30 alle 19.30; mar e gio dalle 9 alle 14.15; lun chiuso.

around the Lagoon: Venice and Jesolo

Quarto D'Altino, a quieter and slightly less upmarket part of the region, is located exactly in the middle between the 'art city' of Treviso, the Lagoon city of Venice, and the beaches of Jesolo. To get to Venice, take a train or the barca tourist boat. The jetty is close to the archaeological museum. You can also take a tourist boat to travel to Treviso on the Sile. Jesolo's many beaches are best accessible by car or bicycle.

Regional cuisine like 2000 years ago

Here could be an inn that has at least one dish on the menu continuously as it was 2000 years ago.

Overnight and camping possibilities in the appendix and in the maps

Questions and information about the subsection

■ Hotline Consorzio di Promozione Turistica Marca Treviso, 0039 0422 54 10 52

■ Hotline Via Claudia Augusta, 0043(0)664 27 63 555

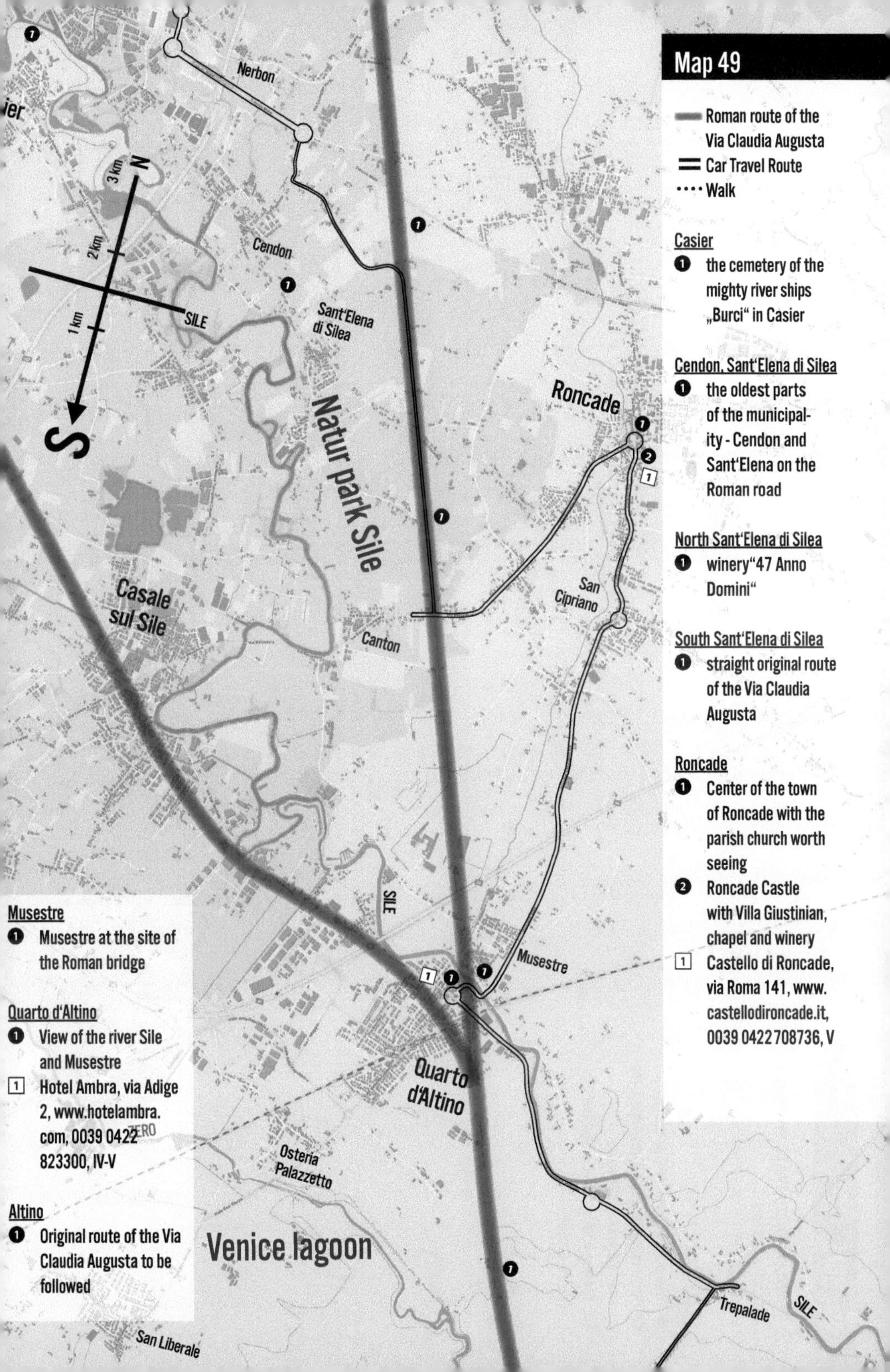

Map 49

Roman route of the Via Claudia Augusta

Car Travel Route

Walk

Casier

❶ the cemetery of the mighty river ships „Burci“ in Casier

Cendon, Sant‘Elena di Silea

❶ the oldest parts of the municipality - Cendon and Sant‘Elena on the Roman road

North Sant‘Elena di Silea

❶ winery“47 Anno Domini“

South Sant‘Elena di Silea

❶ straight original route of the Via Claudia Augusta

Roncade

❶ Center of the town of Roncade with the parish church worth seeing

❷ Roncade Castle with Villa Giustinian, chapel and winery

[1] Castello di Roncade, via Roma 141, www.castellodironcade.it, 0039 0422 708736, V

Musestre

❶ Musestre at the site of the Roman bridge

Quarto d‘Altino

❶ View of the river Sile and Musestre

[1] Hotel Ambra, via Adige 2, www.hotelambra.com, 0039 0422 823300, IV-V

Altino

❶ Original route of the Via Claudia Augusta to be followed

Map 50/1
Roman route of the Via Claudia Augusta
Car Travel Route
Walk
Altino
2 Bike and foot path through the lagoon
3 Archaeological site and museum in the ancient port area of Altino
4 Landing place of the excursion boats to Venice and Treviso
Venezia
1 Venice lagoon city
Marcon
San Liberale
Praello
Zuccarello
DESE
Dese
Altino
Favaro Veneto
Tessera
Campalto
Mestre
MARZENGO
LAGUNA VENETA
Venice lagoon
Burano
Porto Marghera
Murano
Venezia
Cavallino-Treporti
N
S
1 km
2 km
3 km

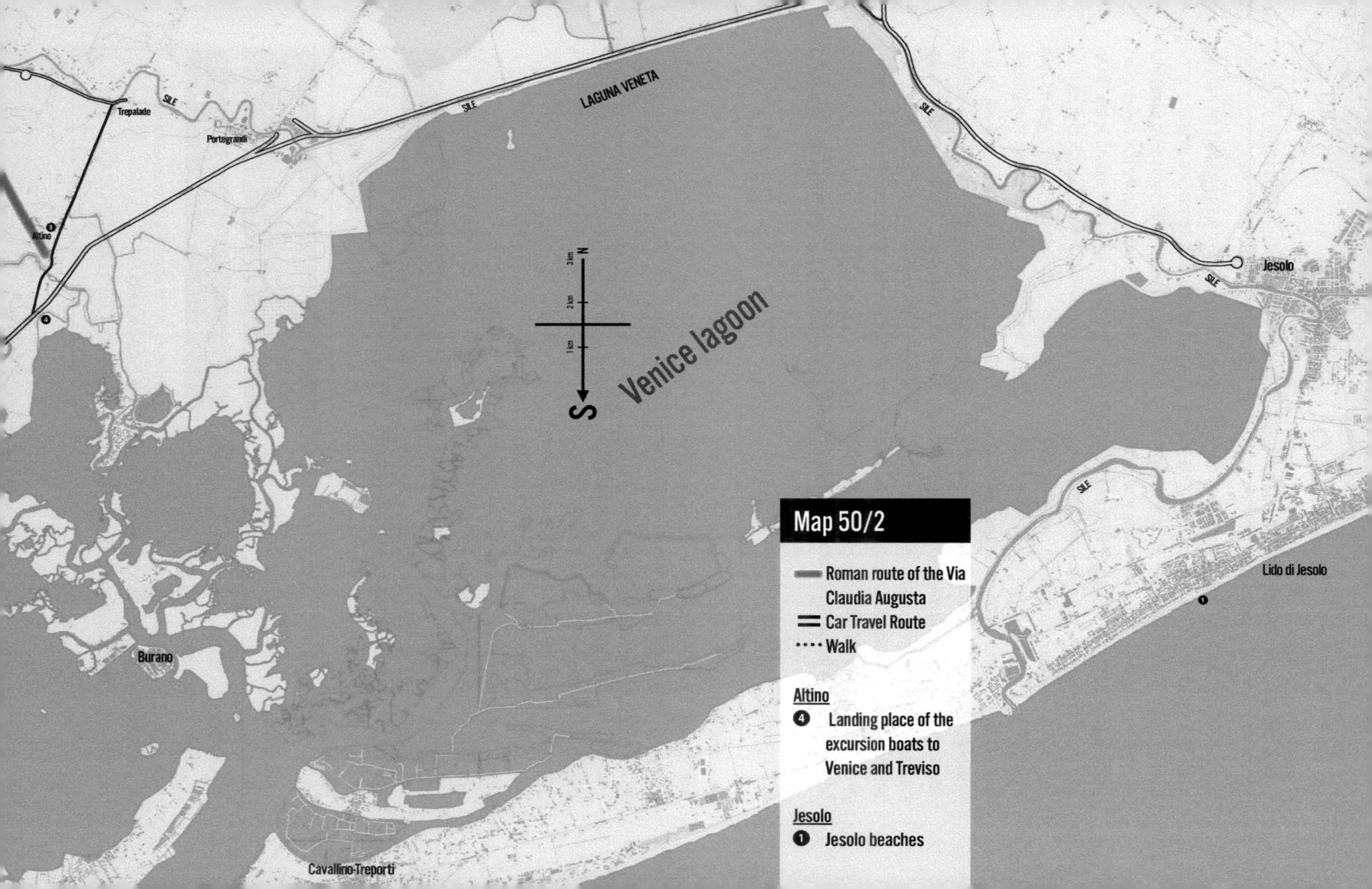

Map 50/2
Roman route of the Via Claudia Augusta
Car Travel Route
Walk
Altino
4 Landing place of the excursion boats to Venice and Treviso
Jesolo
1 Jesolo beaches
Venice lagoon
LAGUNA VENETA
SILE
Trepalade
Portegrandi
Altino
Burano
Cavallino-Treporti
Jesolo
Lido di Jesolo
N
S
1 km
2 km
3 km

Trento / Tridentum, the Roman traffic hub, towards Verona, Ostiglia, Po (map 35, 51)

As the name suggests, Trento has Rhaetian origins. It was already an important traffic hub during their time. The Via Claudia Augusta forked in Tridentum. The road leading to the Adriatic port town of Altinum near Venice was the Via Claudia Augusta Altinate; the road leading to the river port of Ostiglia on the Po river was the Via Claudia Augusta Padana. From there, another road led to Rome. The later historical significance of the city is primarily due to the Council of Trent (1545–1563). It initiated the Counter-Reformation and delineated its intellectual foundations. The map of today's Old Town was shaped significantly during that period. Later, Baroque buildings were added to the Renaissance-style district. Until the invasion of the Napoleonic Troops, the prince-bishops of Trento rules over the city and the surrounding region from the their base in the majestic Buonconsiglio Castle.

Radroute durch Trento nach Verona und Ostiglia

Die Grenze zwischen Lavis und den nördlichen Teilen der Trentiner Landeshauptstadt Trento ist der Avisio, zu dessen Querung die Route nach Lavis, am Talrand , folgt. Danach geht es wieder ans Ufer des Etsch und relativ ruhig und beschaulich fast ins Zentrum der schon in der Römerzeit gegründeten Stadt, in der einst die Weichenstellung für die Gegenreformation fielen. Die Altstadt wurde für das Konzil von Trento im Stil der Renaissance groß herausgeputzt. Auch das Schloss Buonconsiglio erinnert daran. Unter der Stadt sind unterirdische Ausgrabungen der römischen Stadt Tridentum zu bestaunen. Für denjenigen, der sich für die Via Claudia Augusta „Padana" Richtung Verona und Ostiglia am Po entschieden hat geht es anschließend weiter, an der Etsch entlang durch ein Gebiet, das aber der eigentlichen Stadtgrenze eher dünn besiedelt ist.

Additional information about some sights

- At the bridge over the Avisio in Lavis begins the urban area of Trento. Towards Altino near Venice, the old road already led there up the slope towards Valsugana. The itinerary first follows the approximate historical course of the road to the village of Meano, from where the traveler first looks down on the council city. Then it goes back down into the valley and straight to the Renaissance old town.
- A walk through the town is best begun at the tourist information office, near which is also the contemporary town gallery. Not far from there, below Battisti Square, the underground excavations of the Roman Tridentum await. Via Belenzani, lined with Renaissance palazzi, with the Town Hall in Palazzo Thun, the visitor reaches Piazza Duomo. The parallel alleys Via Cavour to the west and Via Oss Mazzurana to the east compete with it. Directly on Piazza Duomo are also the Diocesan Museum and the Cathedral of Vigilio. Finally, the walk leads to the Buonconsiglio Castle, which also houses the Historical Museum of Trento.

Regional cuisine like 2000 years ago

Here could be an inn that has at least one dish on the menu continuously as it was 2000 years ago.

Overnight and camping possibilities in the appendix and in the maps

Questions information on the subsection

■ Hotline tourist board APT Rovereto and Vallagarina, 0039 0464 430 363

■ Hotline Via Claudia Augusta, 0043(0)664 27 63 555

The northern Vallagarina between Trento and Rovereto (map 51, 52)

To the south of Trento lies the southernmost part of the Etschtal valley: the Vallagarina. Its captivating landscape has remained wholly unspoilt despite its location between conurbations and along one of Europe's most important thoroughfares. Historically grown villages nestle in picturesque valleys, mountains and hills lined with sprawling vineyards. Medieval castles punctuate the area.

The south of Trento

The towns of Romagnano and Mattarello to the south of the regional capital still belong to its municipal area.

The north of the Vallagarina

The Vallagarina begins at the Murazzi gorge to the south of Mattarello. Humans have inhabited this area since Roman times or earlier. Pomarolo and Besenello are first mentioned in records from the 12th century. The valley is dotted with fortresses, showing the strategic significance of its location at the southern gateway to the Alps. Some of the fortresses were built by the Austro-Hungarian monarchy. The 12th-century Beseno castle above Besenello is the largest fortress between the Reschenpass and Verona. You can easily spot the impressive structure from afar. Its interior is decorated with many frescoes. The castle complex houses a branch of the museum at Buonconsiglio castle. It is well worth a visit, not least because of the spectacular views of the Vallagarina below.

■ 38060 Besenello, Via al Castello 4, +39 0464 834600, opening hours from mid-March to mid-May: Tue–Sun 9:30 am–5 pm, from mid-May to the beginning of Nov: Tue–Sun 10 am–6 pm, from Nov–mid-March: Sat and Sun only, 9:30 am–5 pm, www.buonconsiglio.it

■ Castel Pietra, 38060 Calliano, Via Castelpietra 1, +39 335 588 28 91, contact the private owners of the castle to arrange a guided tour, www.castelpietra.info.

■ Castello di Castellano, 38060 Castellano, +39 0464 801 177, guided tours by appointment with private owners.

■ Castel Noarna, 38060 Noarna di Nogaredo, Via Castelnuovo 19, daily guided tours with wine tasting by appointment for min. 10 people, www.castelnuoarna.com.

■ Diocesan Museum of Trentino, Palazzo Libera, 38060 Villa Lagarina, Via Garibaldi 10, +39 464 490 374, open Wed - Fri 2 - 6 pm, Sat and Sun 10 - 12:30 and 2 - 6 pm, www.museodiocesanotridentino.it

Regional cuisine like 2000 years ago

Here could be an inn that has at least one dish on the menu continuously as it was 2000 years ago.

Overnight and camping possibilities in the appendix and in the maps

Questions information on the subsection

■ Hotline tourist board APT Rovereto und Vallagarina, 0039 0464 430 363

■ Hotline Via Claudia Augusta, 0043(0)664 27 63 555

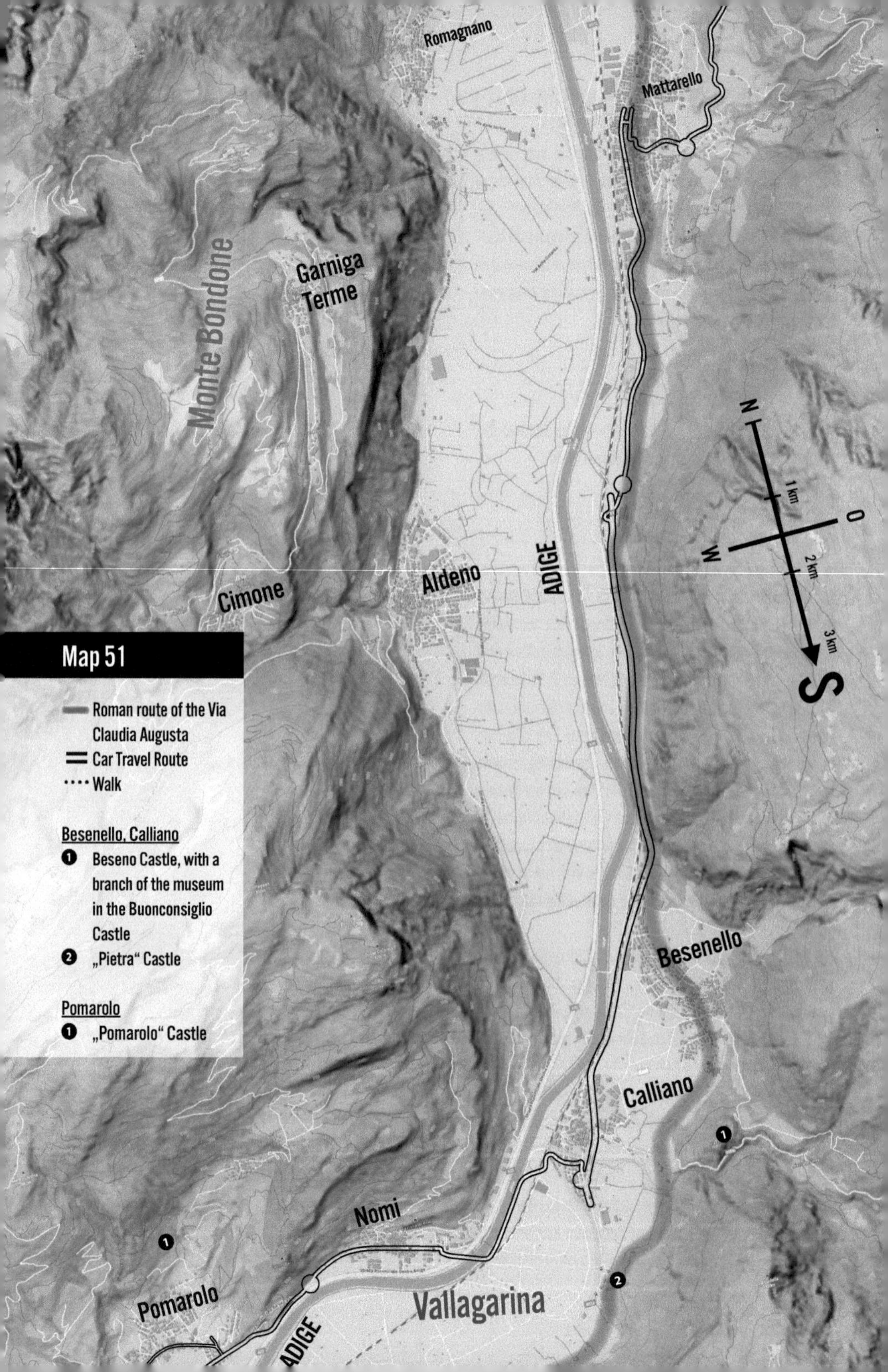
Romagnano
Mattarello
Monte Bondone
Garniga
Terme
Aldeno
Cimone
ADIGE
N
O
W
S
1 km
2 km
3 km
Roman route of the Via Claudia Augusta
Car Travel Route
Walk
Besenello, Calliano
1 Beseno Castle, with a branch of the museum in the Buonconsiglio Castle
2 „Pietra“ Castle
Pomarolo
1 „Pomarolo“ Castle
Besenello
Calliano
Nomi
Pomarolo
Vallagarina
ADIGE
Map 51

Map 52

- Roman route of the Via Claudia Augusta
- Car Travel Route
- Walk

Villa Lagarina

1. Palazzo Libera with part of the Trentino Diocesan Museum

[1] Casa del Noce, Via Zandonai 10, www.casadelnoce.com, 0039 0464 410741, III

Nogaredo

1. „Noarna“ Castle
2. Palazzo Lodron

Castellano

1. „Castellano“ Castle

Rovereto

1. Science and Archeology Museum
2. Birthplace of Antonio Rosmini
3. Palazzo Todeschi-Micheli „Mozart House“
4. City Museum in the Palazzo Alberti
5. „Forbato“ Bridge
6. „Turkish House“
7. Rovereto Castle with Italian War Museum
8. Venetian-style town hall in Palazzo Pretorio from the 15th century
9. Renaissance Palazzo del Ben or dei Conti d'Arco
10. Contemporary Gallery MART and House of Futuristic Art Fortunato Depero
11. Library in the Palazzo Annona
12. „Zandonai“ theatre
13. Neoclassical Palazzo Piomarta

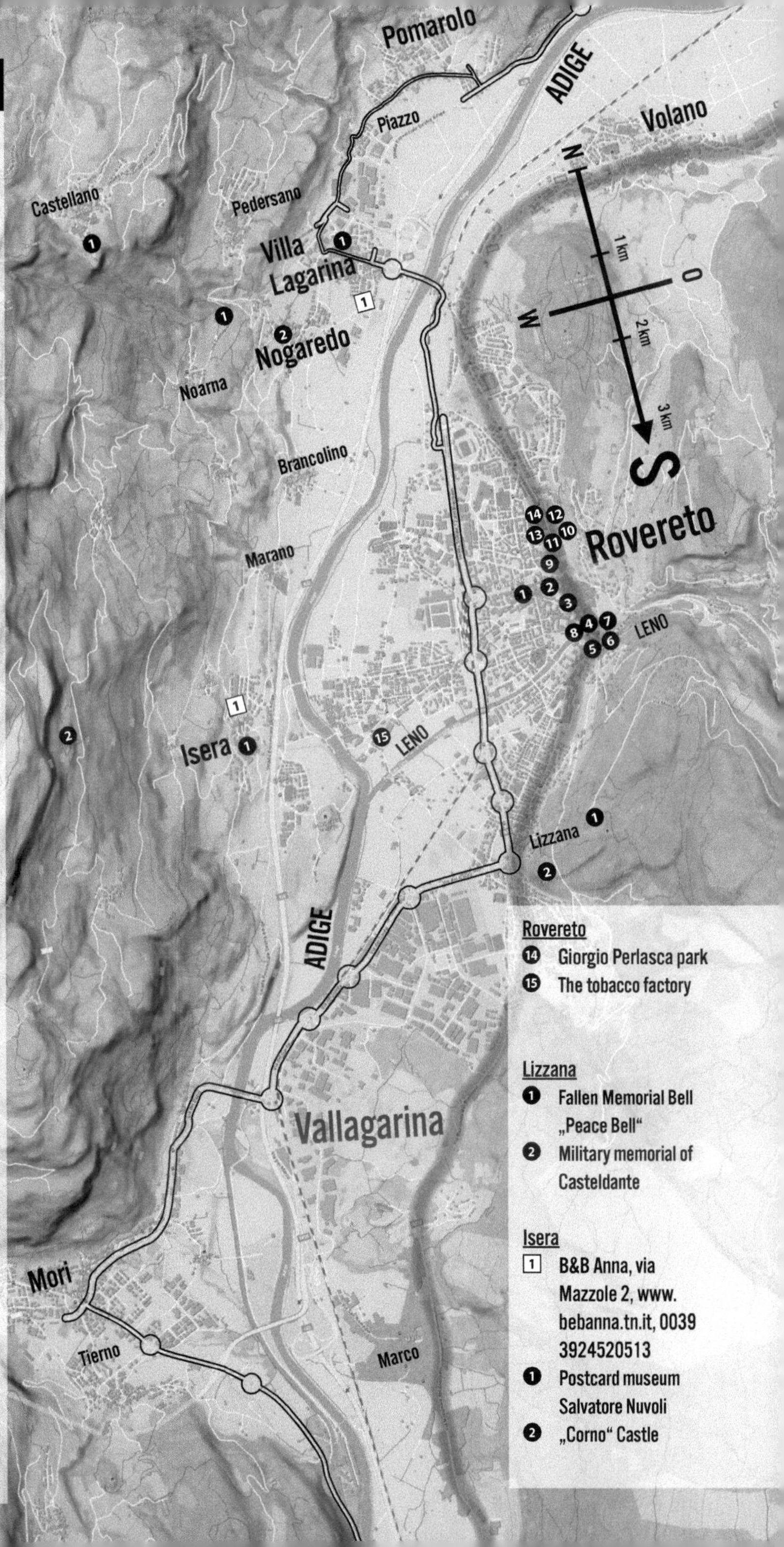

Rovereto

14. Giorgio Perlasca park
15. The tobacco factory

Lizzana

1. Fallen Memorial Bell „Peace Bell“
2. Military memorial of Casteldante

Isera

[1] B&B Anna, via Mazzole 2, www.bebanna.tn.it, 0039 3924520513

1. Postcard museum Salvatore Nuvoli
2. „Corno“ Castle

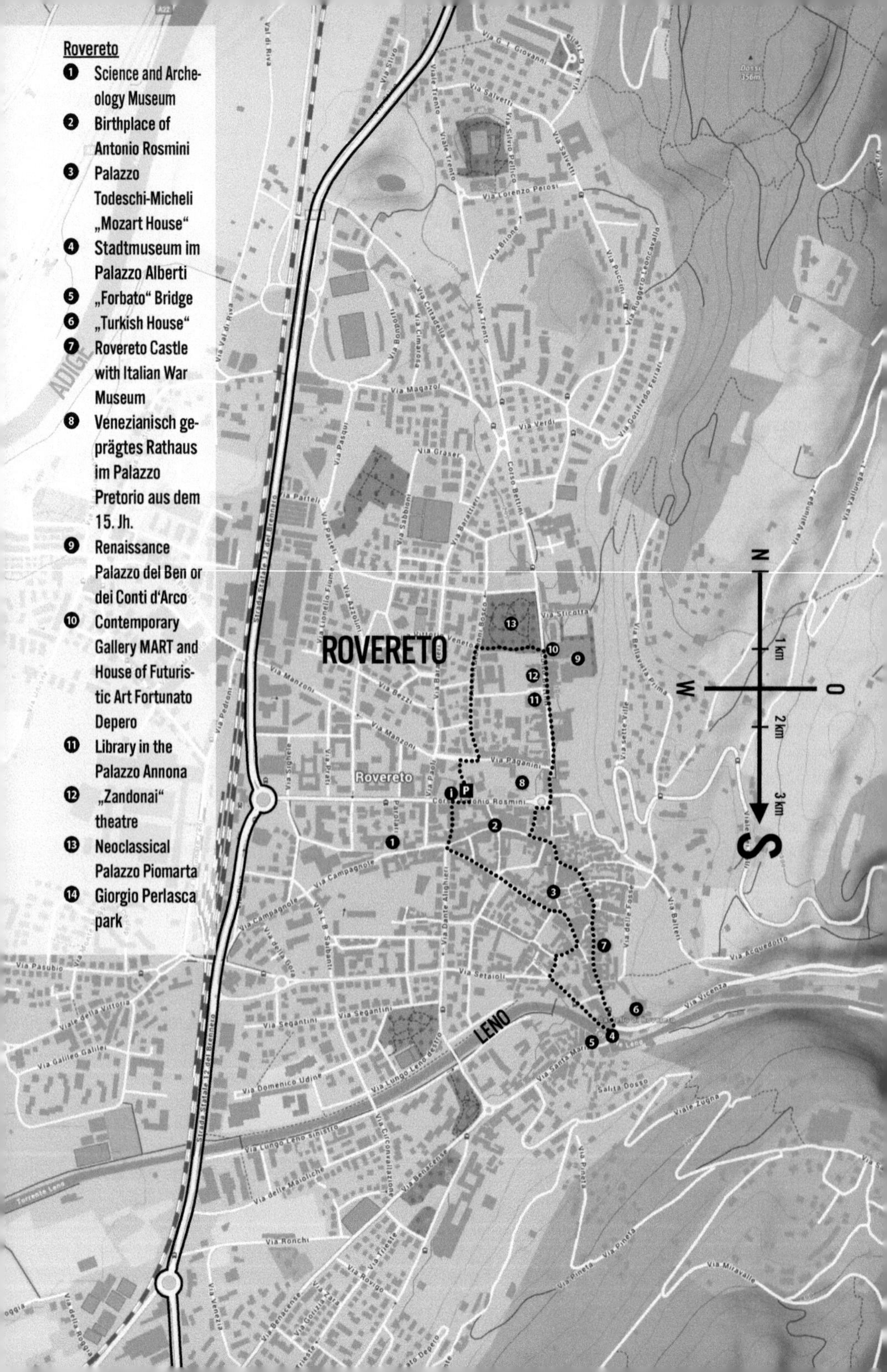
Rovereto
1 Science and Archeology Museum
2 Birthplace of Antonio Rosmini
3 Palazzo Todeschi-Micheli „Mozart House“
4 Stadtmuseum im Palazzo Alberti
5 „Forbato“ Bridge
6 „Turkish House“
7 Rovereto Castle with Italian War Museum
8 Venezianisch geprägtes Rathaus im Palazzo Pretorio aus dem 15. Jh.
9 Renaissance Palazzo del Ben or dei Conti d‘Arco
10 Contemporary Gallery MART and House of Futuristic Art Fortunato Depero
11 Library in the Palazzo Annona
12 „Zandonai“ theatre
13 Neoclassical Palazzo Piomarta
14 Giorgio Perlasca park
ROVERETO
Rovereto
LENO
ADIGE
N
W
O
S
1 km
2 km
3 km
Corso Rosmini
Corso Bettini
Via Manzoni
Via Paganini
Via Setaioli
Via Segantini
Via Campagnole
Via Pasubio
Viale della Vittoria
Via Galileo Galilei
Via Domenico Udine
Via Lungo Leno destro
Via Lungo Leno sinistro
Via delle Maioliche
Via Ronchi
Via Rovigo
Via Benacense
Via Circonvallazione
Via Pineta
Via Miravalle
Viale Zugna
Salita Dosso
Via Vicenza
Via Acquedotto
Via Balteri
Via delle Fosse
Via Dante Alighieri
Via Magazol
Via Graser
Via Verdi
Via Puccini
Via Salvetti
Via Lorenzo Perosi
Via Brione
Viale Trento
Via Cittadella
Via Pasqui
Via Parteli
Via Sabbioni
Via Barattieri
Via Azzolini
Via Bezzi
Via Sighele
Via Prati
Via Pedroni
Via Val di Riva
Strada Statale 12 del Brennero
Torrente Leno
Dosso 356m

The northern Vallagarina seen from Beseno Castle. Photo: APT Rovereto Vallagarina

Besenello. Photo: APT Rovereto Vallagarina Magna Longa

Castellano Castle. Photo: APT Rovereto e Vallagarina

Piazza Romini. Photo: APT Rovereto Vallagarina

The striking roof of the MART art gallery. Photo: Via Claudia Augusta

Adige Valley near Rovereto. Photo: APT Rovereto Vallagarina

33 The Silk City of Rovereto, a memorial for peace (map 52)

Trentino's second city is the capital of the Vallagarina district. Its charming old town and the important MART gallery of contemporary art make it an important tourist attraction. Historians believe that there used to be an Iron Age settlement here. The Romans had a fort here. This important road and the raft factory on the Etsch river between the Alps and Veneto remained a significant economic factor. Rovereto experienced its heyday in the 18th century, when the silk industry, established by the Venetians, was at its height. The region was one of the most fiercely contested areas in the First World War. Countless forts in the mountains to the east of the city serve as war memorials today. They have given the city its image as a 'city of peace'.

A walk through the old town

Rovereto is a lovely labyrinth of narrow alleyways and palaces, many of which have obvious Venetian and Austrian influences. We recommend that you park your car in the parking lot at the corner of Corso Rosmini and Via Poli during your walk. Visit Italy's oldest urban museum for a perfect start to your trip. ■ Borgo Santa Caterina 41, +39 0464 452 800, open Tue–Sun 9:00 am–noon and 3:00 pm–6:00 pm, from 1 July– 16 October also open on Fri and Sun from 8:00 pm to 10:00 pm, closed on Mondays (except public holidays), www.museocivico.rovereto.tn.it. Head a little further and you will find the birthplace of the famous philosopher Anton Rosmini. ■ Via Stoppani 3, +39 0464 420 788, by appointment only. At the Palazzo Todeschi-Micheli at Via Mercerie 14, Mozart played his first successful concert in Italy. The Ponte Forbato over the Leno river was destroyed in a flood in 1797 and rebuilt in 1840. On the opposite shore of the river stands the Casa dei Turchi (Turkish House). The towering Castello Rovereto from the 14th century houses Italy's largest war museum. ■ Borgo Santa Caterina 7, +39 0464 438 100, open Tue–Sun 9:00 am–noon and 3:00 pm–6:00 pm, from 1 July– 16 October also open on Fri and Sun from 8:00 pm to 10:00 pm, closed on Mondays (except public holidays), www.museodellaguerra.it. The elegant Palazzo Pretorio houses the municipal administration. It was built in 1417 in the Venetian style. The Palazzo del Ben (also: dei Conti D'Arco) on the Piazza Rosmini is a gem of Renaissance architecture made available to the public for cultural activities by the Sparkasse Trento and Rovereto bank. A little further, you will find the MART art museum. The Palazzo dell'Annona, which houses a library, is a part of it. ■ MART, Rovereto, Corso Bettini 43, +39 0464 438 887, open Tue–Sun 10:00 am–6:00 pm, Fri 10:00 am–9:00 pm, closed on Mondays (except public holidays), www.mart.trento.it. Opposite the Giorgio Perlasca Park stands Trentino's very first theater: the Theater Zandonai. There is also the Neoclassical Piamarta Palace, better known as the Palazzo della Pubblica Istruzione ('palace of public teaching').

Regional cuisine like 2000 years ago

Here could be an inn that has at least one dish on the menu continuously as it was 2000 years ago.

Overnight and camping possibilities in the appendix and in the maps

Questions and information about the subsection

■ Touristinfo APT Rovereto e Vallagarina, 38068 Rovereto, Piazza Rosmini 16, +39 0464 430 363, during summer moreover at the cycling path: Bike- and Tourist-Info, 38068 Rovereto (TN), Piazzetta della Torre Civica di Borgo Sacco, ciclopoint@visitrovereto.it, 0039 347 098 82 50

■ Hotline Via Claudia Augusta, +43(0)664 27 63 555

The southern part of the Vallagarina and the border area (map 52, 53, 54)

The border between Trentino and Veneto runs south of the Vallagarina. Here, the Etschtal valley turns into the plain of the Pianura Padana. This region used to be heavily contested. Until 1919, it was a part of the Austro-Hungarian Empire. The German names of the local towns and villages date back to that time, and the influence of the German cultural sphere is omnipresent. All over the southern Vallagarina, you will find lovely landscapes and picture-perfect villages.

The south of Rovereto and Isera

There is a bell in the south of Rovereto that tolls a hundred times every evening to commemorate the war dead. The military memorial of Castel Dante contains the mortal remains of 20,000 Italian, Austrian, Czech and Hungarian soldiers. ■ 38068 Rovereto, Via Castel Dante, +39 0464 432 480 or +39 348 7700 541, open Tue–Sat 9 am–12 noon and 2–4 pm. Closed on public holidays. The Manufattura Tabacchi from the mid-19th century recounts the early industrial and social history of the region. ■ Rovereto, Piazza della Manifattura 1, +39 0464 443 313, open to groups, www.progettomanifattura.it. In Isera, the postcard museum showcases 35,000 pictures of Trentino and South Tyrol. ■ Via Galvagni 10, +39 0464 420 840, open Mon–Sat 9 am–12 noon and 2:30–5 pm, www.museodellacartolina.it. The 10th-century Corno castle overlooks the town ■ Località Lenzima, +39 0464 433 792, open 5 Apr–end of September Sat and Sun, 10 am–7 pm

Mori, the gateway to Lake Garda and Monte Baldo

The town of Mori has a population of nearly 10,000. It borders Torbole on Lake Garda and Brentonico on Monte Baldo, a 30-kilometer mountain ridge that separates Italy's largest lake from the Etschtal valley. Its sheltered eastern slope protruded from the ice throughout the entire Ice Age. Today, it is home to unique plants found nowhere else in Europe. Visit the Palazzo Eccheli Baisi for its exhibition of regional plants and fossils. ■ 38060 Brentonico, Via Mantova 4, +39 0464 39 50 59, open from May to Jun: Tue–Sun, 10 am to 12 noon and 4–6 pm, Jul–Sep: Tue–Sun, 10 am–12 noon and 4–6:30 pm.

The border towns of Ala and Avio

The actual border town is Avio – to be precise, its Borghetto district. Ala is another town close to the border. It used to function as a frontier station between Austria and Italy. Both have been shaped by a long history of varying influences. Walk the narrow alleyways of their historical centers to discover numerous palazzi. The Palazzi de' Pizzini in Ala houses the Antique Piano Museum, which is all about the wonders of classical music. ■ 38061 Ala, Via Santa Caterina 1, +39 0464 674 068, open to groups of 15–20 visitors. Avio is overlooked by the ruins of its eponymous castle from the 11th and 13th century.

Regional cuisine like 2000 years ago

Here could be an inn that has at least one dish on the menu continuously as it was 2000 years ago.

Overnight and camping possibilities in the appendix and in the maps

Questions and information about the subsection

■ Touristinfo APT Rovereto e Vallagarina, 38060 Brentonico (TN), Via F. Filzi 23, 0039 0464 430 363

■ Hotline Via Claudia Augusta, 0043(0)664 27 63 555

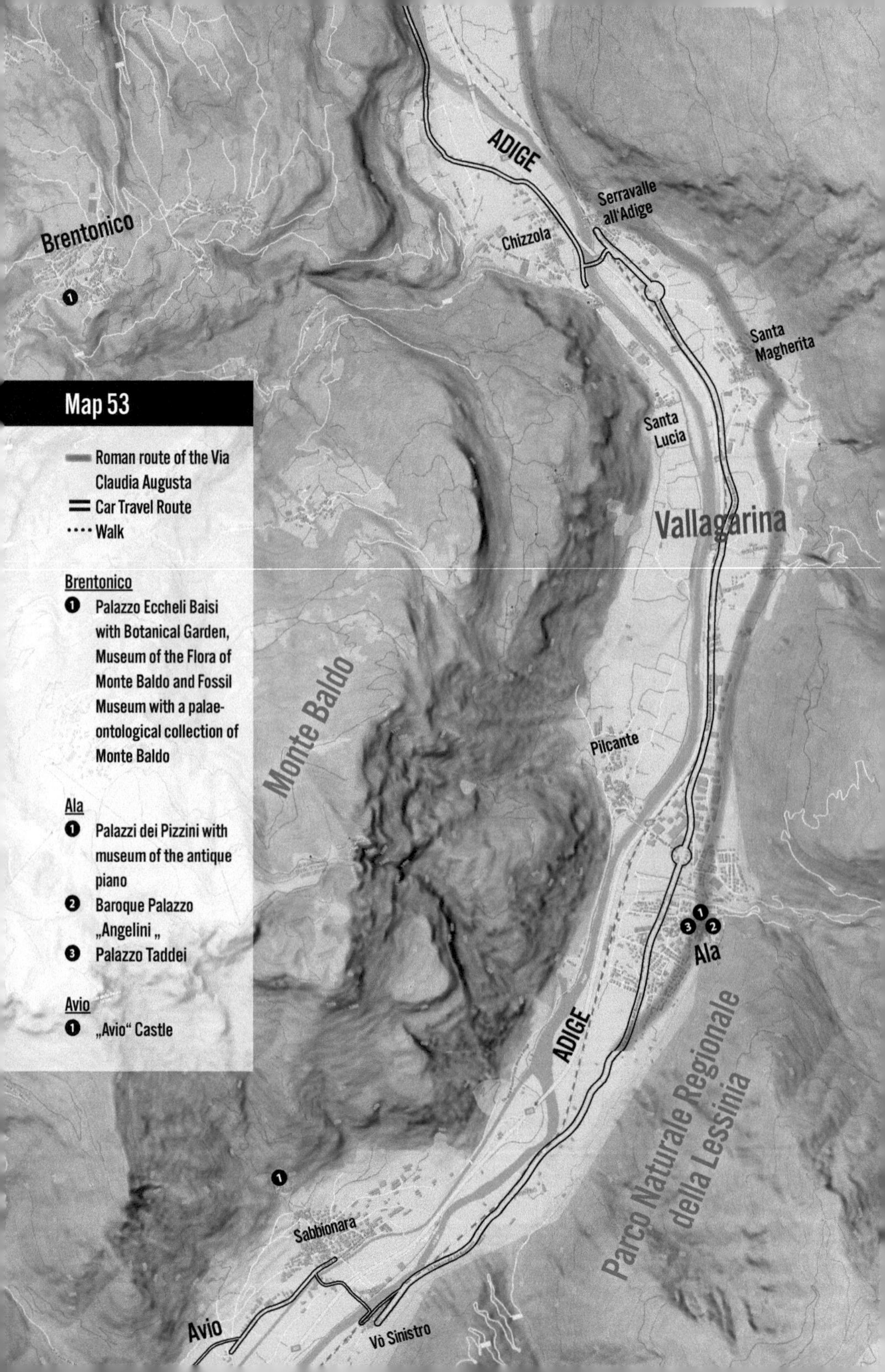
Map 53
Roman route of the Via Claudia Augusta
Car Travel Route
Walk
Brentonico
1 Palazzo Eccheli Baisi with Botanical Garden, Museum of the Flora of Monte Baldo and Fossil Museum with a palae-ontological collection of Monte Baldo
Ala
1 Palazzi dei Pizzini with museum of the antique piano
2 Baroque Palazzo „Angelini „
3 Palazzo Taddei
Avio
1 „Avio“ Castle
Brentonico
ADIGE
Serravalle all'Adige
Chizzola
Santa Magherita
Santa Lucia
Vallagarina
Monte Baldo
Pilcante
Ala
ADIGE
Parco Naturale Regionale della Lessinia
Sabbionara
Avio
Vò Sinistro

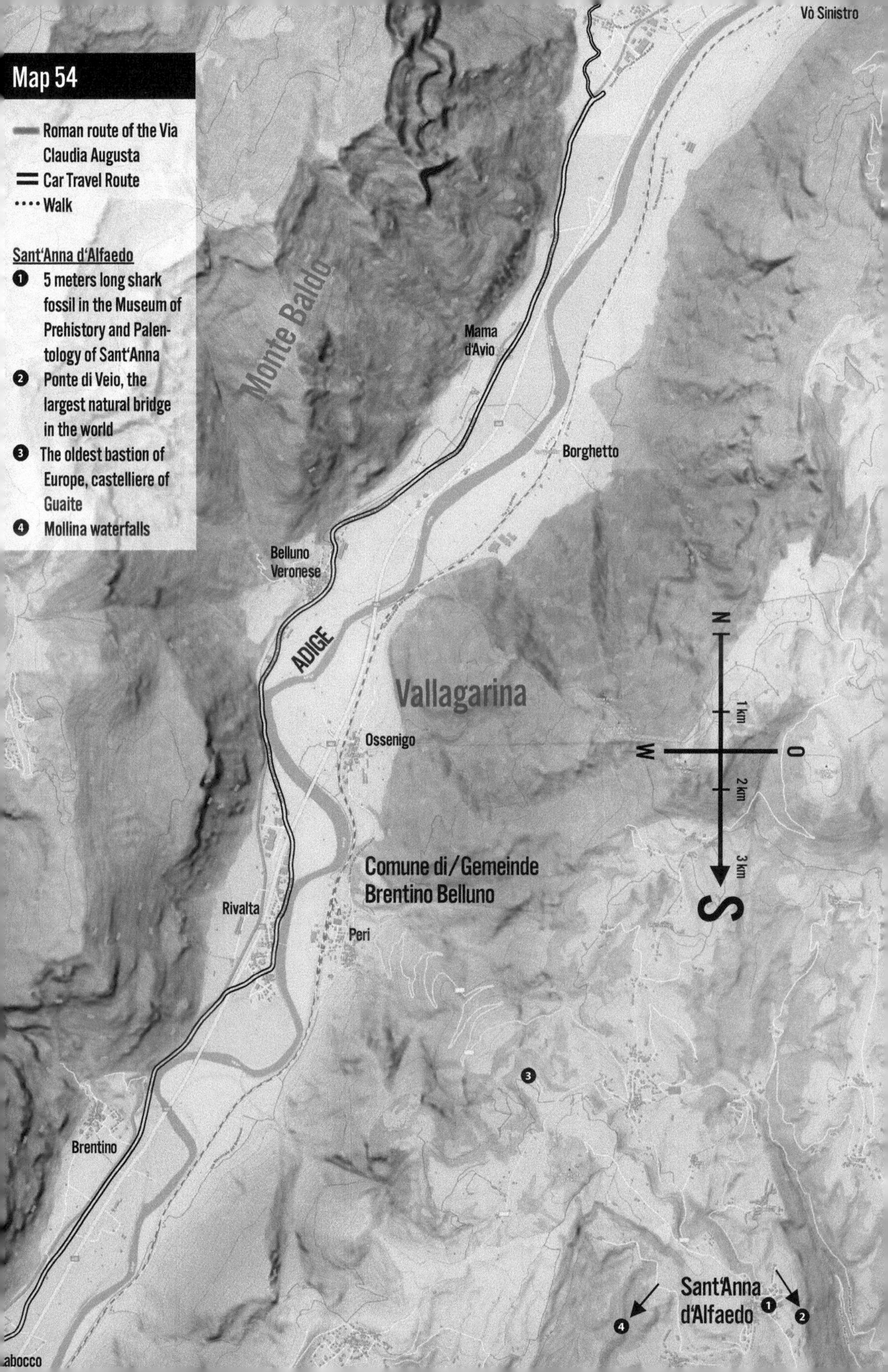
Map 54
Roman route of the Via Claudia Augusta
Car Travel Route
Walk
Sant'Anna d'Alfaedo
1 5 meters long shark fossil in the Museum of Prehistory and Palentology of Sant'Anna
2 Ponte di Veio, the largest natural bridge in the world
3 The oldest bastion of Europe, castelliere of Guaite
4 Mollina waterfalls
Vò Sinistro
Monte Baldo
Mama d'Avio
Borghetto
Belluno Veronese
ADIGE
Vallagarina
Ossenigo
N
W
O
S
1 km
2 km
3 km
Comune di/Gemeinde Brentino Belluno
Rivalta
Peri
Brentino
Sant'Anna d'Alfaedo
abocco

On the border between the provinces of Trentino and Verona.

Sanctuary of the Madonna above Brentino Belluno

Palazzo Pizzini in Ala, Photo: APT Rovereto Vallagarina

Bardolino

Lazise

Lake Garda from Monte Baldo

35 Veronese Vallagarina: Brentino Belluno and Dolcè to the Chiusa di Ceraino.(map 54, 55)

As you leave Borghetto, you enter Veneto – or, to be precise, the Venetian province of Verona. Geographically, the area stretching to the gorge of Rivoli Veronese still belongs to the Vallagarina. It has always been a transit region, and its first settlers arrived here early. The first traces of human activity found here back to the Stone Age. Even the oldest traces of human settlement of the region date to pre-Roman times. At the time of the Via Claudia Augusta, there was a road station in this area. Today, the Veronese Vallagarina is more sparsely populated than the section of the valley that lies in Trentino. The area between Monte Baldo and the Lessinia National Park is a significant wine-growing region and the home of Enantio Wine.

Across the Vallagarina Veronese

At the border between Trentino and the province of Verona, which belongs to Beneto, the Etschtal valley narrows. Our route through the Veronese section of the Vallagarina takes you to the picturesque towns of Belluno Veronese and Rivalta, the main district of the municipality of Brentino Belluno. If you wish to take a detour to Dolcè with its lovely, historical center and three stately palazzi, cross the river at Rivalta, then head back the same way. To this day, there are only very few bridges over the Etsch river in this part of the valley. Continue to the narrowest part of the southern Etschtal valley, the Ceraino close, overlooked by the Austro-Hungarian Wohlgemuth fortress.

Regional cuisine like 2000 years ago

Here could be an inn that has at least one dish on the menu continuously as it was 2000 years ago.

Overnight and camping possibilities in the appendix and in the maps

Questions and information about the subsection

■ Hotline Via Claudia Augusta, 0043(0)664 27 63 555

Rivoli Veronese and Garda Veronese (map 55, 56)

The Ceraino gorge marks the end of the Etschtal valley. On various occasions when the river ran high, it flooded completely and became impassable. That is why the Via Claudia Augusta, much like the modern highway, ran from the Vallagarina up to the plateau on which Rivoli Veronese is situated today. From Rivoli, you have access to the Venetian part of Lake Garda and its famous resort towns, such as Bardolino and Lazise, as well as Verona and the Po Plain. Due to its central location, Rivoli has always been a significant town. Its plateau was the site of a major battle between Napoleon's army and the troops of the Habsburg Monarchy. Later, the House of Habsburg established the Forte Wohlgemuth, which still thrones above the valley to this day.

Radroute Rivoli Veronese (Lago di Garda)

Wie die Römerstraße führt auch die Radroute von der Veroneser Vallagarina hinauf auf das Hochplateau, auf dem Rivoli Veronese liegt. Dafür wurde ein wunderschöner Radweg mit Serpentinen und stetiger Steigung angelegt. Oben angelagt hat man einen herrlichen Blick ins Tal hinunter. Als Besichtigungsziel lockt die österreichisch-ungarische Festung Wohlgemuth. Von Rivoli hat man auch eine gute Möglichkeit in die Badeorte Bardolino und Lazise zu gelangen.

Additional information about some sights

- The end of the Adige valley is formed by the hermitage of Ceraino, which in Roman times, at least for a time, was impassable, forcing the course of the Via Claudia Augusta over the hill where today Rivoli Veronese is located. The hermitage of Ceraino, with its steep rocky walls, has always been fought over. The most recent testimony of this disputed border are the Austro-Hungarian forts, on both sides of the valley, which once formed a complete dam. The fortress „Wohlgemuth“ on the mountain „Castello“ near Rivoli not only gives a good impression of a fortress, of that time, it also includes a military museum with findings from the 2nd World War. Fortress „Wohlgemuth“, 0039 045 728 11 66, open from March - Jan. by appointment and generally on Sun. 2 - 7 pm. Closed in February and August.
- With Bardolino and Lazise, the route also touches two municipalities bordering Lake Garda.
- In Rivoli begins a canal built in the Mussolini era for irrigation, slightly above the Adige towards Verona.
- Immediately after the bridge over the Adige River in the hamlet of Sega in the municipality of Cavaion Veronese, a detour leads into the valley, on the southern side of which lies the Villa del Bene, which is worth seeing and was founded in 1538. ■ Municipality of Dolcè, 0039 045 729 00 22.

Regional cuisine like 2000 years ago

Here could be an inn that has at least one dish on the menu continuously as it was 2000 years ago.

Overnight and camping possibilities in the appendix and in the maps

Questions and information about the subsection

■ Hotline Via Claudia Augusta, 0043(0)664 27 63 555

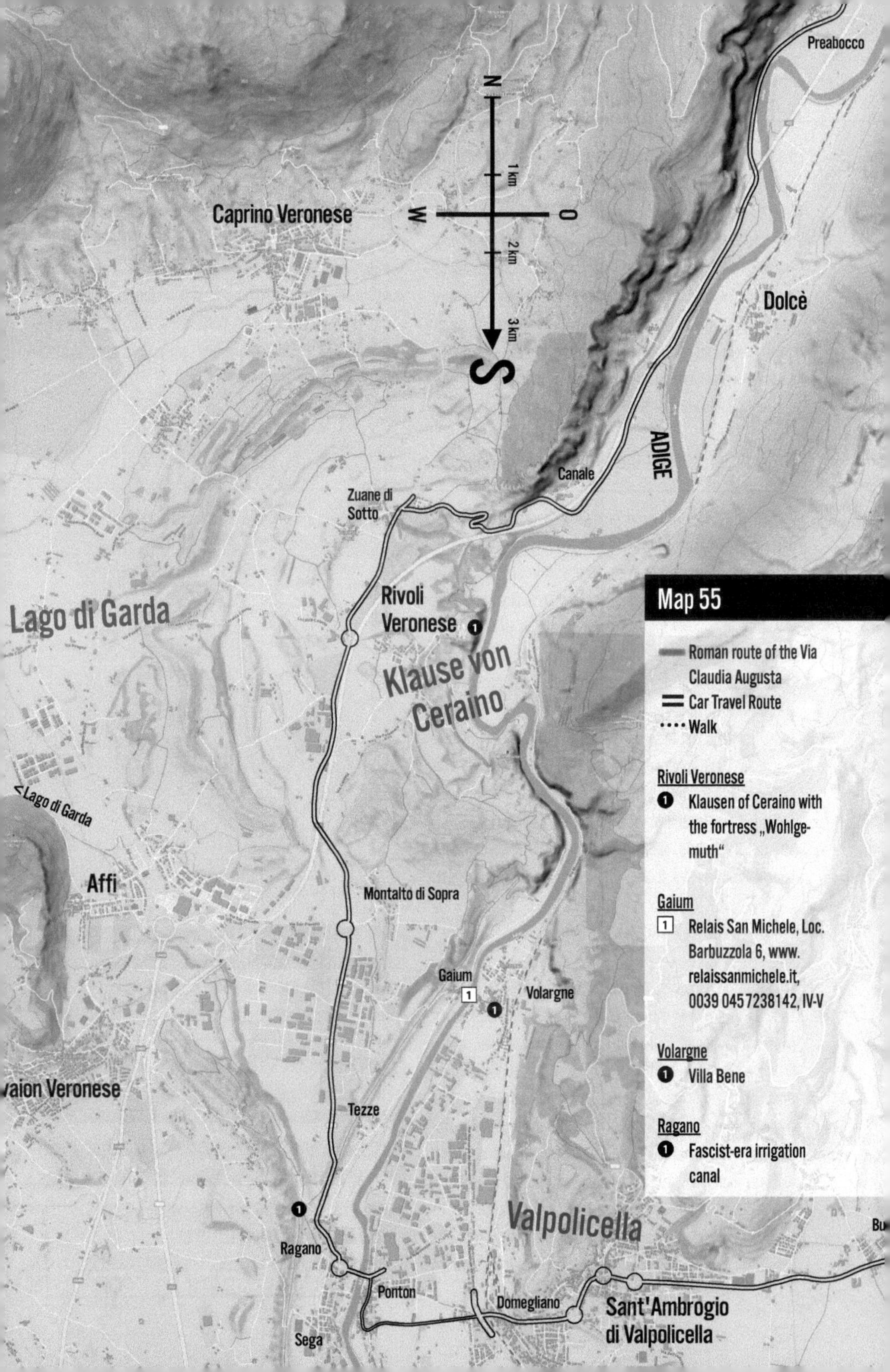

Map 55
Roman route of the Via Claudia Augusta
Car Travel Route
Walk
Rivoli Veronese
1 Klausen of Ceraino with the fortress „Wohlge-muth“
Gaium
1 Relais San Michele, Loc. Barbuzzola 6, www.relaissanmichele.it, 0039 0457238142, IV-V
Volargne
1 Villa Bene
Ragano
1 Fascist-era irrigation canal
N
W
O
S
1 km
2 km
3 km
Preabocco
Caprino Veronese
Dolcè
ADIGE
Canale
Zuane di Sotto
Lago di Garda
Rivoli Veronese
Klause von Ceraino
<Lago di Garda
Affi
Montalto di Sopra
Gaium
Volargne
vaion Veronese
Tezze
Valpolicella
Ragano
Ponton
Domegliano
Sant'Ambrogio di Valpolicella
Sega

37 Valpolicella - Land of 2000 years old wines (map 55, 56, 57)

Mention Valpolicella and you will inevitably think of the Recioto and Amarone, the only surviving wines from antiquity. They have been around for two millennia. Valleys and mountain ridges unfold through the area like the fingers of a hand. These ancient wine-growing landscapes and the traditions associated with it will captivate you at any point of the warm season: from the delicate, fresh shades of green that cover the region in spring to the purples and reds of the grapes that color the area in autumn. The landscape is punctuated by several natural and architectural monuments.

To Rivoli Veronese at the hermitage of Ceraino

Veneto, the Adige Valley becomes increasingly narrow. The narrowest point is the hermitage of Ceraino, which in Roman times, at least for a time, was impassable and forced the course of the Via Claudia Augusta over the hill where Rivoli Veronese is located today. The hermitage of Ceraino, with its steep rocky walls, has always been fought over. The most recent testimony of this disputed border are the Austro-Hungarian forts, on both sides of the valley, which once formed a complete dam. The fortress "Wohlgemuth" on the mountain "Castello" near Rivoli not only gives a good impression of a fortress, of that time, it also includes a military museum with findings from the 2nd World War. ■ Fortress "Wohlgemuth", +39 045 728 11 66, open from March - Jan. by appointment and generally on Sun. 2 -7 pm. Closed in February and August.

Through the Valpolicella wine plain

With Affi the route also touches a municipality that borders Lake Garda. On the way back to the Adige River, the itinerary passes a canal built in the Mussolini era for irrigation, slightly above the Adige toward Verona. Just after the bridge over the Adige River in the hamlet of Sega in the municipality of Cavaion Veronese, a detour leads into the valley, on the southern side of which lies the Villa del Bene, which is worth seeing and was founded in 1538. ■ Municipality of Dolcè, +39 045 729 00 22. The journey then leads through the picturesque southern edge of the Alps and the millennia-old Valpolicella wine plain: there, with the largest natural bridge in the world and the waterfalls of Mollina, natural monuments worth seeing await, points of cultural and historical significance such as the 34,000-year-old grotto of a shaman, and several village centers and architectural monuments worth seeing, including around 100 Ville Venete. In Sant Anna, a prehistoric and paleontological museum with a 5-meter shark fish fossil awaits discovery. ■ Piazza Dalla Bona, 37020 Sant'Anna, +39 349 53 46 074, open early July - early Sept. Wed, Fri, Sat, Sun 10 a.m. - noon and 4 p.m. - 6 p.m.

Regional cuisine like 2000 years ago

Here could be an inn that has at least one dish on the menu continuously as it was 2000 years ago.

Overnight and camping possibilities in the appendix and in the maps

Questions and information about the subsection

■ Touristinfo IAT Valpolicella, Via Ingelheim 7, 37029 San Pietro in Cariano, 0039 045770 19 20
■ Hotline Via Claudia Augusta, 0043(0)664 27 63 555

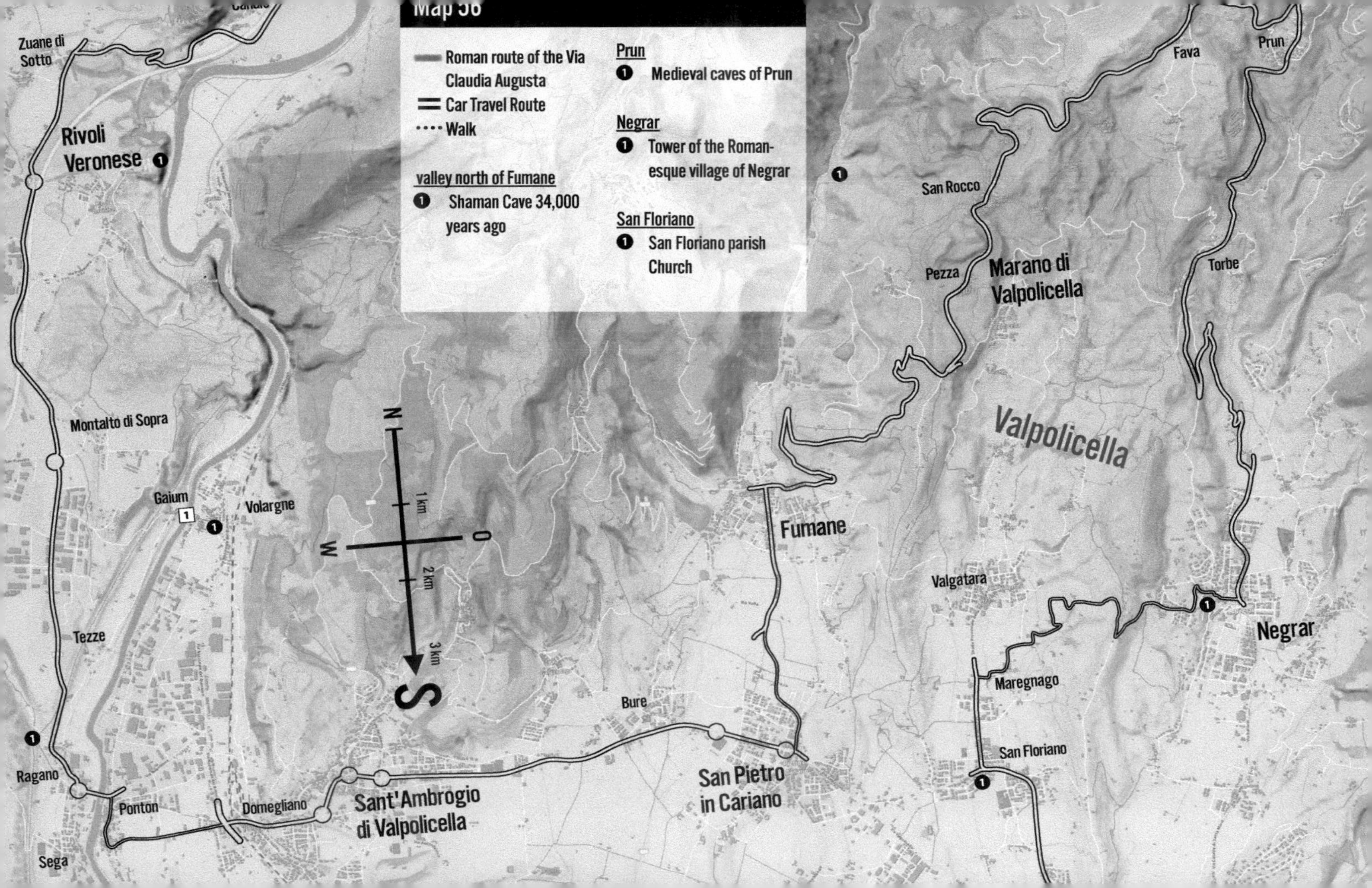
Map 38
Roman route of the Via Claudia Augusta
Car Travel Route
Walk
valley north of Fumane
1 Shaman Cave 34,000 years ago
Prun
1 Medieval caves of Prun
Negrar
1 Tower of the Romanesque village of Negrar
San Floriano
1 San Floriano parish Church
Zuane di Sotto
Rivoli Veronese
Montalto di Sopra
Gaium
Volargne
Tezze
Ragano
Ponton
Sega
Domegliano
Sant'Ambrogio di Valpolicella
Bure
San Pietro in Cariano
Fumane
San Rocco
Pezza
Marano di Valpolicella
Valpolicella
Valgatara
Maregnago
San Floriano
Negrar
Torbe
Fava
Prun
N
W
O
S
1 km
2 km
3 km

Villa Della Torre Cazzola in Fumane. Photo: Province of Verona Tourism Archives

Wohlgemuth Fortress. Photo: Archivio Provincia di Verona Turismo

Bridge of Veja. Photo: Archivio Provincia di Verona Turismo /F. Zane

The house of Julia. Photo: Tschaikner

San Zeno. Photo: Tschaikne

The Arena of Verona. Photo: Tschaikner

The rhaetian city of Verona – Historical center in front of the Alps (map 57, 58)

Verona is the second largest city on the Via Claudia Augusta leading to Augsburg. It was originally founded by the Rhaetians and the Euganei. Around 550 B. C., the Gaulish tribe of the Cenomani conquered the settlement, and in 89 B. C., it became a Roman colony. It was no coincidence that its Roman conqueror was the very same emperor who initiated the construction of the transalpine road and the establishment of an important city at the gateway to the Alps: Augustus. The arena, in which the famous opera festival takes place every year nowadays, was built a little later. It predates the Colosseum in Rome. After the Romans left, an eventful period began. Verona only gained independence in the early 12th century. Its much-visited old town was declared a UNESCO World Heritage Site in 2000.

A walk through a World Heritage Site

The route through Verona gives you a first impression and some lovely views of the city. You get to see the Basilica di San Zeno Maggiore, Ponte Scaligero, Castel San Pietro, the archaeological museum, the remains of the old city wall, the monumental cemetery, and the Arena. If you want to get a slightly more detailed idea of Verona, however, we recommend that you take a walk through the city. You can leave your car at the Arena parking garage. The suggested route leads you past the arena to the Ponte Scaligero and the museum inside the Castelvecchio, where countless paintings and sculptures are exhibited. Afterwards, you meander through picturesque alleyways, taking in several fascinating sacred buildings before reaching the Chiesa San Giovanni in Fonte. The Casa di Giulietta (Juliet's House), Palazzo della Ragione and Torre dei Lamberti are all located in relatively close proximity to each other. Finally, the tour leads you across the Etsch river to the remains of the Roman city walls and the impressive monumental cemetery. After visiting the Tomba di Giulietta (Juliet's Grave), you head back towards the nearby Arena.

■ Museo Castelvecchio, Corso Castelvecchio 2, +39 045 806 26 11, open Mon 1:30 pm–7:30 pm and Tue–Sun 8:30 am–7:30 pm, last entry at 6:45 pm.

■ Archaeological Museum at the Roman Theater, Regaste Redentore 2, +39 045 8000 360, Mon 1:30 pm–7:30 pm and Tue–Sun 8:30 am–7:30 pm. Last entry at 6:45 pm.

■ Casa di Giulietta, Via Cappello 23, +39 045 803 4303, open Mon 1:30 pm–7:30 pm and Tue–Sun 8:30 am–7:30 pm, last entry at 6:45 pm.

■ Torre dei Lamberti, Via della Costa 2, +39 045 927 30 27, open Mon–Sun, 9:30 am–7:30 pm.

■ Tomba di Giulietta, Via Luigi da Porto 5, +39 045 8000 361, open Mon 1:30 pm–7:30 pm and Tue–Sun 8:30 am–7:30 pm, last entry at 6:45 pm.

■ Arena, Piazza Bra, +39 045 800 3204, open Mon 1:30 pm–7:30 pm and Tue–Sun 8:30 am–7:30 pm, last entry at 6:30 pm.

Regional cuisine like 2000 years ago

Here could be an inn that has at least one dish on the menu continuously as it was 2000 years ago.

Overnight and camping possibilities in the appendix and in the maps

Questions and information about the subsection

■ Touristinfo IAT Verona, Via Degli Alpini 9 (Piazza Bra), 37121 Verona, 0039 045 806 86 80

■ Hotline Via Claudia Augusta, 0043(0)664 27 63 555

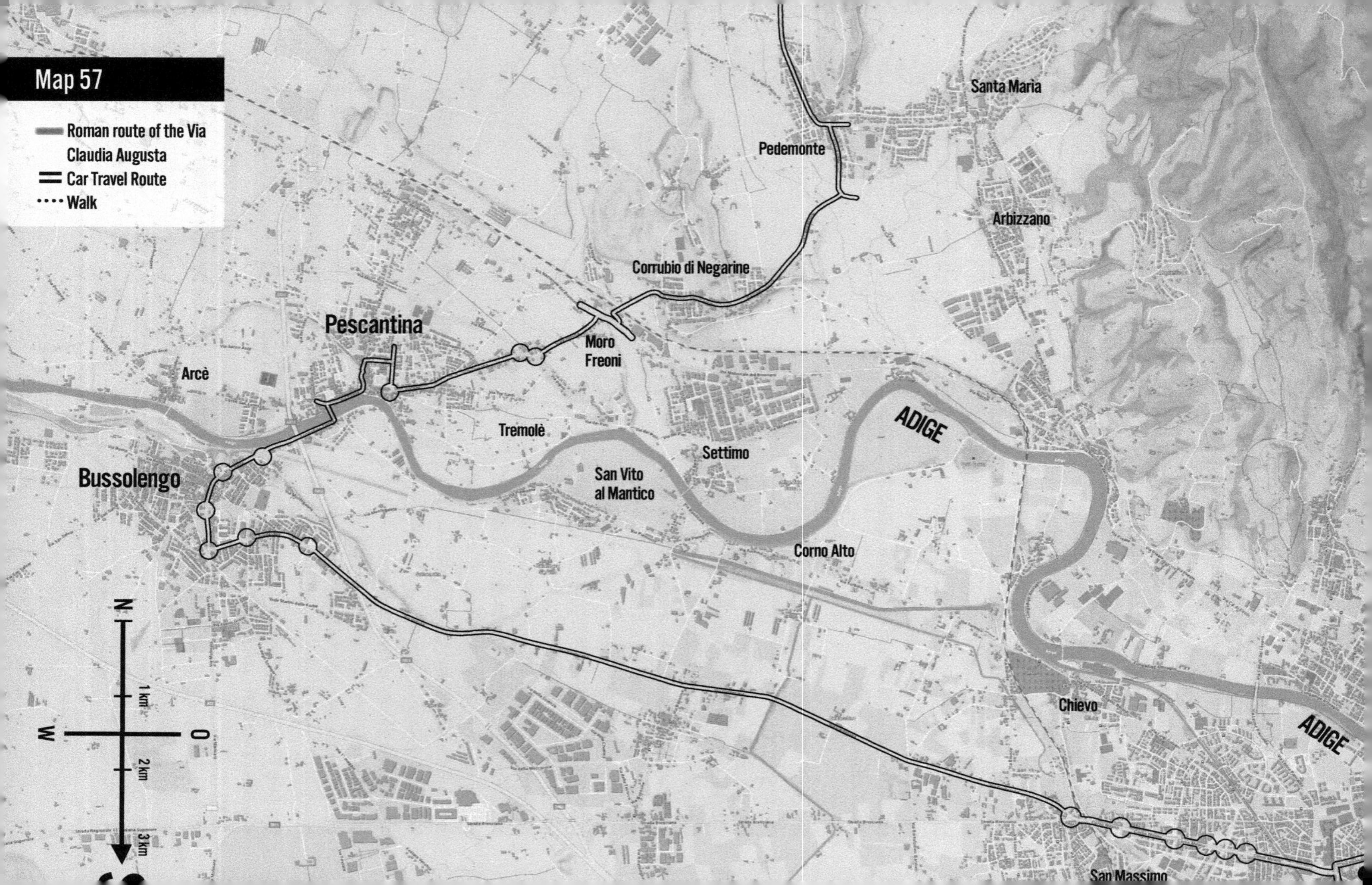
Map 57
Roman route of the Via Claudia Augusta
Car Travel Route
Walk
Santa Maria
Pedemonte
Arbizzano
Corrubio di Negarine
Pescantina
Moro
Freoni
Arcè
Tremolè
ADIGE
Settimo
San Vito
al Mantico
Bussolengo
Corno Alto
Chievo
ADIGE
San Massimo
N
W
O
1 km
2 km
3 km

39 The Po plain: the breadbasket of Italy (map 58, 59, 60, 61, 62)

The wide plain stretching towards the horizon on both sides of the Po river is one of Italy's most fertile and, in turn, most densely populated areas. Due to the relatively cold winters, tropical fruit have never been grown here on a large scale. Today, sugar beets, sweetcorn, wheat, and wine make up most of the crops cultivated along Italy's largest river. The agricultural fields surrounding Verona bear a wider variety of produce, as they have always supplied the city itself. Historically and culturally, the towns are closely connected to the city, too. There are especially many connections to the Scaligeri, the ruling family of Verona in the late Middle Ages. The historical route of the Via Claudia Augusta is said to correspond to today's railway track from Verona to Ostiglia. That is why our travel route takes you through the towns along that railway line – after a quick detour through the wine-growing region surrounding Custoza and the 'fruit and vegetable garden' of the city.

The western and southern environs of Verona

The rice route passes the airport of Verona to the north on its way to Sommacampagna, where a little church from the fifth century stands witness to early human settlement. Grapes grow all around Custoza, waiting to be made into 100,000 hl of DOC white wine. A tower-shaped ossuary marks the Battle of Custoza. Villafranca was founded as a Roman camp along the Via Postumia. Today, it is the second-largest town in the Province. The well-preserved Scaligero fortress dates back to the refoundation of the town as a colony of Verona in the 12th century. It is likely that humans have inhabited the region along the Via Claudia Augusta since prehistoric times. The names of Castel d'Azzano and Vigasio come from Latin. They imply that there used to be a pre-Roman settlement built by the Attic people, which belonged to the Veneti. The name of Castel d'Azzano also refers to the Villa Violini Nogarola or 'Il Castello'. Isola refers to the extensive swamps surrounding the Tartaro river, which only had a few inhabitable islands. In the municipality of Nogara, evidence of pile dwellings from the Bronze Age has been found. Vigasio is mentioned in records from 1014, which describe it as a rest station between Mantua and Verona. Later, Benedictines settled in the area and began to make it arable.

Regional cuisine like 2000 years ago

Here could be an inn that has at least one dish on the menu continuously as it was 2000 years ago.

Overnight and camping possibilities in the appendix and in the maps

Questions and information about the subsection

- Hotline IAT for south of Verona, 0039 045 861 91 63
- Hotline IAT Legnago, 0039 0442 200 52
- Hotline Via Claudia Augusta, 0043(0)664 27 63 555

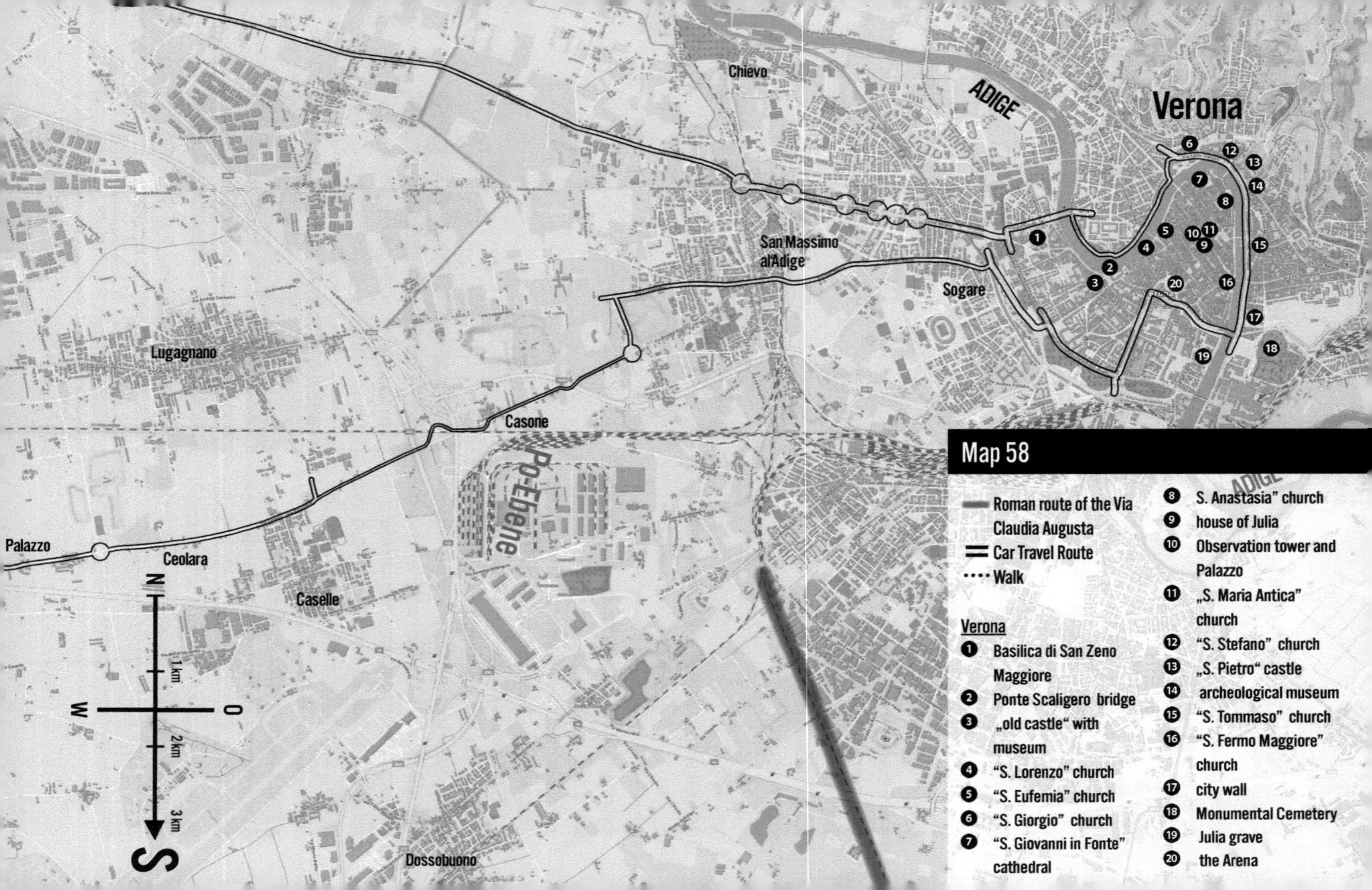
Verona
ADIGE
Chievo
San Massimo al'Adige
Sogare
Lugagnano
Casone
Po-Ebene
Palazzo
Ceolara
Caselle
Dossobuono
N
S
W
O
1 km
2 km
3 km
Map 58
Roman route of the Via Claudia Augusta
Car Travel Route
Walk
Verona
1 Basilica di San Zeno Maggiore
2 Ponte Scaligero bridge
3 „old castle“ with museum
4 “S. Lorenzo” church
5 “S. Eufemia” church
6 “S. Giorgio” church
7 “S. Giovanni in Fonte” cathedral
8 S. Anastasia” church
9 house of Julia
10 Observation tower and Palazzo
11 „S. Maria Antica” church
12 “S. Stefano” church
13 „S. Pietro“ castle
14 archeological museum
15 “S. Tommaso” church
16 “S. Fermo Maggiore” church
17 city wall
18 Monumental Cemetery
19 Julia grave
20 the Arena

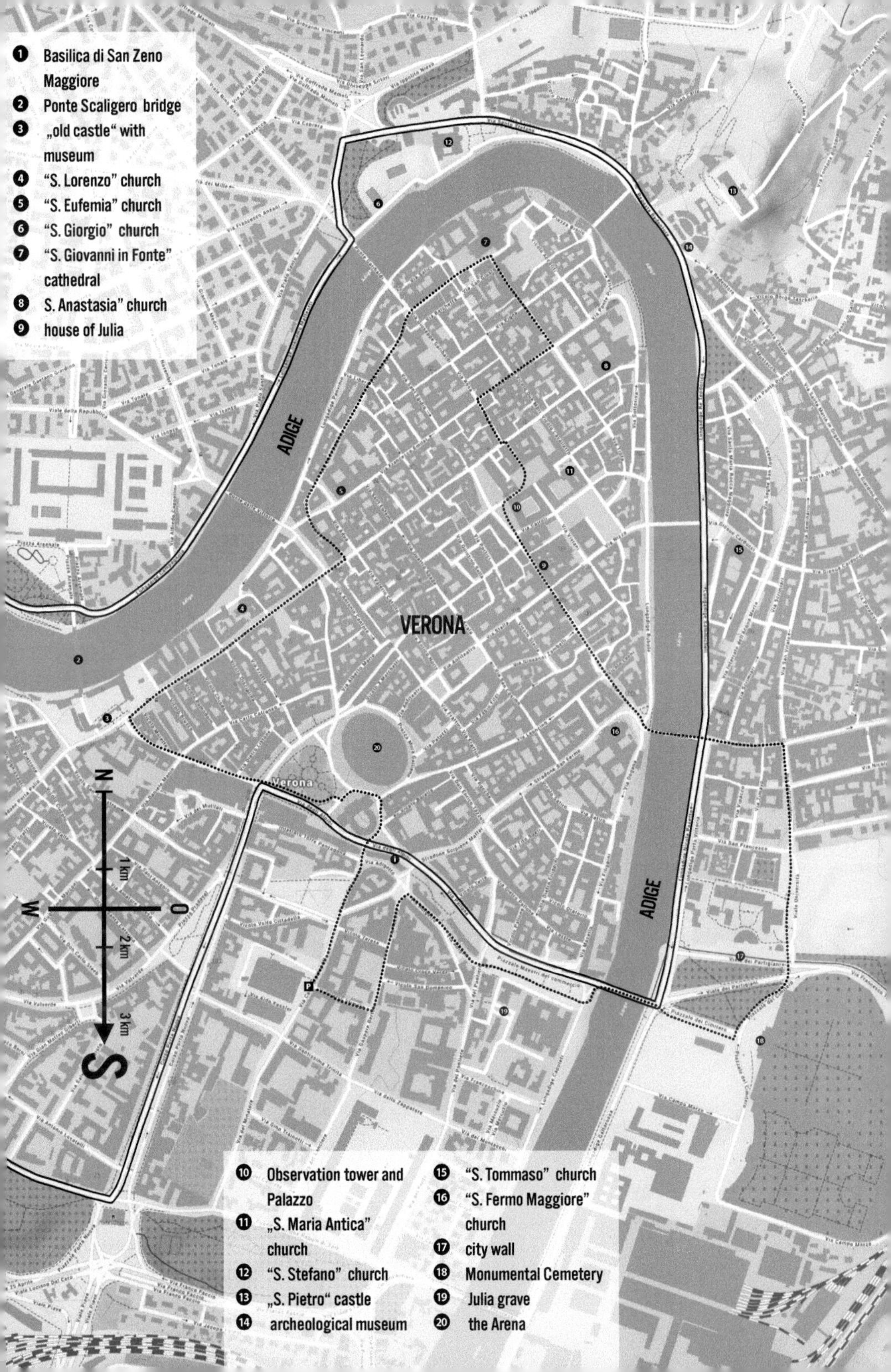

1 Basilica di San Zeno Maggiore
2 Ponte Scaligero bridge
3 „old castle“ with museum
4 “S. Lorenzo” church
5 “S. Eufemia” church
6 “S. Giorgio” church
7 “S. Giovanni in Fonte” cathedral
8 S. Anastasia” church
9 house of Julia
ADIGE
VERONA
ADIGE
N
1 km
W
O
2 km
3 km
S
10 Observation tower and Palazzo
11 „S. Maria Antica“ church
12 “S. Stefano” church
13 „S. Pietro“ castle
14 archeological museum
15 “S. Tommaso” church
16 “S. Fermo Maggiore” church
17 city wall
18 Monumental Cemetery
19 Julia grave
20 the Arena

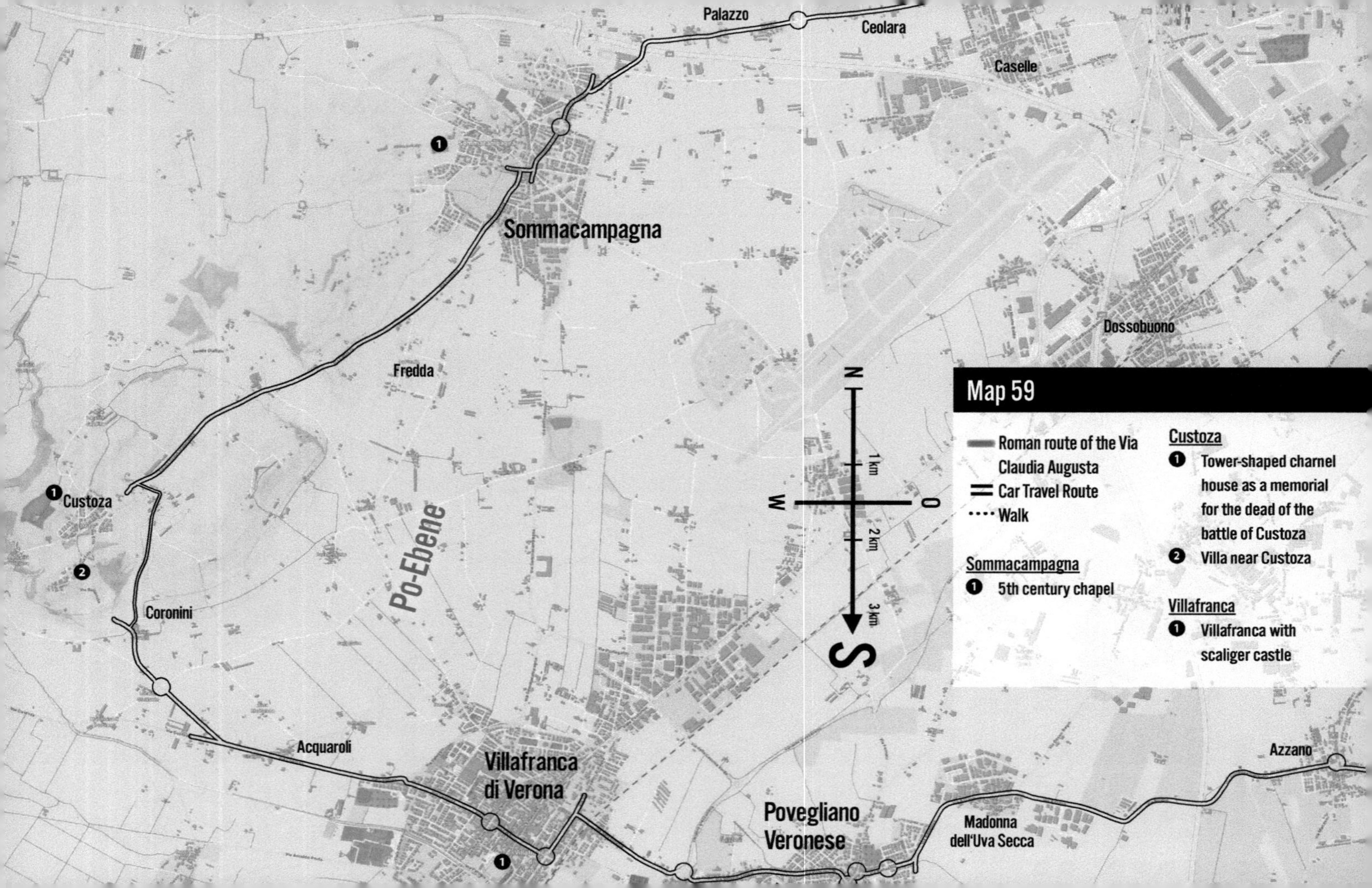

Map 59
Roman route of the Via Claudia Augusta
Car Travel Route
Walk
Sommacampagna
1 5th century chapel
Custoza
1 Tower-shaped charnel house as a memorial for the dead of the battle of Custoza
2 Villa near Custoza
Villafranca
1 Villafranca with scaliger castle
N
O
S
W
1 km
2 km
3 km
Palazzo
Ceolara
Caselle
Dossobuono
Sommacampagna
Fredda
Po-Ebene
Custoza
Coronini
Acquaroli
Villafranca di Verona
Povegliano Veronese
Madonna dell'Uva Secca
Azzano

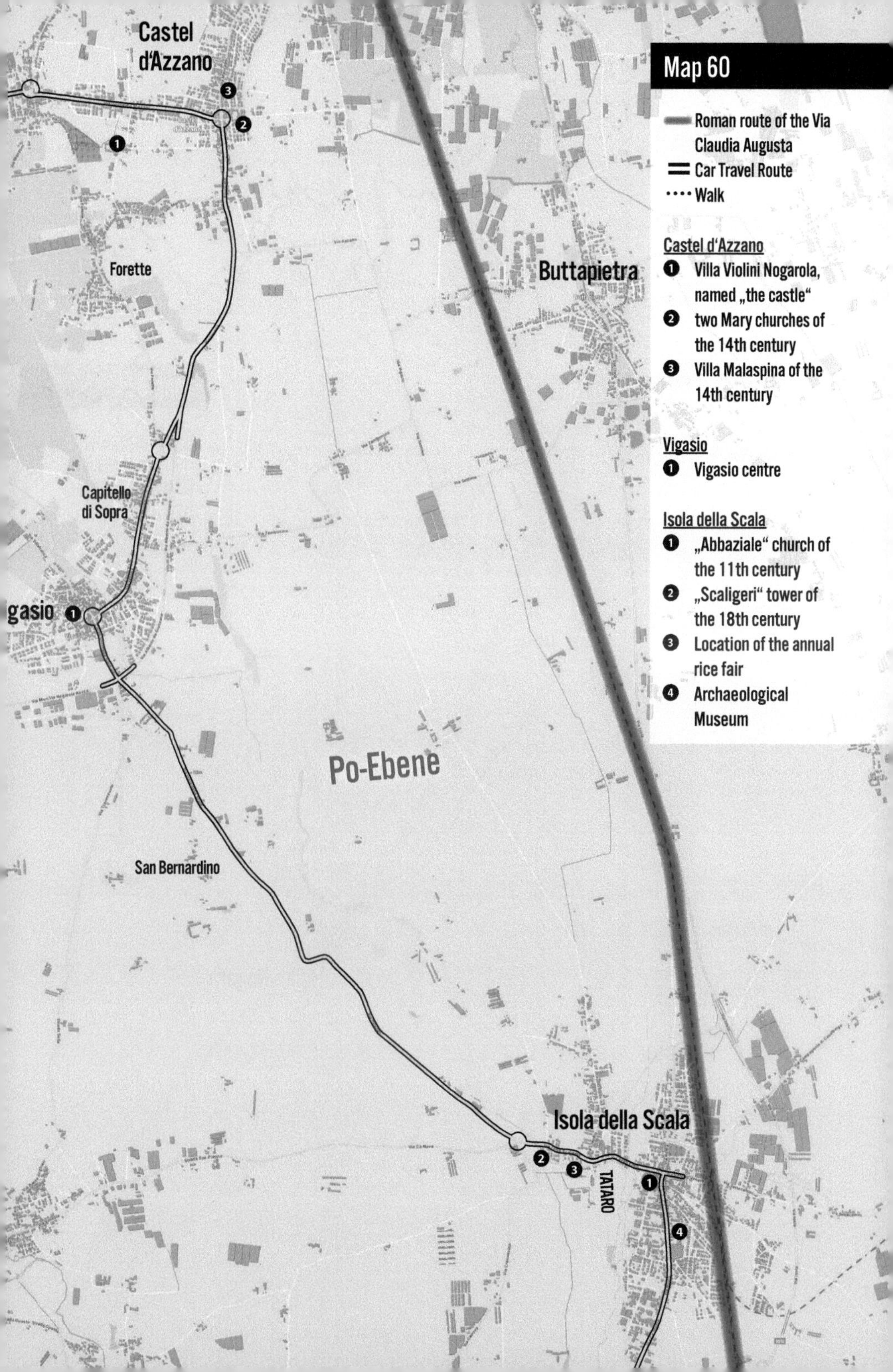
Map 60
Roman route of the Via Claudia Augusta
Car Travel Route
Walk
Castel d'Azzano
❶ Villa Violini Nogarola, named „the castle“
❷ two Mary churches of the 14th century
❸ Villa Malaspina of the 14th century
Vigasio
❶ Vigasio centre
Isola della Scala
❶ „Abbaziale“ church of the 11th century
❷ „Scaligeri“ tower of the 18th century
❸ Location of the annual rice fair
❹ Archaeological Museum
Castel d'Azzano
Forette
Buttapietra
Capitello di Sopra
gasio
Po-Ebene
San Bernardino
Isola della Scala
TATARO

Po-Ebene
Map 61
Roman route of the Via Claudia Augusta
Car Travel Route
Walk
Pellegrina
TATARO
Motta
no
Bonferraro
TATARO
Nogara
TIONE
N
3 km
2 km
1 km
S

The Garden of Italy. Photo: Archivio Provincia di Verona Turismo / F. Zanetti

Villa Dionisi. Photo: Archivio Provincia di Verona Turismo / F. Dall'Aglio

Fortress „Scaligero" in Villafranca. Photo: Archivio Provincia di Verona Turismo

Rice field in Isola della Scala. Photo: Archivio Provincia di Verona Turismo

The Palazzo Bonazzi, which is now the town hall. Photo: Lois Lammerhuber.

The Po near Ostiglia in the evening hours. Photo: Tschaikner

40 Ancient river port of Ostiglia in the risotto rice region (map 62)

In Roman times, Ostiglia was called Hostilia. It was an important river port on the Po. According to the milestone of Rabland/Rablà, it is the starting point of the Via Claudia Augusta. From here, goods were transported downriver and across the river, from where the Via Claudia Augusta continued to the south. Today, Ostiglia is still a traffic hub, where the state road 482 'Alto Polesine', coming from Mantua, crosses with the state road 12 dell'Abetone e del Brennero , coming from Verona. In the 17th century, the people of this region began to grow rice, which the Italians use to make their beloved risotto.

Rice fair Isola della Scala

In the center of the rice-growing area there is an annual rice fair. Rice is no longer as important as it used to be, but Italy is still the country with the largest crop in Europe. Padania specializes mainly in the cultivation of varieties for the traditional risotto rice dishes, which are deeply rooted in the regional culture. Many popular festivals are unthinkable without the great risotto rice dish, and the gastronomy also upholds the kitchen tradition. Rice in Padania is bought from the farmer you trust.

Nogara, Gazzo Veronese and the Paludi (marshes)

Grave finds show that the border area between Veneto and Lombardy has been inhabited for at least 5000 years. The Roman tower from the 4th century and the churches of Santa Maria Maggiore and Ceson di San Pietro in Valle from the 10th and 11th centuries show that the area continued to be inhabited beyond Roman times and in the early Middle Ages. The history is documented in the Archaeological Museum of the municipality. Gazzo and Ostiglia, which is already in the Lombardai, share vast marshes (paludi) with a fascinating fauna and flora.

■ Visitors Center Nature Reserve „Oasi del Busatello", +39 0422 550 219.

■ Archaeological Museum, 37060 Gazzo Veronese, Via Piazza Gazzo 14, +39 347 43 20 270.+39 0422 550 219.

Ostiglia on the Po dam and the Po bridge

The Romans were followed by turbulent times under the Goths, Byzantium, the Longobards and the Franks. In the late Middle Ages there was a fortress on the Po, of which the tower is still preserved. Under Austria Ostiglia lost its strategic importance and Charles VI ordered its demolition and the use of the building material for the fortification of Mantua. Ostiglia is impressive as a town, but also for its position on the embankment of the Po River. The two museums of Ostiglia were unfortunately damaged in the earthquake of 2012 and are currently closed.

Regional cuisine like 2000 years ago

Here could be an inn that has at least one dish on the menu continuously as it was 2000 years ago.

Overnight and camping possibilities in the appendix and in the maps

Questions and information about the subsection

■ City Hall Ostiglia, Via Gnocchi Viani 16,
0039 0386 300211 (italian and english)

■ Hotline Via Claudia Augusta, 0043(0)664 27 63 555

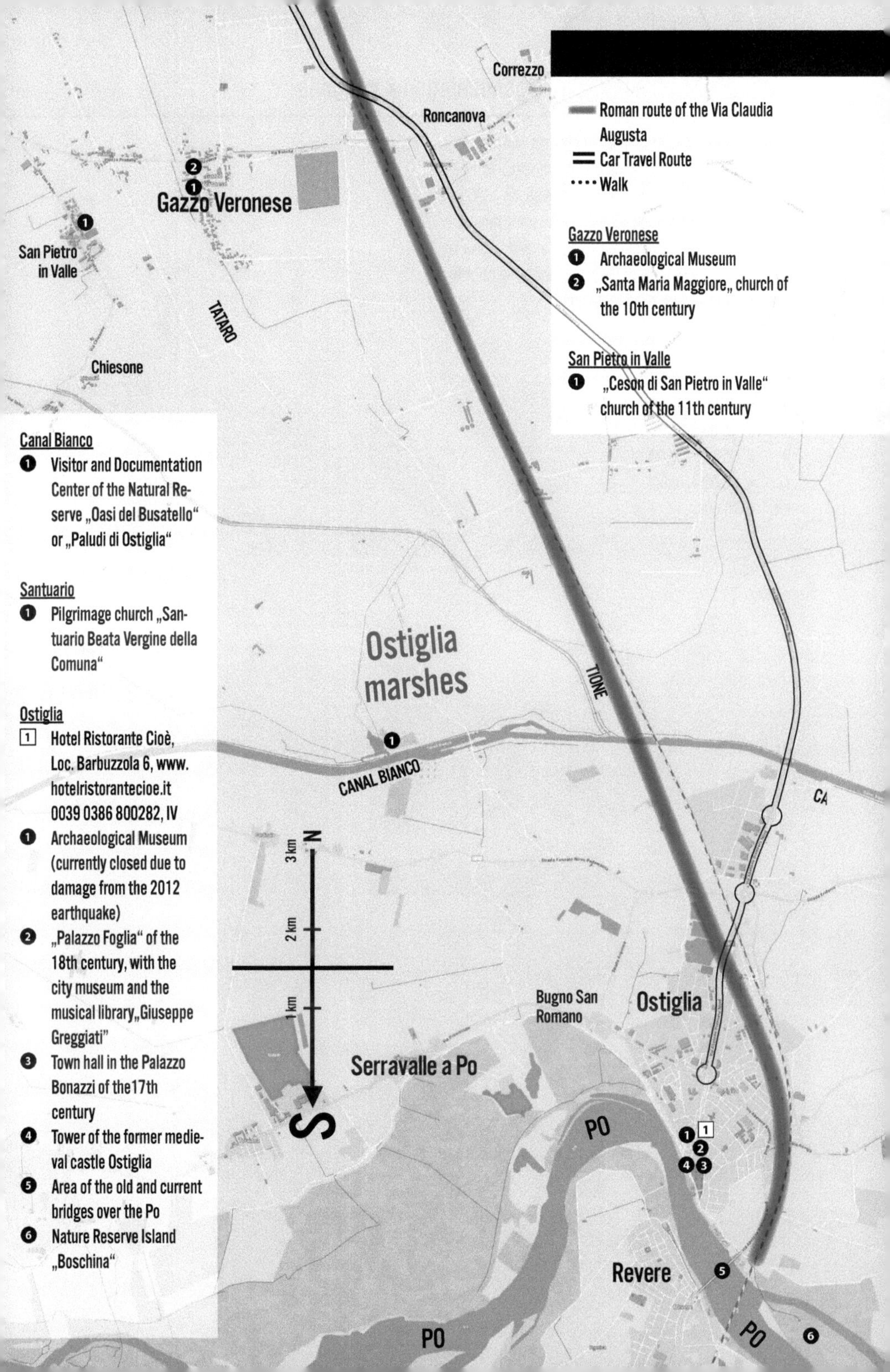
Roman route of the Via Claudia Augusta
Car Travel Route
Walk
Gazzo Veronese
1 Archaeological Museum
2 „Santa Maria Maggiore„ church of the 10th century
San Pietro in Valle
1 „Ceson di San Pietro in Valle" church of the 11th century
Canal Bianco
1 Visitor and Documentation Center of the Natural Reserve „Oasi del Busatello" or „Paludi di Ostiglia"
Santuario
1 Pilgrimage church „Santuario Beata Vergine della Comuna"
Ostiglia
1 Hotel Ristorante Cioè, Loc. Barbuzzola 6, www.hotelristorantecioe.it 0039 0386 800282, IV
1 Archaeological Museum (currently closed due to damage from the 2012 earthquake)
2 „Palazzo Foglia" of the 18th century, with the city museum and the musical library „Giuseppe Greggiati"
3 Town hall in the Palazzo Bonazzi of the17th century
4 Tower of the former medieval castle Ostiglia
5 Area of the old and current bridges over the Po
6 Nature Reserve Island „Boschina"
Correzzo
Roncanova
Gazzo Veronese
San Pietro in Valle
TATARO
Chiesone
Ostiglia marshes
TIONE
CANAL BIANCO
CA
N
3 km
2 km
1 km
S
Bugno San Romano
Ostiglia
Serravalle a Po
PO
Revere
PO
PO

Accomodation & camping

All hosts are specially adapted to cyclists and hikers, but also other travelers along the Via Claudia Augusta. Those with the bowl have at least one dish, as 2000 years ago, on the menu or menu plan.I-VII - the price ranges in the following advertisements are intended to give an approximate impression of the price range and refer to one night per person in a double room.

I < 15,00
II = 15,00 – 23,00
III = 23,00 – 30,00
IV = 30 00 – 35,00
V = 35,00 – 50,00
VI = 50,00 – 70,00
VII > 70,00.

FSC
www.fsc.org
MIX
Papier aus verantwortungsvollen Quellen
Paper from responsible sources
FSC® C105338